IMAGES
of America

Assyrian American Association of Chicago: 100 Years

I0805797

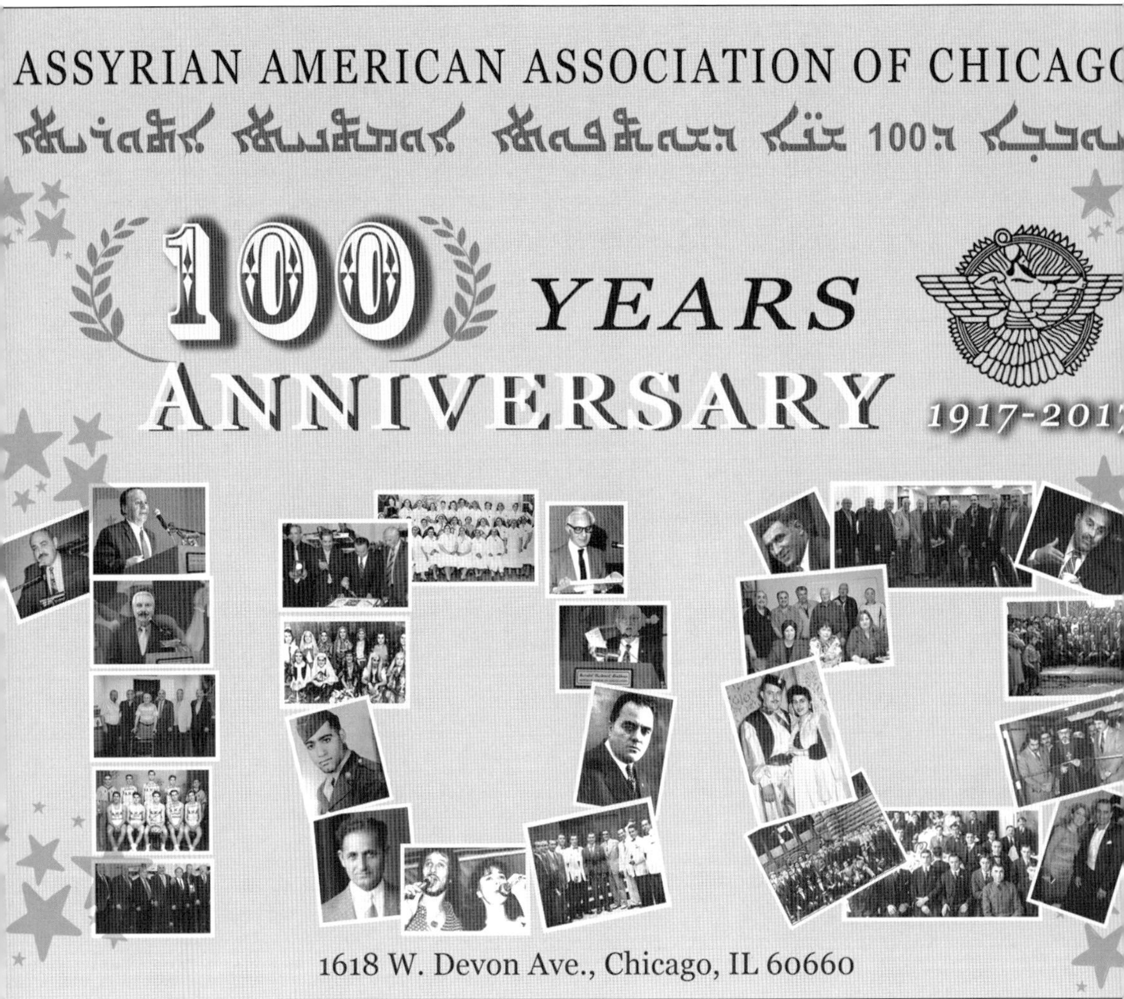

This greeting card celebrates the 100th anniversary of the Assyrian American Association of Chicago in 2017. (Author's collection.)

ON THE COVER: Pictured is the ground-breaking ceremony for the Assyrian American Association's new building at 2108 North Halsted Street in Chicago in 1938. (Courtesy of Sarah N. Benjamin.)

IMAGES
of America

Assyrian American Association of Chicago: 100 Years

Vasili Shoumanov

ARCADIA
PUBLISHING

ISBN 978-1-4671-0275-9

Published by Arcadia Publishing
Charleston, South Carolina

Printed in the United States of America

Library of Congress Control Number: 2018952266

For all general information, please contact Arcadia Publishing:
Telephone 843-853-2070
Fax 843-853-0044
E-mail sales@arcadiapublishing.com
For customer service and orders:
Toll-Free 1-888-313-2665

Visit us on the Internet at www.arcadiapublishing.com

This book is dedicated to my kids, Gavreel and Adam. It is a wonderful opportunity to teach them about the incredible accomplishments of the Assyrian people in America and abroad.

Contents

ACKNOWLEDGMENTS

I want to express my gratitude to the many individuals whose contributions made this book possible. A year ago, the *Nineveh* magazine of the Assyrian Foundation of America in Berkeley, California, published my article "Assyrian American Association of Chicago." My friends inspired me to continue my research and write a book. Arcadia Publishing was the absolute ideal publisher for such project.

First, I would like to thank Jack David Jr., who gave me access to his priceless family archives. I want to thank the Assyrian American Association of Chicago and members Guiliana Younan, Edward Nadirsha, Emmanuel Isho, Raman Oshana, Sam Oushana, Sarah N. Benjamin (1922–2018), Gary E. Daniels, Germaine Malik, Fransis Yousif, Sankhareb Abraham, Eddie Zomayah, Linda Dekelaita, and Teena Khaee.

I deeply appreciate the Illinois Humanity Council for funding this book. I thank the Ashurbanipal Library of the Assyrian Universal Alliance Foundation (AUAF) and especially, Ninos Nirari and Awayah Isho.

I thank Fred Sarkiso, Dr. Norman Solhkhah, Marina Benjamin, Joey Joseph, Michael Mammo, Ninos Elnaya, Rev. Charles Klutz, Edward Hasso, Wilson Younan (SBS Australia), Henri Charr, His Grace Mar Paulus Benjamin, Rev. Antwan Lachin, Emanuel Solomon, Sargon Isaac, Sam Darmo, Maegan BetGivargis-McDaniel, Ninwe Maraha, Suzanne Shamoun, Abboud Zeitoune, Andrew Bet-Shlimon, Tony S. Kalogerakos, Dankha Zomaya, and Ashur Gabriel.

Also, I would like to thank my friends for giving me their valuable advice: Hieromonk Stefan Sado; Roland Bidjamov, PhD; Anahit Khosroeva, PhD; Ruben Aleksanov; Joe Rasho; Michael Tarelko, PhD; Alexey Tamrazov, PhD; Giwargis Badare, and David Raphael.

Introduction

Assyrians or Syriacs—some of them self-identify as Arameans or as Chaldeans—are an indigenous people of Mesopotamia (modern Iraq) dating to 2500 BC. The Assyrians are a Semitic people who originally spoke and wrote Akkadian before the easier-to-use Aramaic language became more popular. The Assyrians are named after Ashur, a city in northern Mesopotamia that lay at the center of their homeland, today's Iraq. The ancient Assyrian Empire is often called "the Cradle of Civilization." There had been a number of different capitals of Assyria throughout its history, and the region was not always a kingdom in its own right, sometimes split up or called various other names. In addition to Ashur, the great cities of Assyria included Nimrud, Kalhu, Dur-Sharrukin, Harran, Ekallatum, Carchemish, Kar-Tukulti-Ninurta, and Nineveh. Ashur was the capital of the first original empire. The last capital of Assyria was Nineveh, one of the oldest and greatest cities in antiquity.

Assyrian religion was polytheistic, accepting the existence of many different deities, both male and female, though it was also henotheistic. The head of the Assyrian pantheon was the god Ashur.

The last great Assyrian king, Ashurbanipal, constructed a great library at the city of Nineveh. He collected clay tablets from all over the world, including books on history, religion, geography, poetry, music, medicine, astronomy, and more. The Assyrians were perhaps most famous for their professional army. They were a warrior society, in which fighting was a part of life. It was how they survived. Two things that made the Assyrians great warriors were their chariots and their iron weapons, which were stronger than copper or tin.

After the fall of Nineveh, Assyria remained as a geopolitical region, ethnic entity, and colonized province under Achaemenid, Macedonian/Seleucid, Parthian, Roman, Sassanid, Arab, Mongol, and Ottoman empires.

The Assyrians were the first nation to accept Christianity, during the first century AD. Their Apostolic church was established by Thomas the Apostle, Thaddeus of Edessa, and Bartholomew the Apostle. They successfully preached Christianity in Persia, India, China, Socotra and Ceylon, Turkestan, Mongolia, and Sri Lanka. The language of the first three centuries of the Christian era is also known as classical Assyrian (Syriac). The Assyrian language became the lingua franca of the Middle East.

The Assyrians mostly adhere to the East and West Syrian form of Christianity. The churches that constitute the East Syrian rite include the Assyrian Church of the East, Ancient Church of the East, and Chaldean Catholic Church, whereas the churches of the West Syrian rite are the Syriac Orthodox Church and Syriac Catholic Church. Both rites use classical Assyrian (Syriac) as their liturgical language. Indigenous Assyrians gradually became a minority in their own homeland; they became subject to severe religious, ethnic, and cultural discrimination. They suffered a number of severe massacres.

In the 19th century, the Assyrians came into contact with the Western world. During this time, they experienced a new cultural renaissance and played an instrumental role in the economic, political, and educational development in Iran and Turkey.

The Assyrians had political and military contacts with European countries before and after World War I. Britain, France, and Russia promised Assyrians an independent homeland in the area of northern Iraq. Their promises never materialized.

Most of the Assyrians today live around their traditional homeland, which comprises parts of northern Iraq, Syria, Turkey, and Iran. There are almost two million Assyrian people in the world. Members of the Assyrian diaspora are spread out all over the world, including 800,000 in the United States. Assyrian immigration to the United States occurred in four major waves. The first wave of immigrants arrived mainly from the late 1800s up to World War I. They came to America mainly for economical, but also political and religious, reasons.

The earliest Assyrian Americans settled in New York, Chicago, Boston, Los Angeles, Worcester, Flint, Bristol, Paterson, Elizabeth, New Britain, and Gary.

Initially, Assyrian immigration to Chicago was primarily a male phenomenon. Young men and boys came to escape extreme poverty in the Turkish-occupied territories. The vast majority planned to return to their homeland with enough money to pay off family debts and provide for future life. Some Assyrians moved to the United States with their families. Many of them were illiterate and unskilled laborers. Assyrian immigration to America mostly came to a halt due to the Immigration Act of 1924, which effectively cut off legal immigration to the United States for Assyrians.

The second large wave of immigration occurred in the 1960s and 1970s, mainly from Iraq due to conflicts and persecution by the Baathist government.

The third wave of immigrants started arriving in the late 1970s and the early 1980s from Iraq, Syria, and Lebanon.

The new fourth wave started recently, in 2014, due to the persecution of Christians by ISIL (ISIS) in Iraq and Syria. ISIL demanded that Assyrian Christians living in Arab countries convert to Islam, pay tribute, or face execution. Hundreds of Assyrians were captured and kidnapped, and many were killed. Many Assyrian monuments and churches have been damaged or destroyed.

Today, the largest population of the Assyrian diaspora is located in Chicago, around 80,000. Chicago's Assyrian community cultivated a rich social and cultural life, establishing clubs, organizations, and churches. One of them is the Assyrian American Association of Chicago (AAAC). It was formed in 1916 and officially registered in 1917. For generations, the association has offered an array of comprehensive programming and support services to families and individuals centered on educational and social enrichment, employment and wellness, and cultural exchange. The organization is a diverse alliance of artistic people—writers, musicians, radio and TV speakers, singers, and supporters—who believe that working together as a pan-ethnic, multidisciplinary community is essential to nurturing the development of artists and providing meaningful and innovative ways for civic engagement in society. The Assyrian American Association of Chicago demonstrates Chicago's values by empowering residents to build better lives, stronger families, and more informed communities.

One

The Homeland

By the 20th century, the Assyrians and other Christian communities, including the Greeks and Armenians, were significant minorities in the Ottoman Empire. Some Assyrians in Turkey were self-governing, divided into tribes known as Ashirate: Upper and Lower Tyari, Tkhumi, Tal, Diz, Baz, and Jilu, in the region of the Hakkari Mountains. There were many districts containing numbers of Assyrian Rayas (semi-independent) in Gawar, Somai, Chara, and Mamoodiah. The tribes were also divided into clans, which were made up of some families. The tribes were ruled by tribal leaders (Maliks) and were united politically and religiously under the administration of Mar Shimun, the Assyrian patriarch of the Church of the East, with headquarters in the town of Qodchanis. Mar Shimun was under the authority of the Turkish government. The other Assyrians were located in regions of Sapna Valley, Mosul, Diyar Bakir, Mardin, Tur Abdin, and Midyat. The Assyrians in Persian Azerbaijan lived in compact villages along the three rivers of Nazlu, Shahar, and Baranduz along the western shore of Lake Urmia, on the border with Ottoman Turkey.

In the middle of the 19th century, western missionaries came to the Urmia region. In 1834, Rev. Justin Perkins and his wife, Charlotte, arrived in Persia and established a mission with headquarters at Urmia. In addition to Reverend Perkins, American missionaries Fidelia Fiske, Joseph Cochran, Frederick Coan, David Stoddard, Austin Wright, and William Stocking founded educational institutions and hospitals in Iran. A number of key missionaries in Iran were Chicagoans, including Rev. William Shedd. They established schools and hospitals. By 1906, there were a total of 201 schools and 5,084 Assyrian students in Urmia. The missionaries prompted Assyrians to come to America. Most early Assyrian immigrants were young men sent by missionaries for religious training. They dreamed of getting some education, making some money to support their families, and returning to their homeland, but many stayed forever.

An outbreak of anti-Assyrian violence took place in the 20th century. In 1914–1915, the Ottoman Empire under the Young Turk regime declared a holy war on the British, French, and Russian empires. Hundreds of Christian villages were looted and destroyed. A large portion of the Christian population fled to the Caucasus and Russia. Most of the Christians who remained took refuge in the American, French, and Russian missions. Rev. William Shedd tried to protect the Assyrian people from the genocide. He reported to the US minister to Persia that one fifth of the total population of Christians in the Urmia region had perished in the first five months of 1915 alone and that the vast majority of families had had all their property stolen. During and after World War I, newspapers in London, Paris, New York, and Los Angeles regularly reported on the desperate straits imposed on Assyrian Christians in the Ottoman Empire. The *Times of London* and the *Los Angeles Times* confirmed that 200,000 to 250,000 Assyrians had lost their lives in the Ottoman Christian genocide. Assyrian refugees flowed out of the Ottoman Empire into Europe and the United States.

In 1919, delegates from 32 countries met in Paris to make peace after World War I. The Assyrian delegates traveled to participate in the conference. It was called the Assyro-Chaldean Delegation and delegates from Turkey, Iran, the United States, and Russia were included. Among them, Joel Werda, president of the Assyrian National Associations of America, represented the Assyrians of America. There was a glimmer of hope for establishing an Assyrian homeland and an expectation that, at the very least, Assyrians would be compensated for the massacres and destruction of their homes, churches, and monasteries. The conference did not fulfill any of these expectations.

In 1921, the Kingdom of Iraq was created under British Mandate. At the same time, the British administration established the first military base to control Iraq. It was made up mostly of Assyrian, Armenian, Turkmen, and Kurdish forces and British officers and was used mostly for guarding Royal Air Force bases in Iraq. In 1932, when the British Mandate officially ended, King Faisal I proclaimed independence from Iraq, and Assyrians refused to become part of the newly formed state of Iraq. The Assyrian leader Mar Eshai Shimun XXI, the patriarch of the Assyrian Church of the East, asked the League of Nations to recognize their right to govern the area known as the "Assyrian Triangle" in northern Iraq. In August 1933, Iraqi forces massacred Assyrian civilians in the Simele village. Around 3,000 civilians were killed and residential areas were destroyed. August 7 has been designated Memorial Day for Assyrian people.

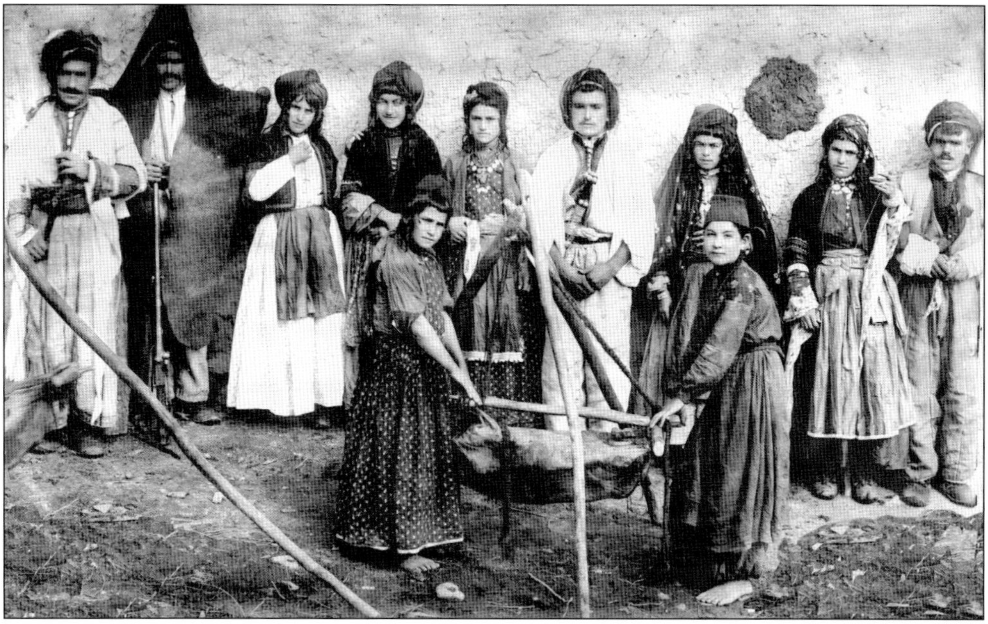

Assyrian village people in the Urmia region of Iran are pictured in the early 1900s. The Assyrians were industrious and educated inhabitants of the region. (Courtesy of Library of Congress.)

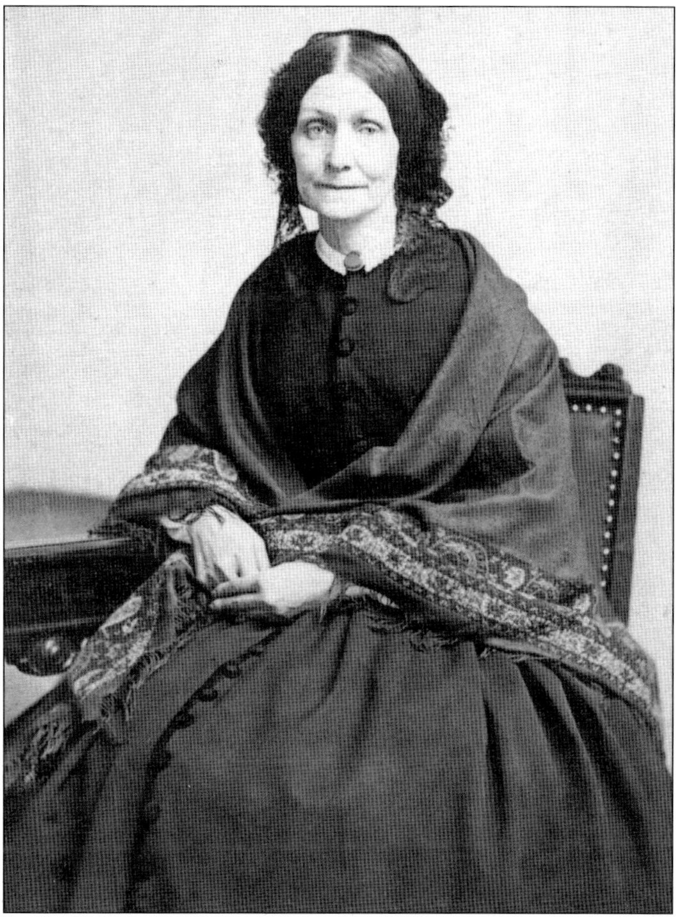

Fidelia Fiske (1816–1864) was the first woman missionary in Persia and founder of the Assyrian Female Seminary. The purpose of the seminary was to make Assyrian girls better wives and mothers and revive their Christian faith. The school had grown to an enrollment of some 40 pupils by 1858 when ill health forced Fiske to return to the United States. (Courtesy of Mount Holyoke College.)

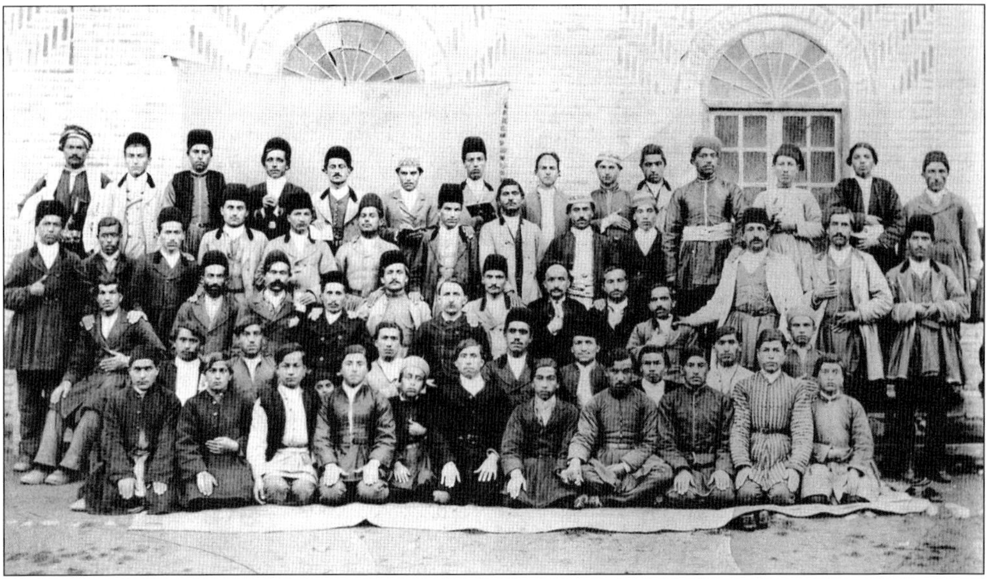

Assyrian students are pictured here at the American Mission College in Urmia. The college prepared hundreds of doctors, teachers, preachers, nurses, and other professional Assyrians. (Courtesy of Jack David Jr.)

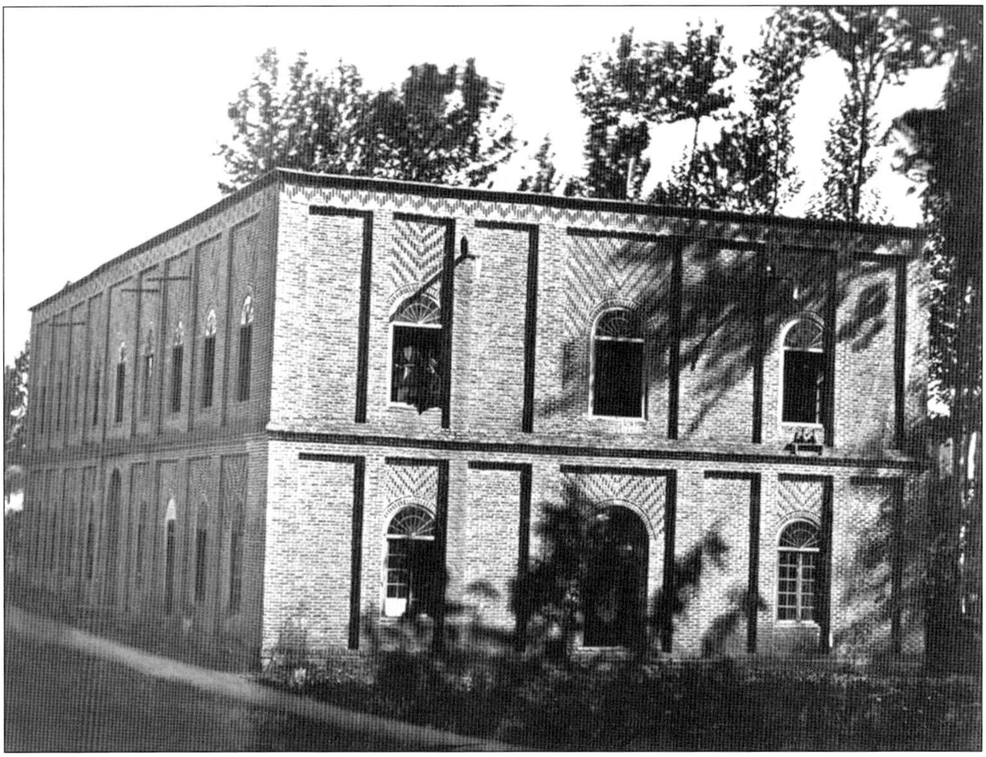

This is a view of the Urmia American Mission College. The American mission had grown to include doctors, linguists, and preachers. (Courtesy of Jack David Jr.)

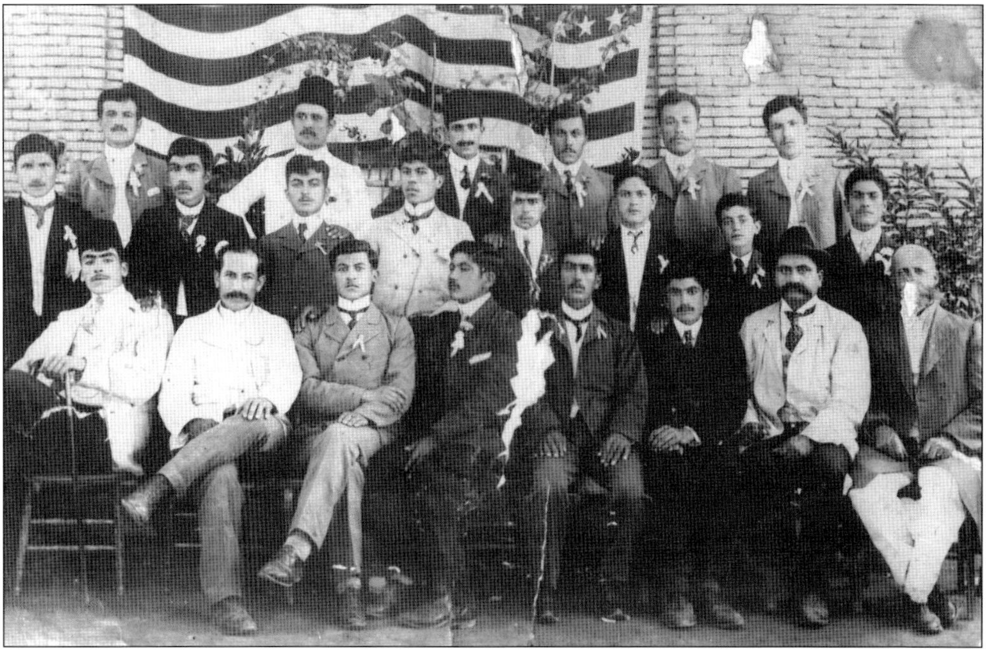

Frederick G. Coan is pictured (first row, far right) with Assyrian students. He was a Christian missionary who was a witness to the Assyrian Genocide. In 1904, Coan took charge of Urmia College, a position he held until 1912. (Courtesy of Jack David Jr.)

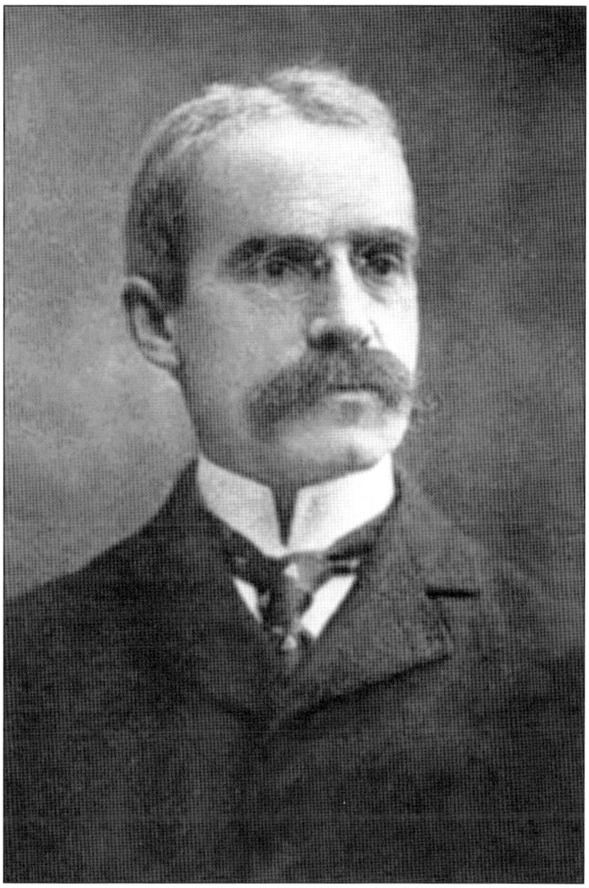

Dr. Joseph Plumb Cochran (1855–1905) was an American Presbyterian missionary. Born in Urmia, he studied medicine at New York Medical College. At his request, the Board of Assyrian Missionaries purchased a 15-hectare garden, which became the site of a 100-bed hospital named Westminster Hospital, in 1879. Cochran learned the Assyrian, Azerbaijani, and Kurdish languages. (Courtesy of Ashurbanipal Library, AUAF.)

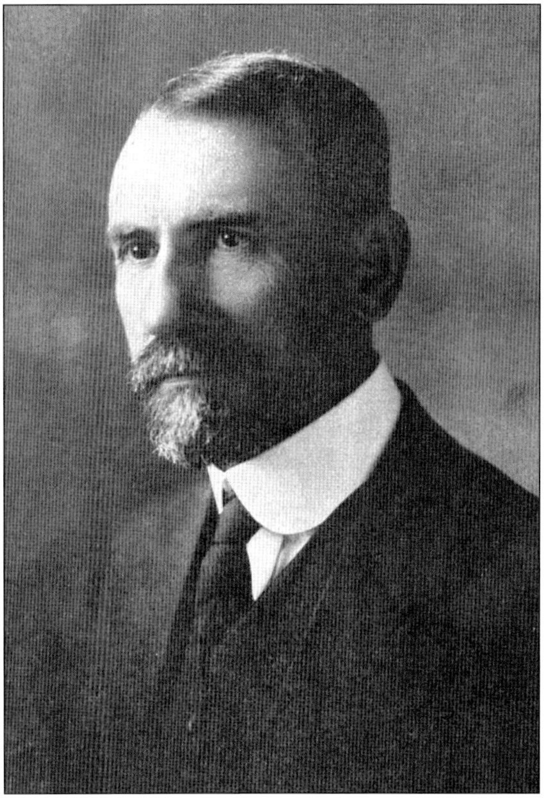

William Ambrose Shedd (1865–1918) was a US Presbyterian missionary who served in Urmia and tried to protect the Assyrian people from the genocide. He spent the rest of his life among the Assyrian Christians of northwestern Iran. (Courtesy of Ashurbanipal Library, AUAF.)

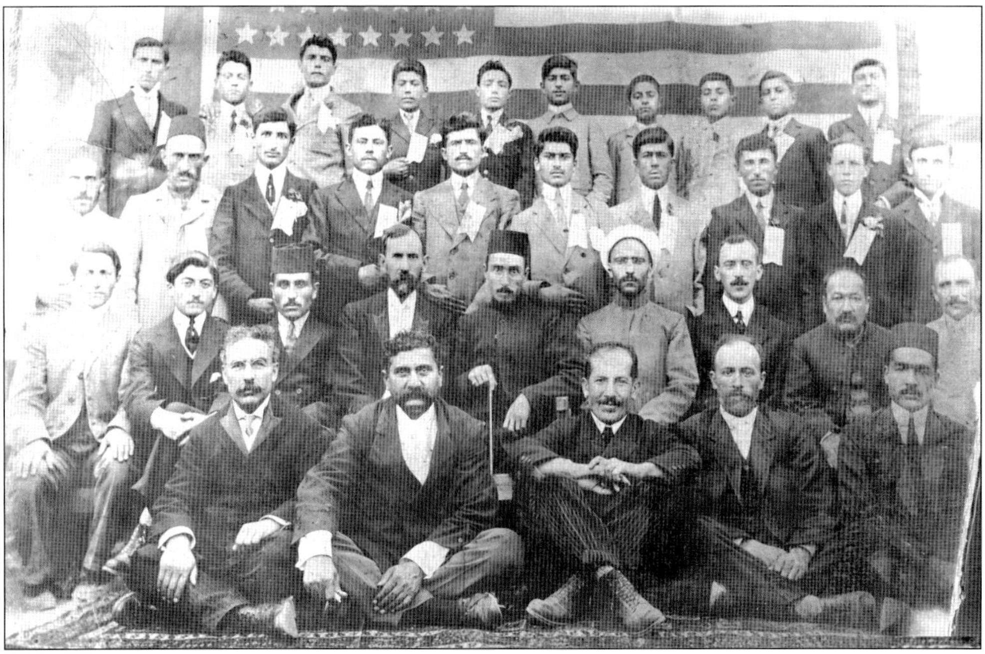

A number of key missionaries in Iran were Chicagoans, including William Shedd, pictured here seated (second row, fourth from left) with Assyrians and Persians in Urmia, Iran. The missionary school continued to educate students up to the 1930s. (Courtesy of Jack David Jr.)

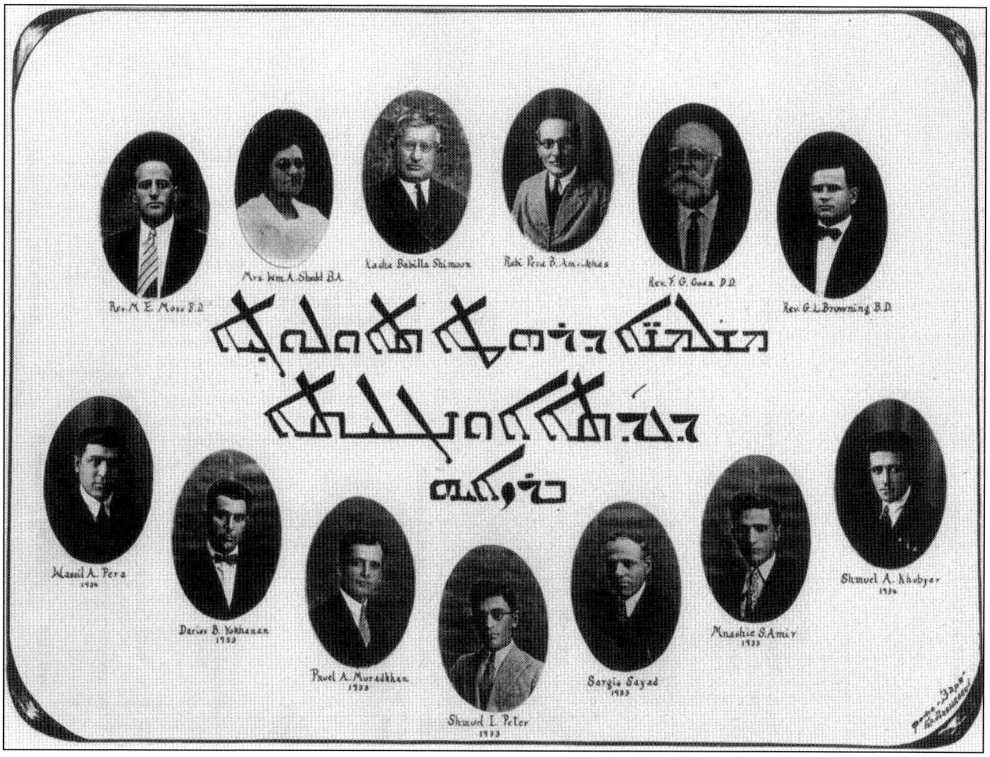

This is a composite photograph of Assyrian graduates and teachers of the missionary college in Urmia for the 1933–1934 school year. The photographs were taken by the Davidovs brothers of the Zarya studio. (Courtesy of Jack David Jr.)

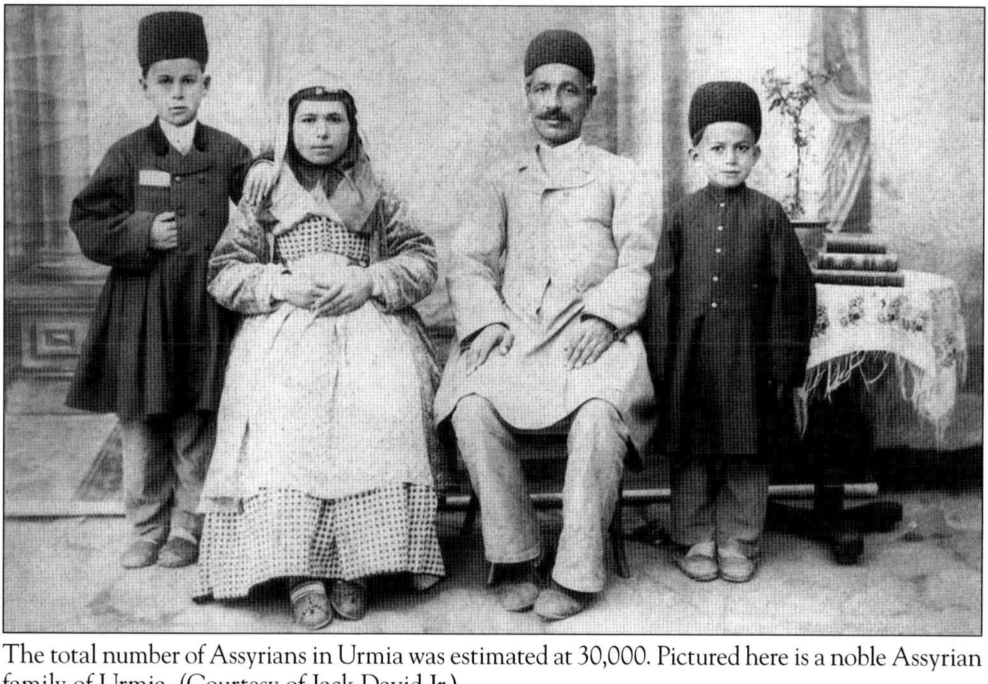

The total number of Assyrians in Urmia was estimated at 30,000. Pictured here is a noble Assyrian family of Urmia. (Courtesy of Jack David Jr.)

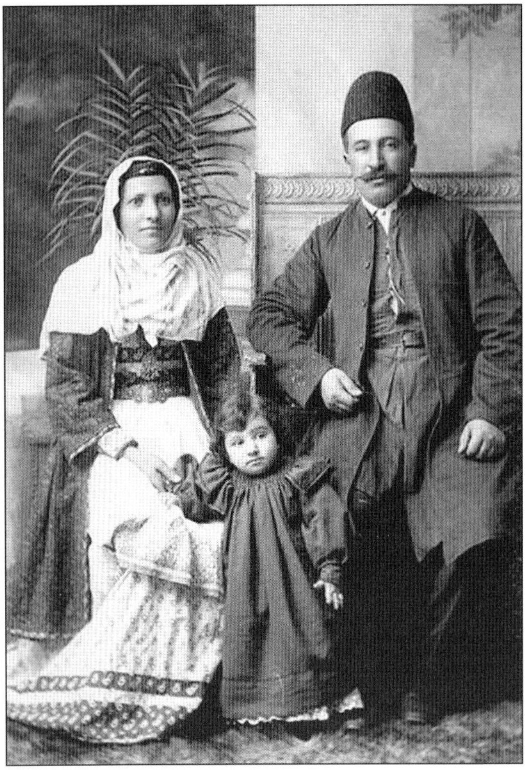

Joseph Khnanisho of the Supurgan village is seen here with his wife, Sarah, in 1899. The American-educated Assyrians, such as Joseph Khnanishu and his father, Muradkhan Khnanisho, played an important role in the Assyrian culture in Iran. He founded schools in Urmia. (Courtesy of Jack David Jr.)

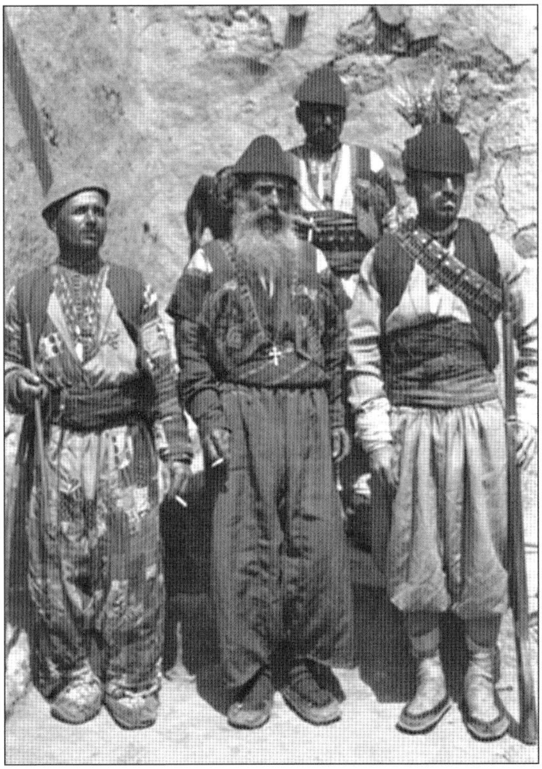

An Assyrian priest and two deacons in traditional Assyrian clothing are pictured in Jerwan (Dohuk Region, Iraq) in 1933. (Courtesy of the Oriental Institute of the University of Chicago)

This is a photograph of an unknown Chaldean man of Turkey in 1869. Chaldeans, also called East Syriacs (Assyrians), were associated with the Assyrian Church of the East formed in 1552. (Photograph by Abdullah Freres, courtesy of Library of Congress.)

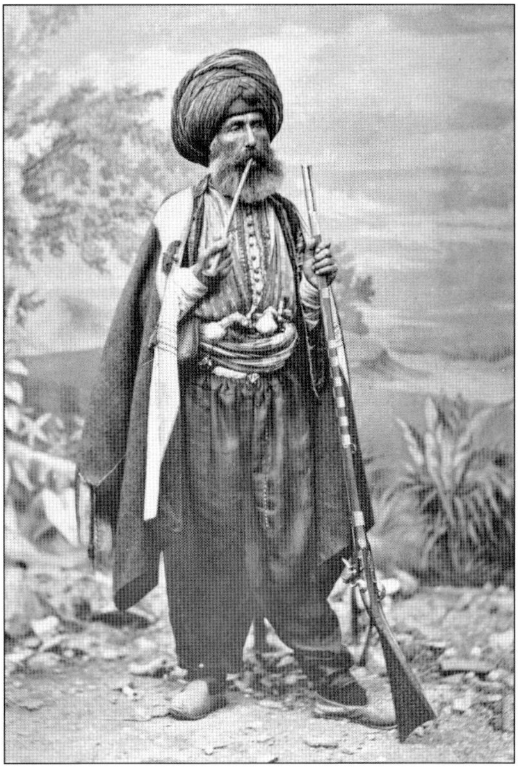

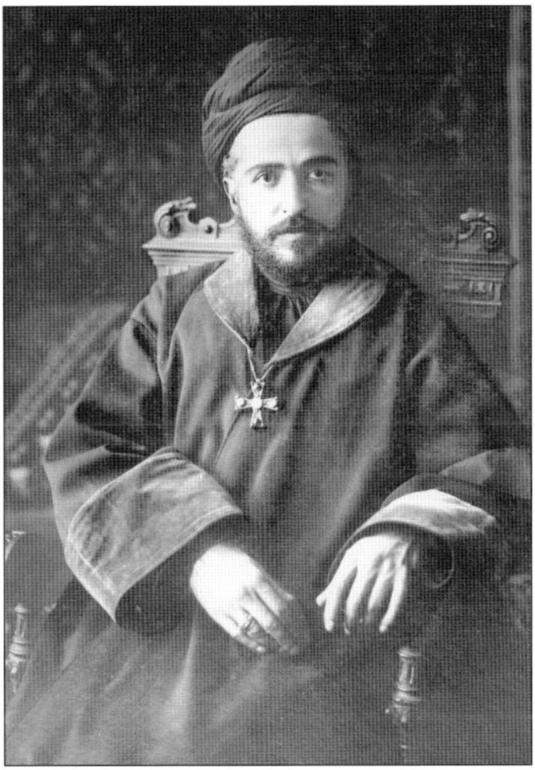

Mar Shimun XXI Benyamin (1887–1918) was a catholicos-patriarch of the Assyrian Church of the East. He was assassinated by Ismail Agha (Simko), the Kurdish chieftain, in 1918. (Courtesy of Hieromonk Stefan Sado.)

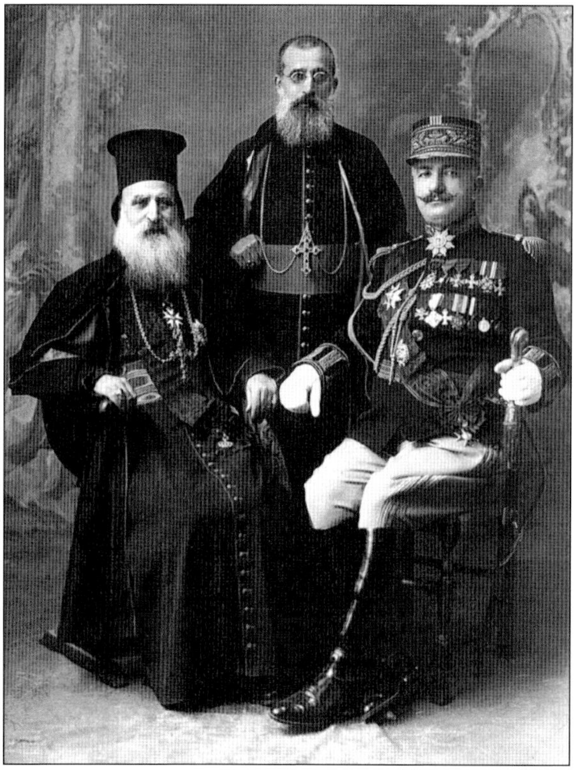

This photograph was taken during a historic meeting in Rome in 1917. From left to right are Mar Ignatius Ephrem II Rahmani, patriarch of the Syriac Catholic Church; Mar Eugen Manna, bishop of the Chaldean Catholic Church, writer, and linguist; and Agha Patros Elia, Assyrian military leader during World War I. (Courtesy of Sargon Abuna.)

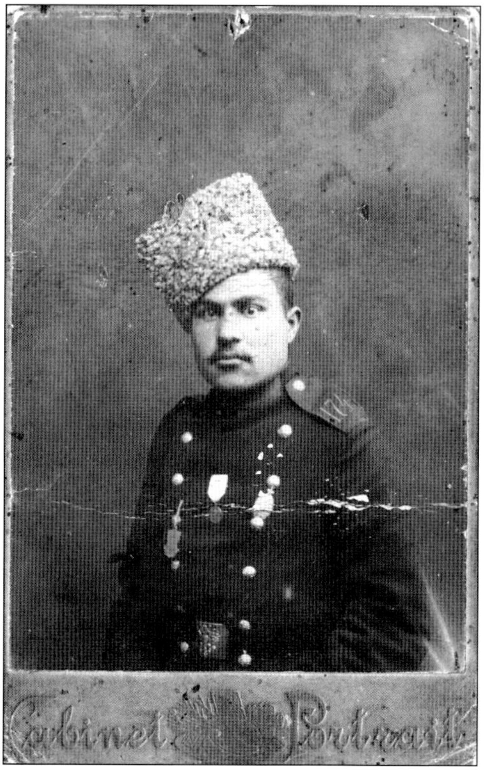

During the Russo-Turkish wars (or Ottoman-Russian wars) in the 20th century, Assyrians joined the war on the side of Russia. Pictured here around 1914–1917 is Gilyana Suleiman in a Russian World War I uniform. (Author's collection.)

Assyrians wore various kinds of uniforms throughout the years. One of the most popular, seen here, was called the Cherkesska, a uniform of the indigenous people of North Caucasus. Pictured is Asko Semionov (left), a member of the Assyro-Chaldean Battalion in the early 20th century. (Author's collection.)

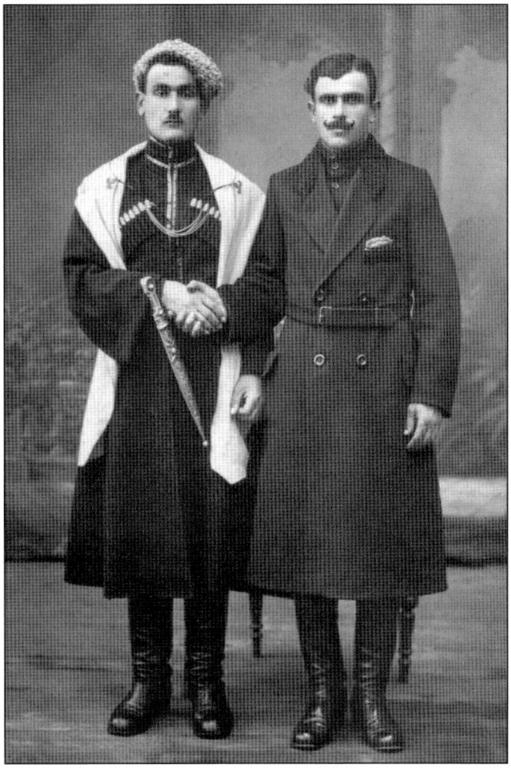

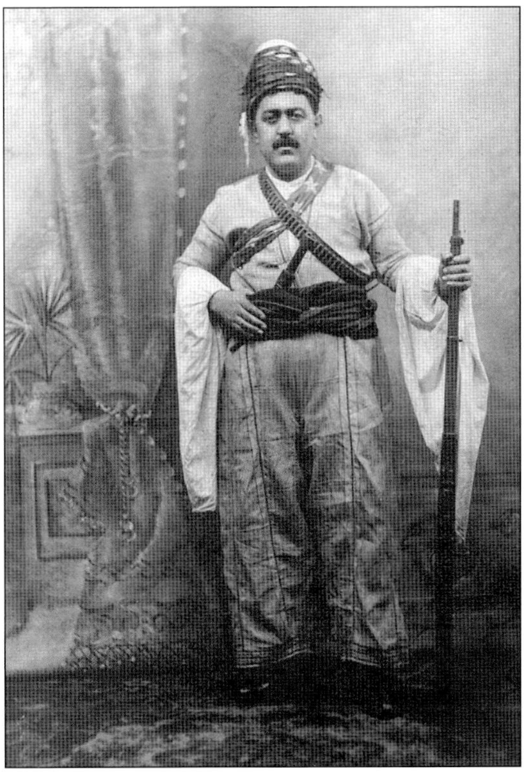

In 1914–1915, general massacres of Christians were underway. Assyrians found themselves the focus of public contempt and attacks. Assyrians started to form self-defense units in border villages, and received training and some surplus rifles from the Russian army. Pictured here is an armed Assyrian of Urmia in the 1900s. (Courtesy of Jack David Jr.)

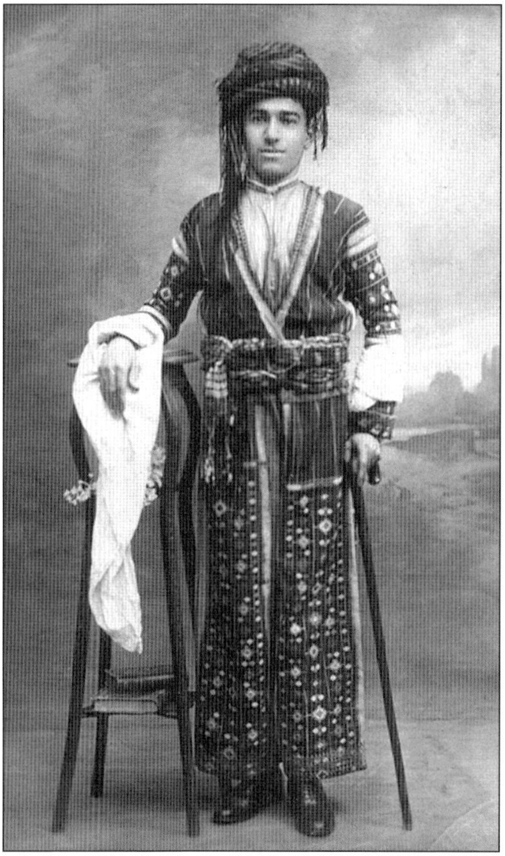

As a result of massacres in Iran and Turkey, Assyrians dispersed throughout the world, with many escaping to Europe and America. Pictured here is an Assyrian man in national costume in Marseille, France, in the early 20th century. (Courtesy of Iosif Ivanov.)

A group of Assyrian tribal chiefs and clerics are seen around 1899. From left to right are Malik Werda (father of Malik Qambar) of Zerini in Greater Jeloo; Samuel of the Mar Shimun, from Qudshanis; Mar Yosip Sargis, bishop of Jilu, Baz, Rekan, and Tkhooma. (Courtesy of Juliana Jawaro.)

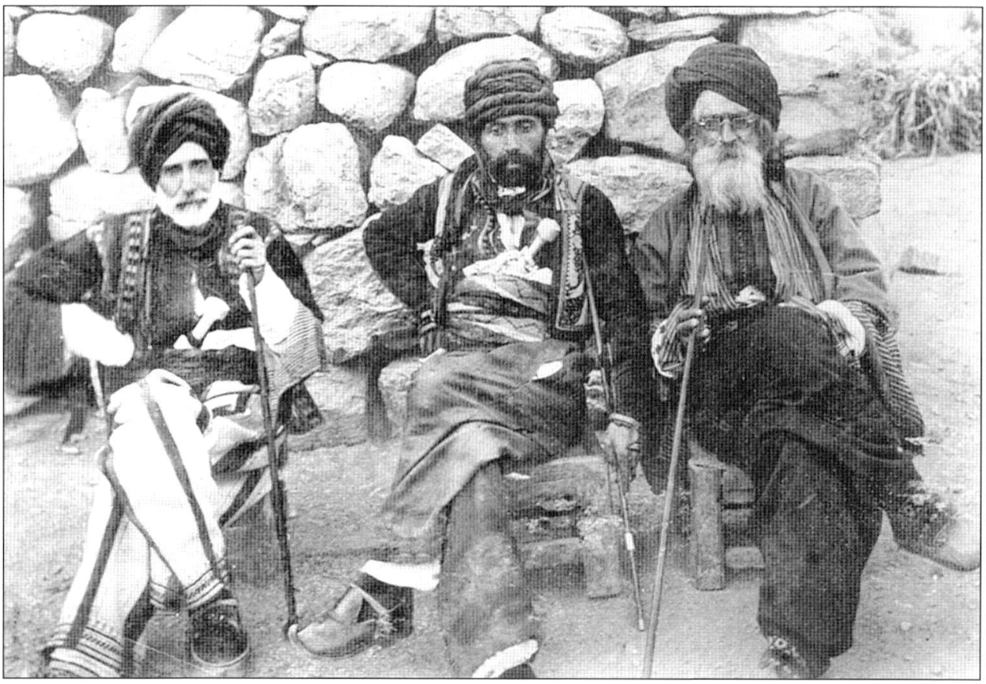

Pictured are Rab-Emma Nadirsha Gorgo (left) and Lieutenant Sargon of Mar Shumun, the brother of the Assyrian patriarch Mar Eshai Shimun XXI. They both were born in the Qudchanis village of the Hakkari district in Turkey. After settlement in Iraq, Nadirsha joined the Iraqi Levies in 1923 and was commissioned rab-emma (commander of 100). In 1979, he moved to the United States. (Courtesy of Edward Nadirsha.)

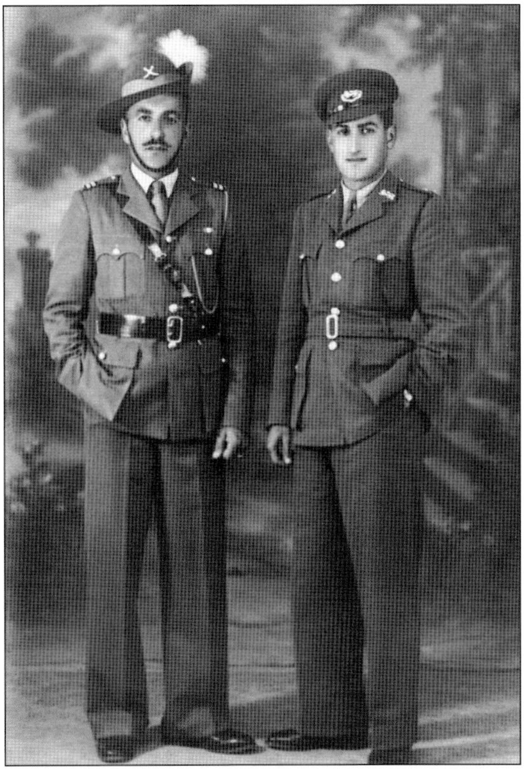

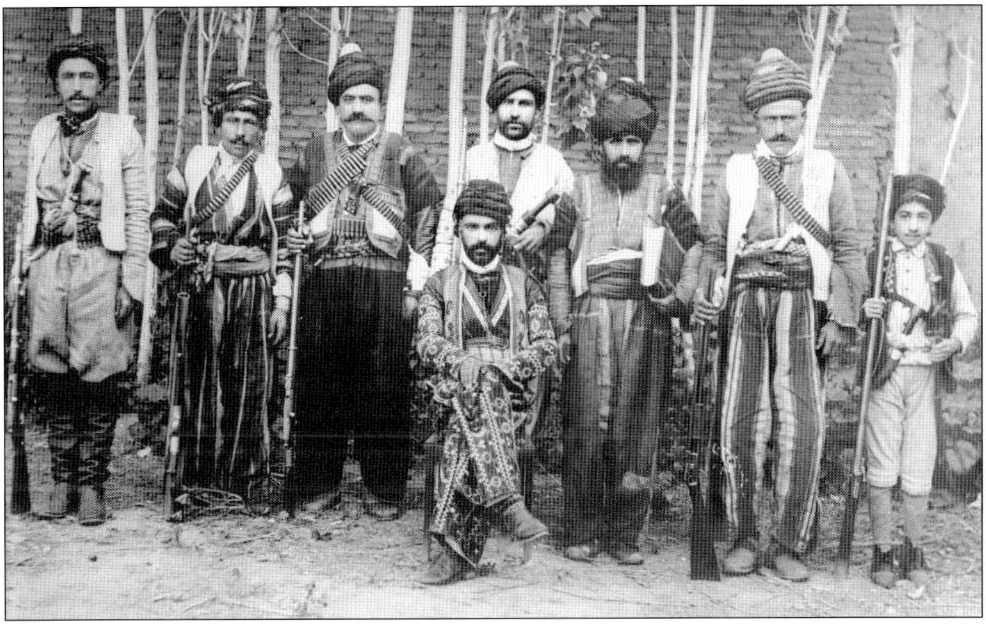

Pictured is a group of Assyrian Mountaineers from the Hakkiary region of Turkey in 1894. Seated in front is Ishai Shimon, father of patriarch Mar Benyamin Shimun. From left to right in the second row are deacon Yonan Qambar of Eiel; Rayees Yako Yukhannan of Gawar; Gullo Pikho of Qodchanis; Oukhi Qelaita of Mar Bisho; priest Taha (Ataya) of Qodchanis; Hinaro Daniel of Qodchanis; and Joseph Neesan, son of Yaroo Neesan of Shamsdinan. (Courtesy of Edward Nadirsha.)

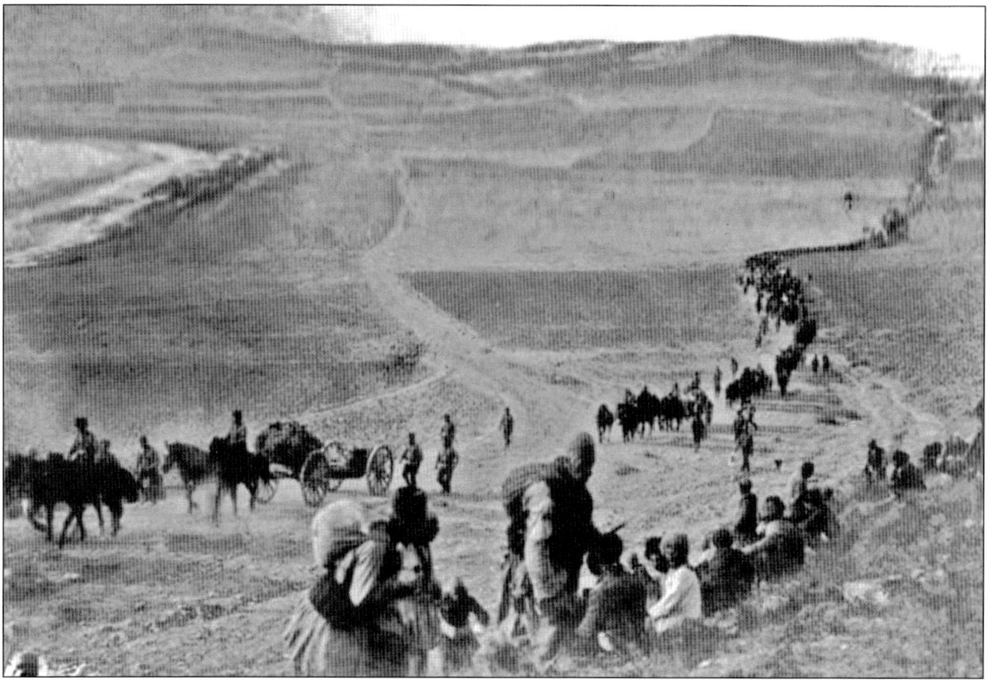

More than 500,000 people were forced to flee their homes in a time known as "the Caravan of Sorrow." They escaped to Russia, Armenia, Georgia, France, and finally, America. (Courtesy of Dr. Anahit Khosroeva.)

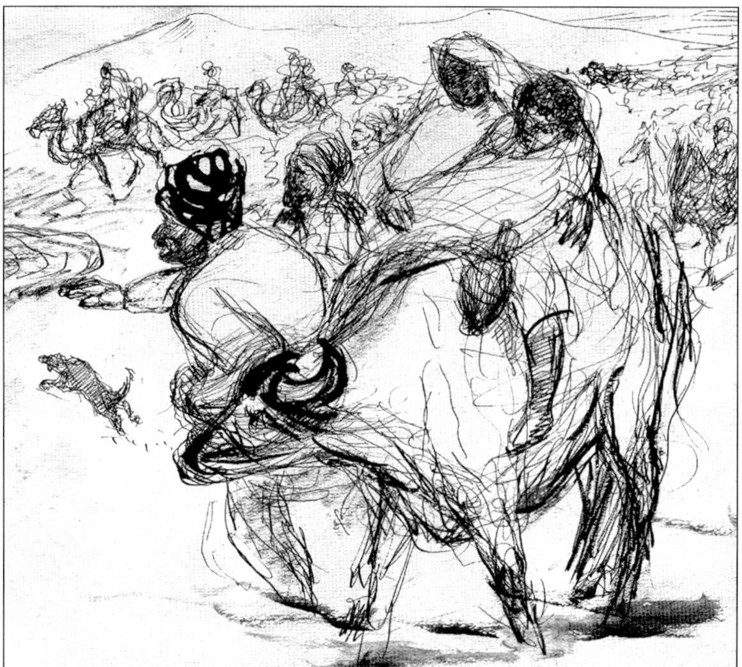

This charcoal drawing by Khnania Brindarov is titled "Assyrian Refugees." (Courtesy of Anna Brindarova.)

Two

THE ASSOCIATION'S EARLY YEARS

Assyrian immigrants settled initially in the center of their new cities in order to be near their churches and places of work. The social organizations established by Assyrians tended to have a narrow focus, uniting immigrants from a region, subregion, or even a single village. Assyrian periodicals of that time name several organizations and clubs, including the Ardishai Society, Seiri Society, Society of Geogtapa, Sepurghan Association, and others. But tribal organizations did not meet the social and political criteria of that time. In 1916, the *Assyrian American Courier* (*Izgadda*) and the *Assyrian-American Herald* stated that the Assyrians of Chicago formed a new organization called the National Association of Syrians (Syriacs) in Chicago, but it was officially registered by the secretary of state of Illinois on October 2, 1917, as the Assyrian National Association (ANA) of Chicago. The idea of unity came up when Rev. Joel Werda visited Chicago. He asked Pera S. Benjamin, assistant editor of the *Assyrian American Courier*, to work among the Assyrians for the purpose of arranging the ANA. Reverend Werda explained the advantage and benefits of national harmony in the association. The ANA was founded by Rev. Joel Werda, Pera Benjamin, and Chicago inventor David Yadgir. The first ANA president was Sargis Baaba, a successful businessman born in the village of Golpatalikhan, Iran. The Assyrian National Association of Chicago became a branch of the Assyrian National Association of America. Assyrians called it "Shotaputa" (Association) for short.

In 1917, the United States joined World War I and declared war on Germany. The United States played a major role until victory was achieved on November 11, 1918. Two thirds of the American soldiers participating in the war returned back home. Among them were many Assyrian soldiers and officers. On December 20, 1918, the association held a sumptuous banquet celebrating the victory.

In 1919, the ANA of America had branches in 15 cities of the United States, Russia, and Canada. Also in that year, Joel Werda attended Paris Peace Conference as the representative of the Assyrian people. The newly elected organization's officers rented their first office on 1805 Hammond Street in Chicago.

Twentieth-century life in Chicago was a period of great change within the Assyrian culture. For years, Assyrians placed a strong emphasis on the importance of art. It was a way to feel a sense of belonging in a strange place, understand life in a new world, and preserve the culture of the homeland. They have been involved in the local theater as writers and actors. In a broad range of styles, from lively musical folk plays to intellectual theatrical performances, the Assyrian theater was a center of community life. On April 1, 1916, the association made its first performance of *The Merchant of Venice*, written by William Shakespeare and translated to Assyrian by Jonathan S. Colia. The popular players of the Assyrian theater were Bob Bacus, Sarah Benjamin, Mary Lazar, Bob Benjamin, Joel Pera, Murassa Georges, Bob Sargis, and David Karalary. In 1929, Murassa Georges released the first recording of Assyrian songs. Sarah Benjamin was a great singer; her voice was heard not only at Assyrian parties, but also in public American rallies and celebrations.

The ANA produced theater dramas, including *Scheherazade d'Azerbaijan*, *One Thousand and One Nights*, *Molla Nasraddin*, and *Ashik Kareb*.

On November 4, 1933, the Assyrian American National Federation (AANF) was established. The Assyrian Association of Chicago was the first organization to join the AANF as an affiliate.

In 1938, the association made a plan to erect a new building. A ground-breaking ceremony was held at 2108 North Halsted Street, where the new home was to be built.

Along with school, home, and charity activities, the association was an active supporter of the Assyrian American women's movement. In 1936, the Ladies Auxiliary was established. The auxiliary was chartered to aid, assist, and promote welfare, social, and patriotic work of the association, its members, and their families.

Assyrians always had a close tie with their mother church, the Assyrian Church of the East, officially the Holy Apostolic Catholic Assyrian Church of the East. In 1940, His Holiness Mar Eshai Shimun XXI, catholicos-patriarch of the Assyrian Church of the East, visited Chicago. A testimonial banquet was given in his honor on October 20 at the new building at 2108 North Halsted Street.

During World War II, the Assyrian American Association encouraged Assyrian women to volunteer for the Red Cross as part of the war effort to help the American Army, and many did so.

In the 1950s, the association moved to a new location at 5400 North Clark Street.

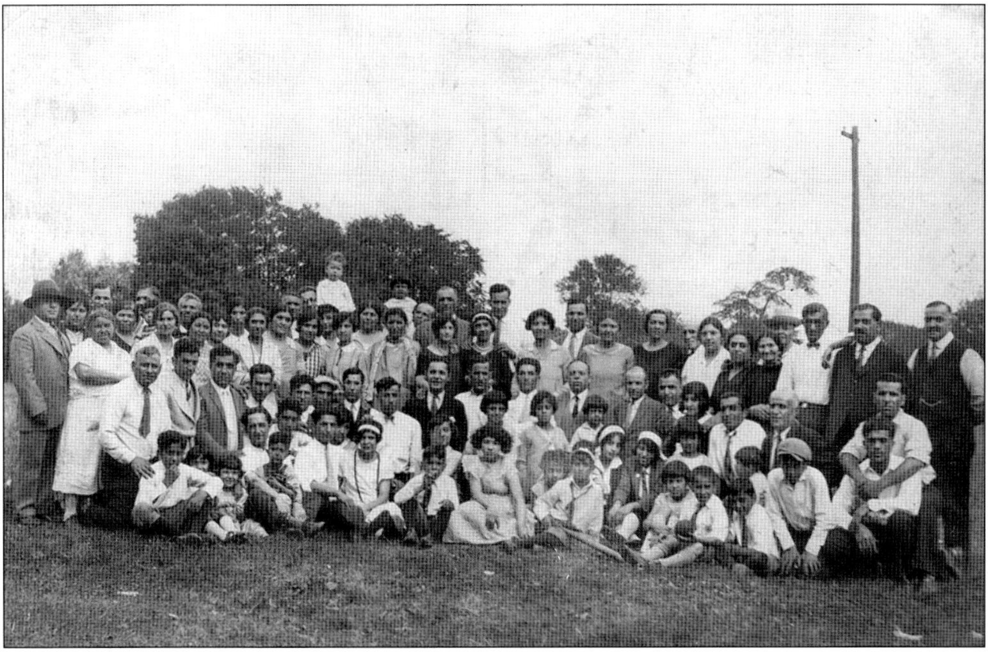

Pictured is Chicago's Little Assyria community in the 1920s. The main group of Assyrians was from Persian villages of the Urmia district: Geogtapa, Taka Ardishai, Seer, Sepurgan, Charbash, Gulpashan, and Alwach. Some of them came from the mountains of Hakkiari, Turkey, and villages such as Tkhoome, Tyare, and Jeloo. (Courtesy of Jack David Jr.)

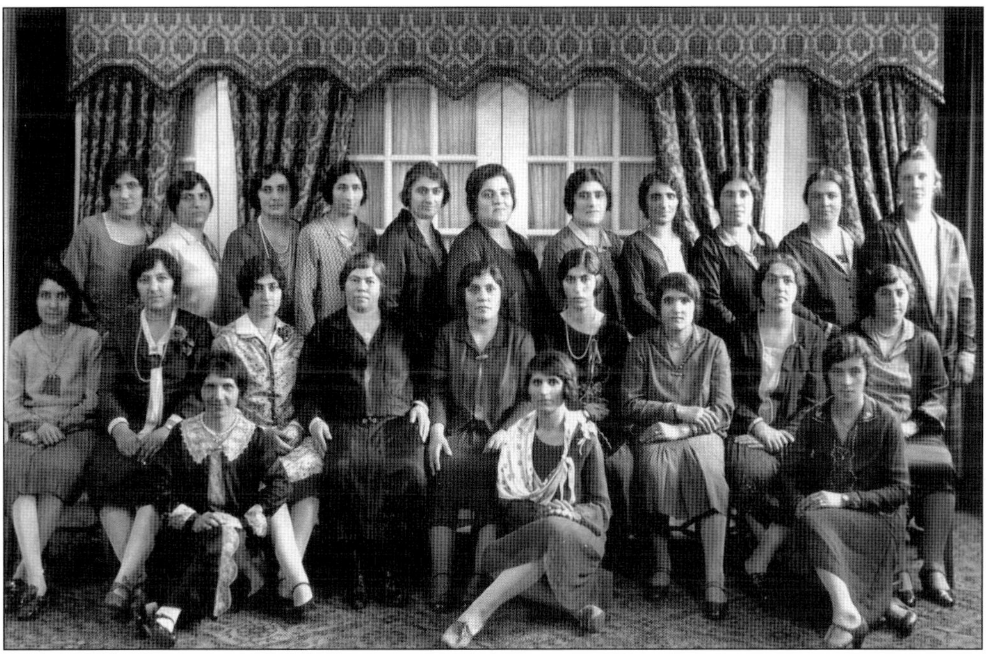

The association was an active supporter of the Assyrian American women's movement. Pictured here is an Assyrian ladies' sewing bee in the 1920s. (Courtesy of Jack David Jr.)

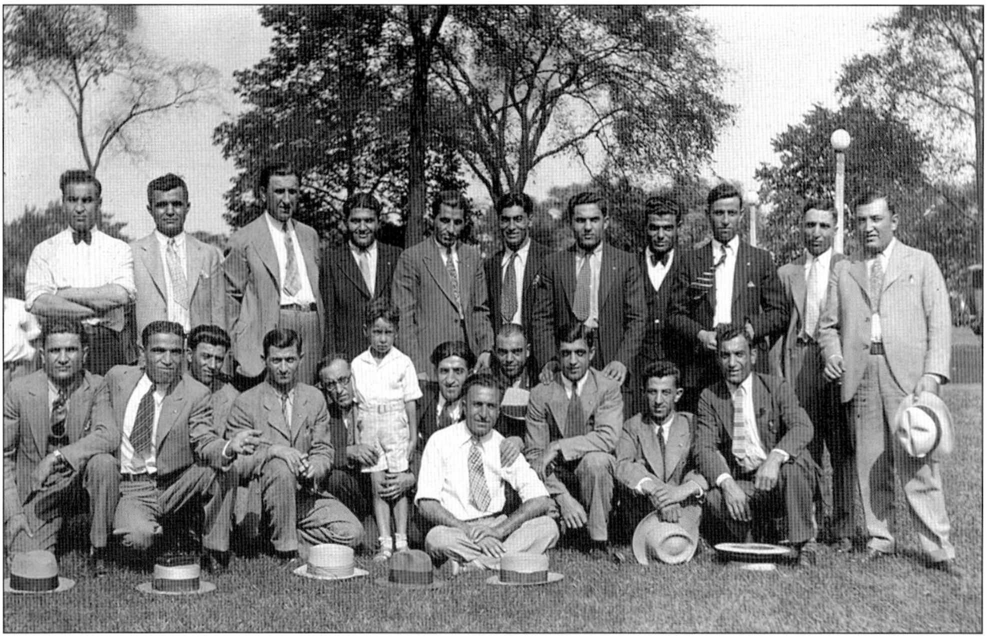

Assyrians settled around the neighborhoods of Lincoln Park and Lake View. They were employed as hotel and restaurant workers and janitors. (Courtesy of Jack David Jr.)

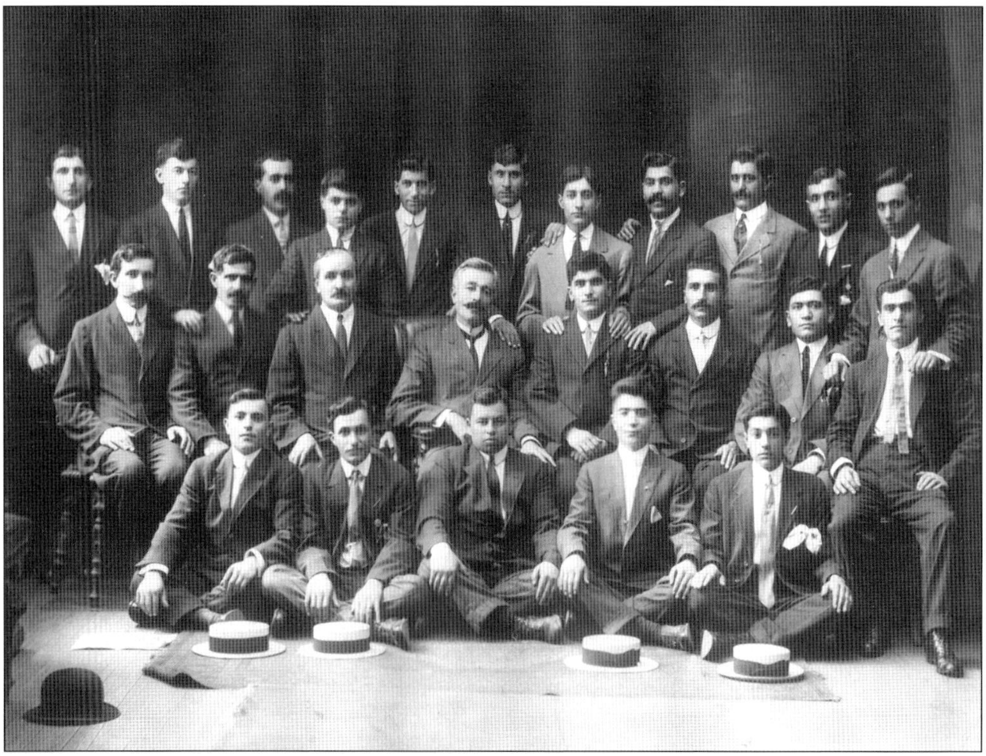

Assyrians established village-based organizations and clubs. This is the Seir Society around the 1930s. In the second row, third from left, is Joseph Nimrod, Sen. John Nimrod's father. (Courtesy of Helen Schwarten.)

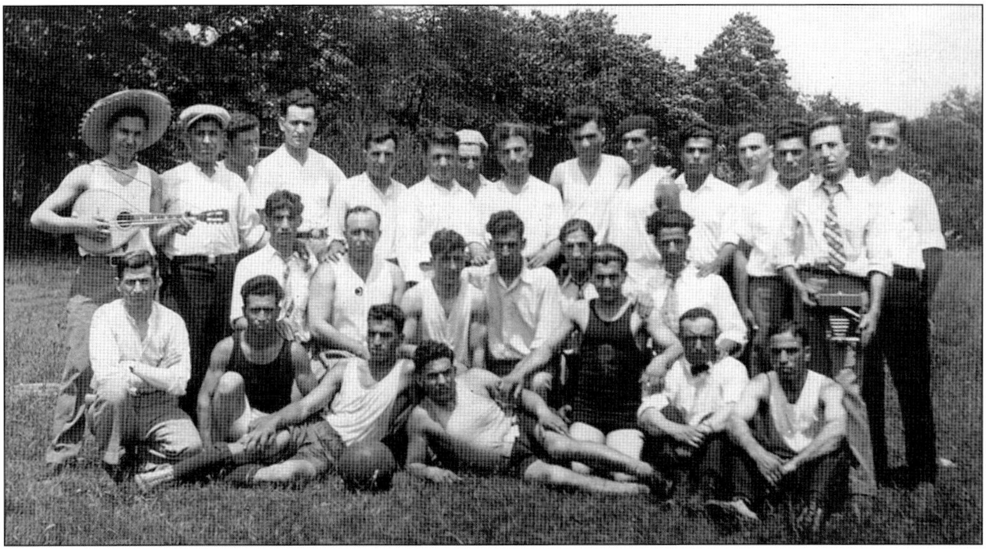

Following the 1920s, Garfield Park's field house became the center of Assyrian recreational activities. Pictured here is the Assyrian National Association picnic at Garfield Park in 1928. (Courtesy of Jack David Jr.)

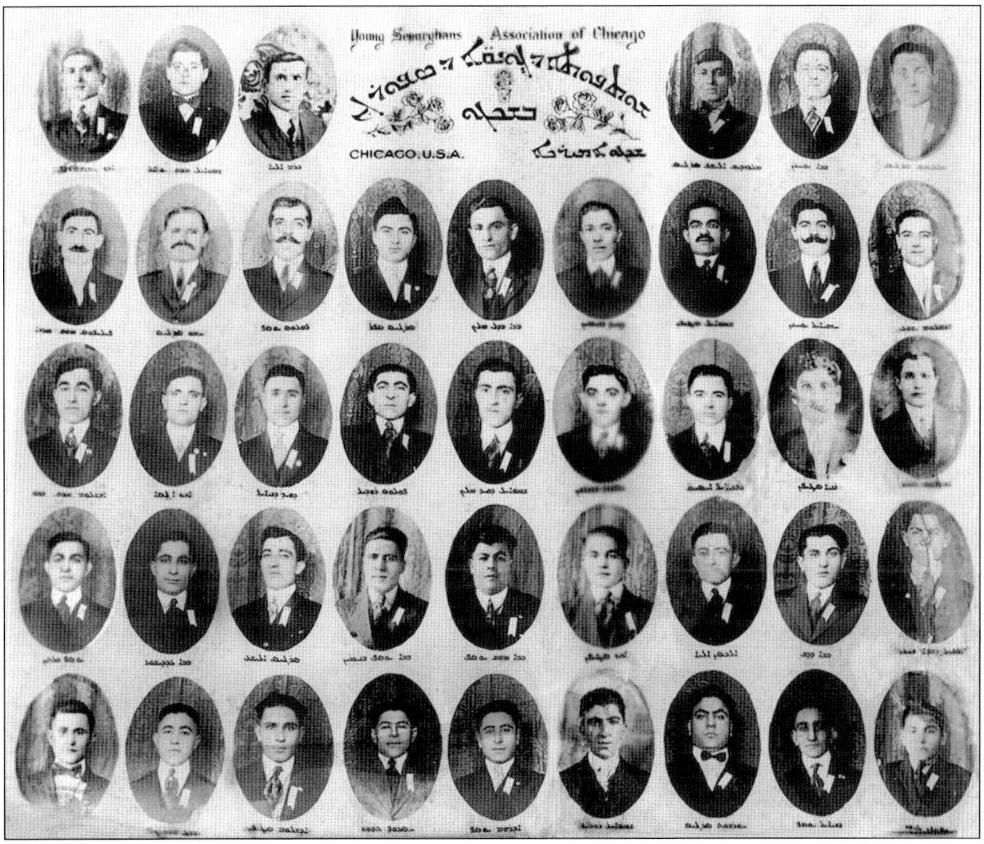

Pictured here is the Young Sepurghan Association of Chicago. The name indicates that they were natives of the village of Sepurgan in Urmia. (Courtesy of Dr. Norman Solhkhah.)

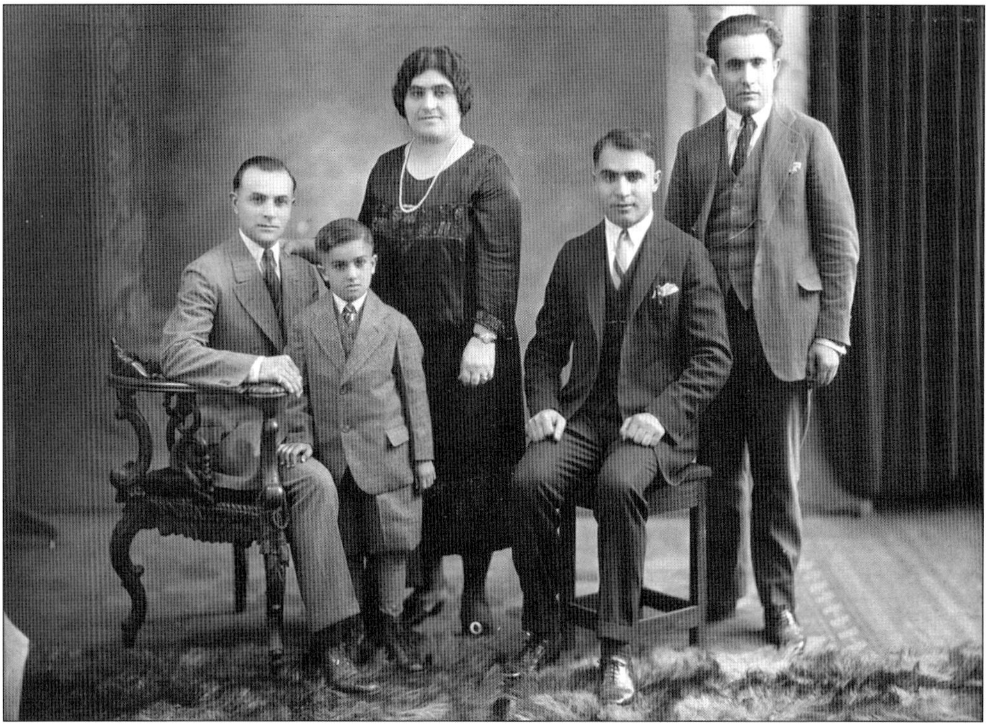

This photograph of an Assyrian family in Chicago was taken at Alitto Studio at 678 North Clark Street. From left to right are Uroo, Raymond, Carmen Baba, Khanimjon Benjamin, and Yonathan. (Courtesy of Jack David Jr.)

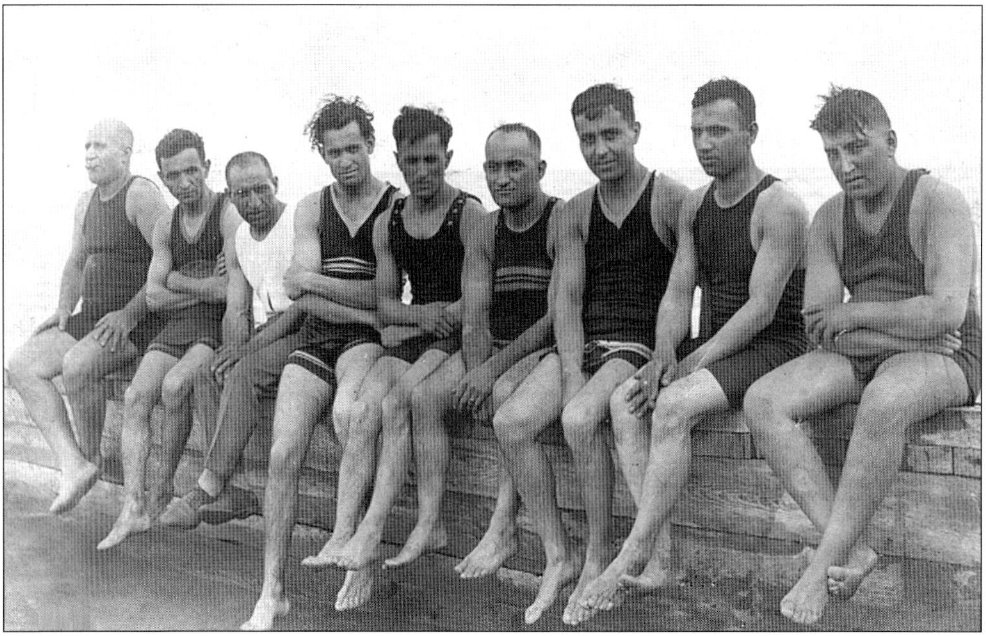

This 1928 photograph shows a picnic by Lake Michigan in Chicago. Seen here are members of the association; from left to right are John Elia, Joel Davajon, Pete Yonan, Jack David, Alex Johns, Sam Thomas, Joe Sargis, and Jimmy Adams. (Courtesy of Jack David Jr.)

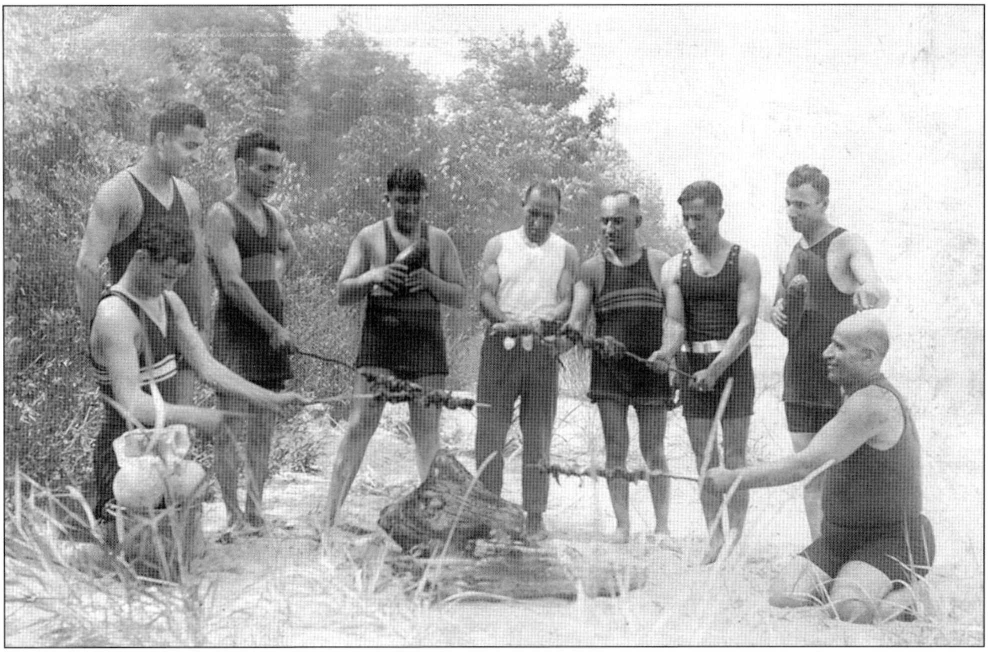

This photograph, also from 1928, was taken during a picnic by Lake Michigan in Chicago. The men are grilling traditional shish kebabs. From left to right are Jack David, Joe Davajon, Jimmy Adams, Pete Yonan, Sam Thomas, Alex Johns, Joe Sargis, and John Elia. (Courtesy of Jack David Jr.)

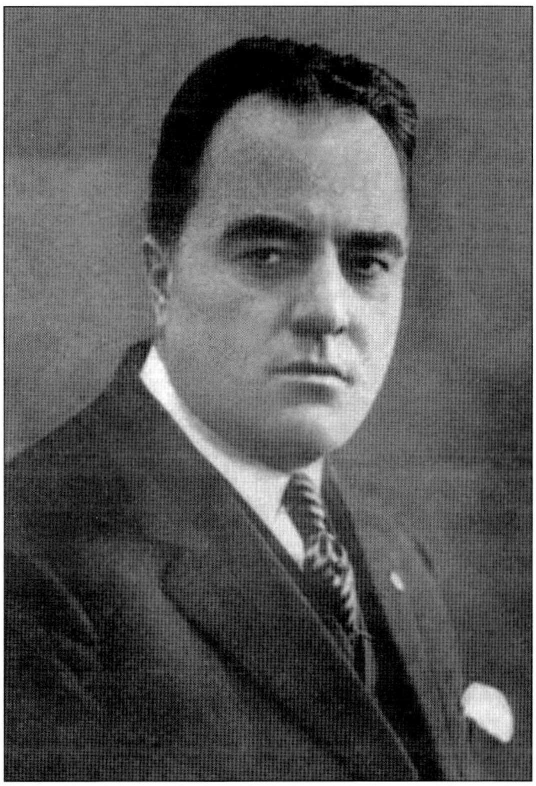

Rev. Joel Werda was one of the founders and ideologists of the Assyrian National Association of America in 1914, and co-founder of the Chicago branch in 1917. He was an editor and publisher of the *Assyrian American Courier* and the *New Assyria* magazine and author of *The Flickering Light of Asia*. Reverend Werda was an Assyrian delegate from America to the Paris Peace Conference in 1919. This image is from the *Assyrian American Courier*, vol. 2, No. 3, published in 1918. (Author's collection.)

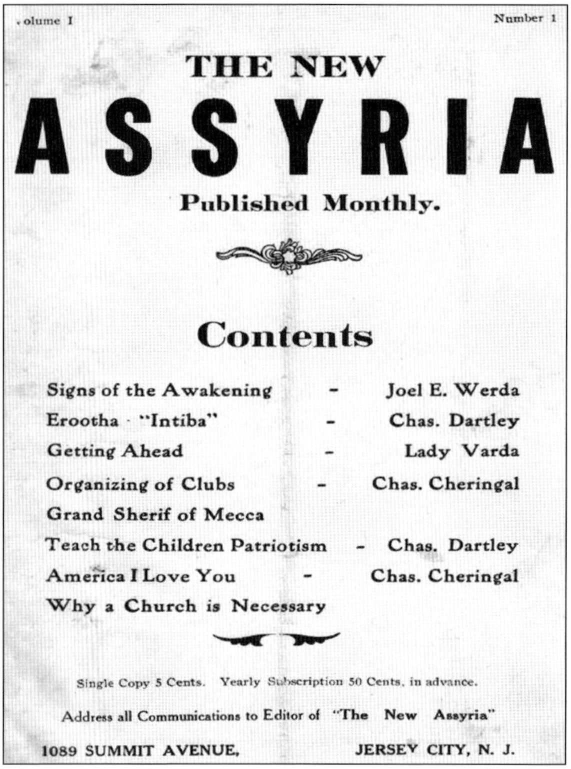

Volume I Number 1

THE NEW

ASSYRIA

Published Monthly.

Contents

Single Copy 5 Cents. Yearly Subscription 50 Cents, in advance.

Address all Communications to Editor of "The New Assyria"

1089 SUMMIT AVENUE, JERSEY CITY, N. J.

This is the cover of the first issue of *The New Assyria* magazine edited by Rev. Joel Werda. *The New Assyria* was published by the New Assyria Publishing Company in Jersey City, New Jersey, from 1916 to 1919. (Courtesy of Ashurbanipal Library, AUAF.)

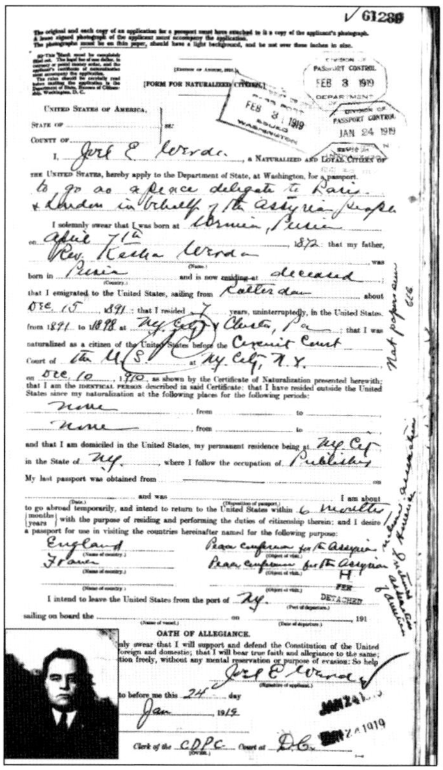

61289

[FORM FOR NATURALIZED CITIZEN.]

UNITED STATES OF AMERICA,
STATE OF
COUNTY OF

I, Joel E. Werda, a NATURALIZED AND LOYAL CITIZEN OF THE UNITED STATES, hereby apply to the Department of State, at Washington, for a passport.

I solemnly swear that I was born at Urmia, Persia on April 7th, 1872; that my father, Rev. Kasha Werda was born in Persia and is now deceased; that I emigrated to the United States, sailing from Rotterdam about Dec. 15, 1891; that I resided 7 years, uninterruptedly, in the United States, from 1891 to 1898 at NY City & Chester, Pa.; that I was naturalized as a citizen of the United States before the Circuit Court of the U.S. at NY City, N.Y. on Dec. 10, 1910, as shown by the Certificate of Naturalization presented herewith; that I am the IDENTICAL PERSON described in said Certificate; that I have resided outside the United States since my naturalization at the following places for the following periods: none

and that I am domiciled in the United States, my permanent residence being at NY City, in the State of NY, where I follow the occupation of Publishing.

My last passport was obtained from

I am about to go abroad temporarily, and intend to return to the United States within 6 months with the purpose of residing and performing the duties of citizenship therein; and I desire a passport for use in visiting the countries hereinafter named for the following purpose:

England — Peace Conference for the Assyrians
France — Peace Conference for the Assyrians

I intend to leave the United States from the port of NY

OATH OF ALLEGIANCE.

Further, I do solemnly swear that I will support and defend the Constitution of the United States against all enemies, foreign and domestic; that I will bear true faith and allegiance to the same; and that I take this obligation freely, without any mental reservation or purpose of evasion: So help me God.

Joel E. Werda

Sworn to before me this 24th day of Jan 1919.

Joel Werda applied for his US passport on January 24, 1919, to attend the Paris Peace Conference, also known as the Versailles Peace Conference. This is his passport application. (Courtesy of ancestry.com.)

The *Assyrian-American Herald* published an article by Iskhaq Murhach about the Assyrian National Association of Chicago and its goals on March 25, 2016. The first organizing meetings were held between February 1 and 26, 1916. The association was called the National Association of Syrians (Syriacs) of Chicago. (Courtesy of Ashurbanipal Library, AUAF.)

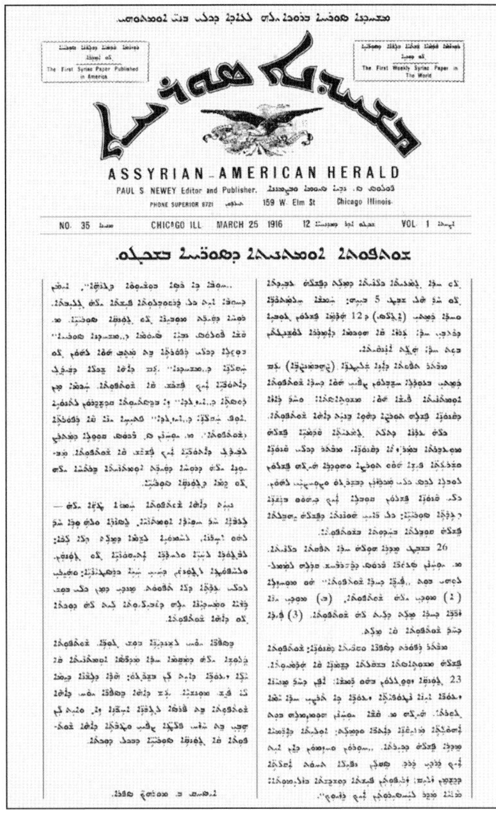

The First Syriac Paper Published in America

The First Weekly Syriac Paper in The World

ASSYRIAN-AMERICAN HERALD

PAUL S. NEWEY Editor and Publisher.

PHONE SUPERIOR 8721 159 W. Elm St Chicago Illinois.

NO. 35 CHICAGO ILL MARCH 25 1916 VOL. 1

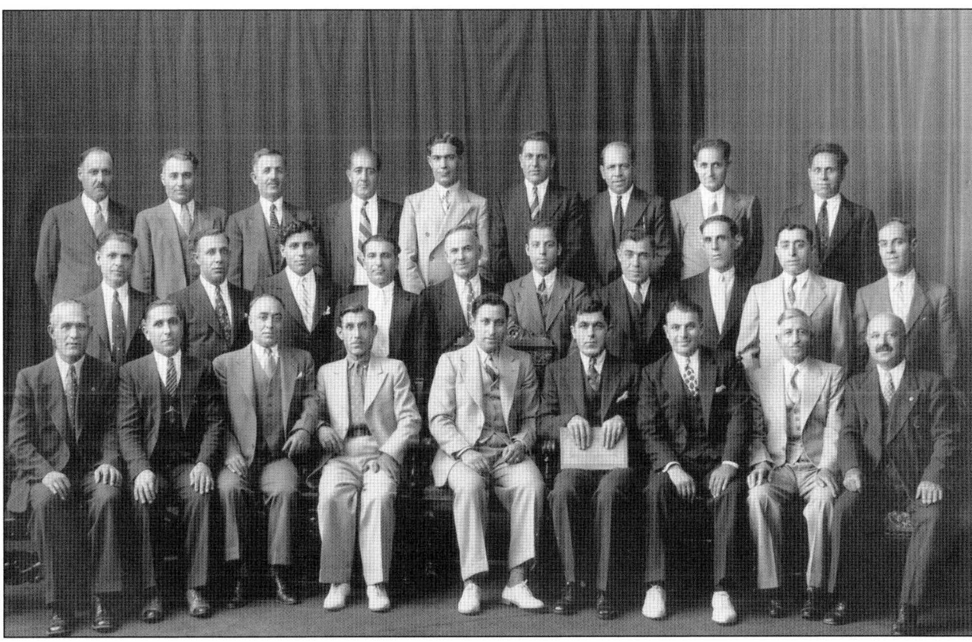

Pictured here are the founding members of the Assyrian National Association of Chicago. The association's meetings were held at 1805 Hammond Street in Chicago. (Courtesy of Jack David Jr.)

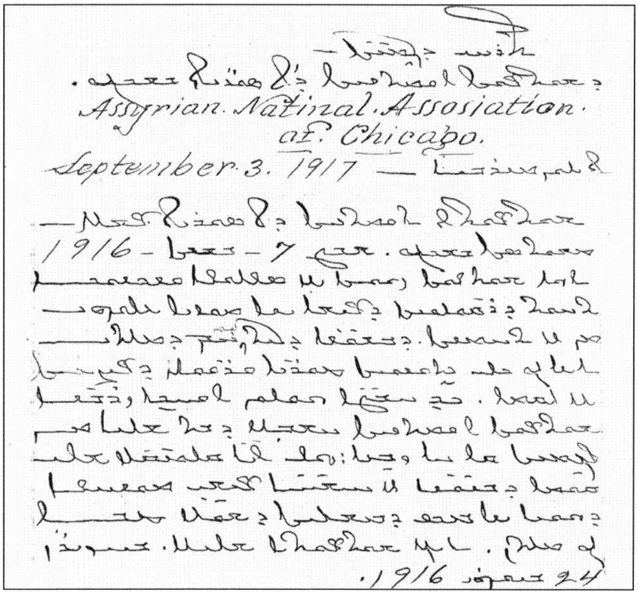

Assyrian National Association
of Chicago.
September 3. 1917 —
1916 – – 7
1916 24

This is a report of a meeting of the Assyrian National Association on September 3, 1917. This document states that the organization was founded on February 7, 1916. On June 24, 1916, for some reason, it ceased its activity and delayed registration until 1917. (Courtesy of Ashurbanipal Library, AUAF.)

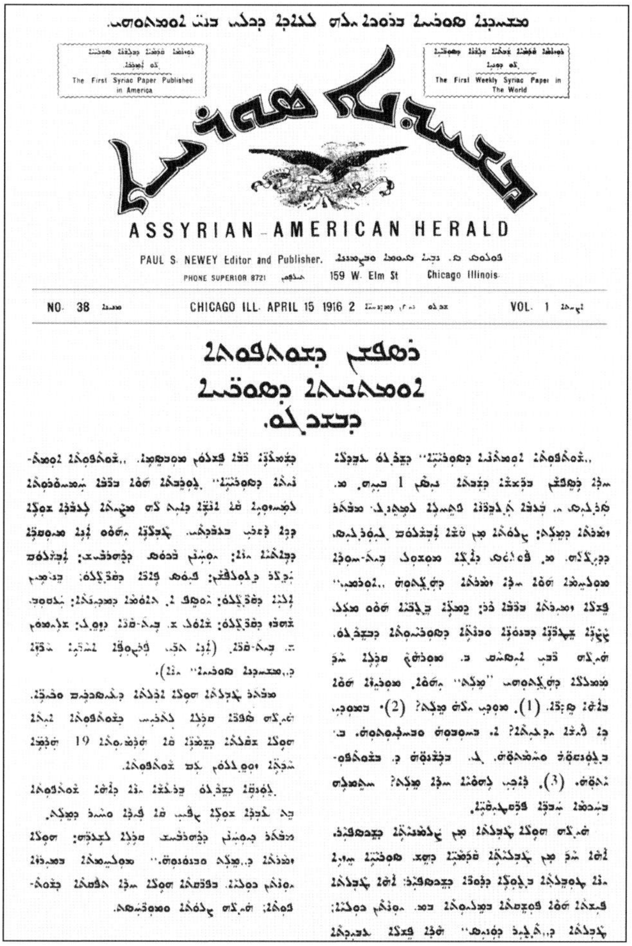

The First Syriac Paper Published in America

The First Weekly Syriac Paper in The World

ASSYRIAN-AMERICAN HERALD

PAUL S. NEWEY Editor and Publisher.

PHONE SUPERIOR 8721 159 W. Elm St Chicago Illinois.

NO. 38 CHICAGO ILL. APRIL 15 1916 2 VOL. 1

The *Assyrian-American Herald* of April 15, 2016, featured an article about the association's first reception meeting, where Sargis Baaba was elected president. (Courtesy of Ashurbanipal Library, AUAF.)

This is the certificate of registration for the Assyrian National Association and the Assyrian American Protective League issued by the Illinois secretary of state on October 2, 1917, and October 20, 1917. (Courtesy of Jack David Jr.)

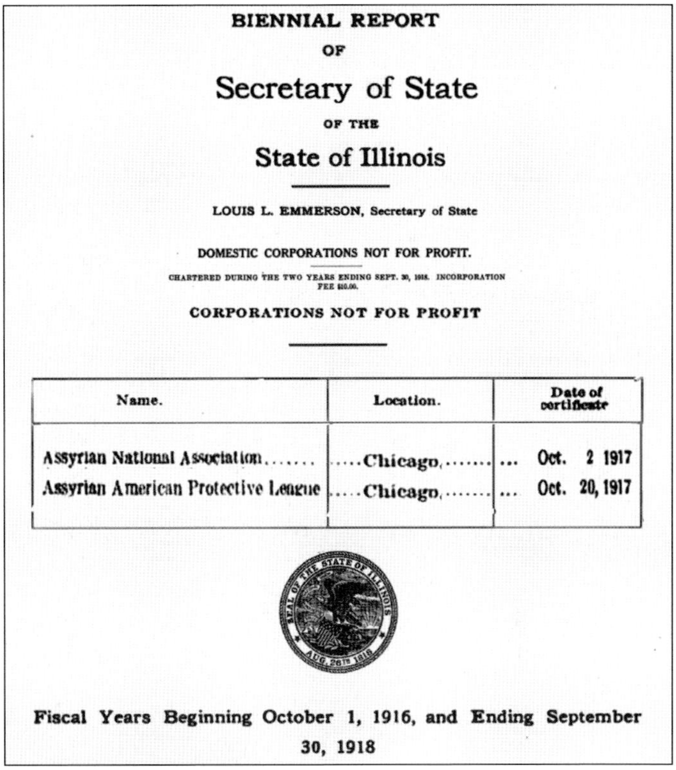

BIENNIAL REPORT

OF

Secretary of State

OF THE

State of Illinois

LOUIS L. EMMERSON, Secretary of State

DOMESTIC CORPORATIONS NOT FOR PROFIT.

CHARTERED DURING THE TWO YEARS ENDING SEPT. 30, 1918. INCORPORATION FEE $10.00.

CORPORATIONS NOT FOR PROFIT

Name.	Location.	Date of certificate
Assyrian National Association.......	....Chicago,.......	... Oct. 2 1917
Assyrian American Protective League	....Chicago,.......	... Oct. 20, 1917

Fiscal Years Beginning October 1, 1916, and Ending September 30, 1918

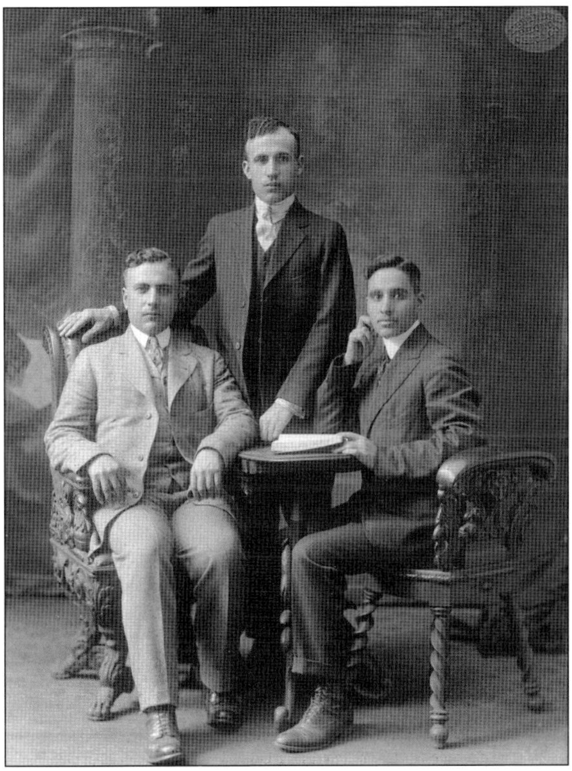

These are the founders of the Assyrian National Association of Chicago. From left to right are Pera Benjamin, David Yadgar, and Sargis Baaba. (Courtesy of Jack David Jr.)

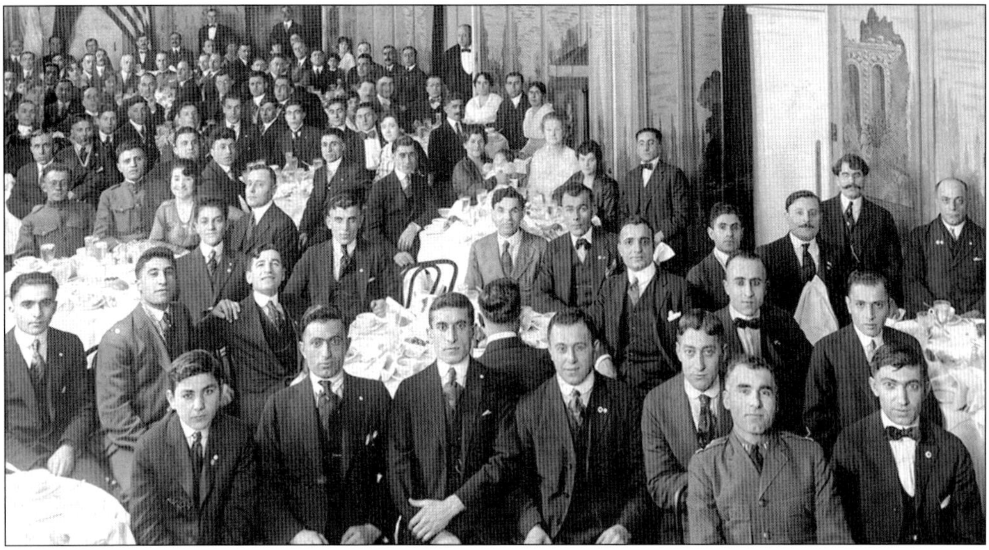

On December 20, 1918, AAAC held a banquet celebrating the end of World War I. More than 150 members of the Assyrian National Association came to a victory banquet at the Morison Hotel. Rev. Joel Werda of New York attended the dinner. (Courtesy of Jack David Jr.)

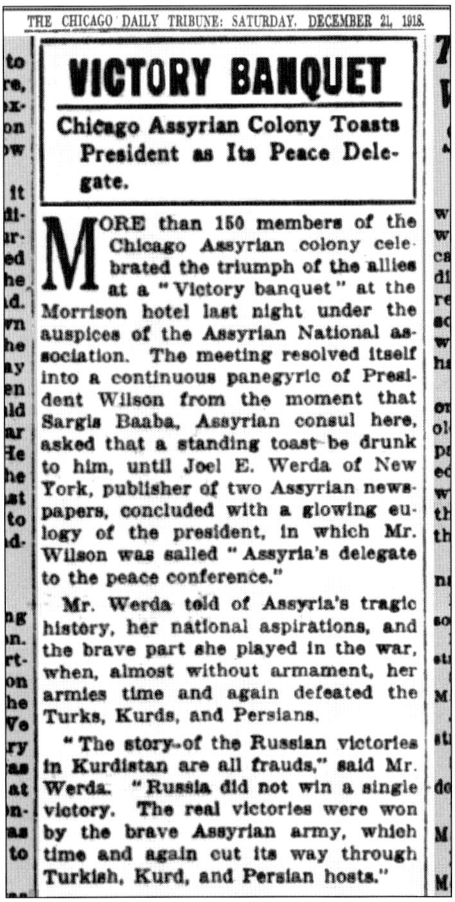

THE CHICAGO DAILY TRIBUNE: SATURDAY, DECEMBER 21, 1918.

VICTORY BANQUET

Chicago Assyrian Colony Toasts President as Its Peace Delegate.

MORE than 150 members of the Chicago Assyrian colony celebrated the triumph of the allies at a "Victory banquet" at the Morrison hotel last night under the auspices of the Assyrian National association. The meeting resolved itself into a continuous panegyric of President Wilson from the moment that Sargis Baaba, Assyrian consul here, asked that a standing toast be drunk to him, until Joel E. Werda of New York, publisher of two Assyrian newspapers, concluded with a glowing eulogy of the president, in which Mr. Wilson was salled "Assyria's delegate to the peace conference."

Mr. Werda told of Assyria's tragic history, her national aspirations, and the brave part she played in the war, when, almost without armament, her armies time and again defeated the Turks, Kurds, and Persians.

"The story of the Russian victories in Kurdistan are all frauds," said Mr. Werda. "Russia did not win a single victory. The real victories were won by the brave Assyrian army, which time and again cut its way through Turkish, Kurd, and Persian hosts."

This *Chicago Daily Tribune* article is about the victory banquet on December 21, 1918. The article reads, "More than 150 members of the Chicago Assyrian colony celebrated the triumph of the allies at a 'Victory banquet' at the Morison Hotel under the auspices of the Assyrian National Association. The meeting resolved itself into a continuous panegyric of President Wilson from the moment that Sargis Baaba, Assyrian consul here, asked that a standing toast be drunk to him, until Joel E. Werda of New York, concluded with a glowing eulogy of the president, in which Mr. Wilson was called 'Assyria's delegate to the Peace Conference.' " (Courtesy of the Chicago Historical Society archives.)

Ilyas Awshalum (left) was a member of the Assyrian National Association. He joined the US Army to become an American citizen. (Courtesy of Jack David Jr.)

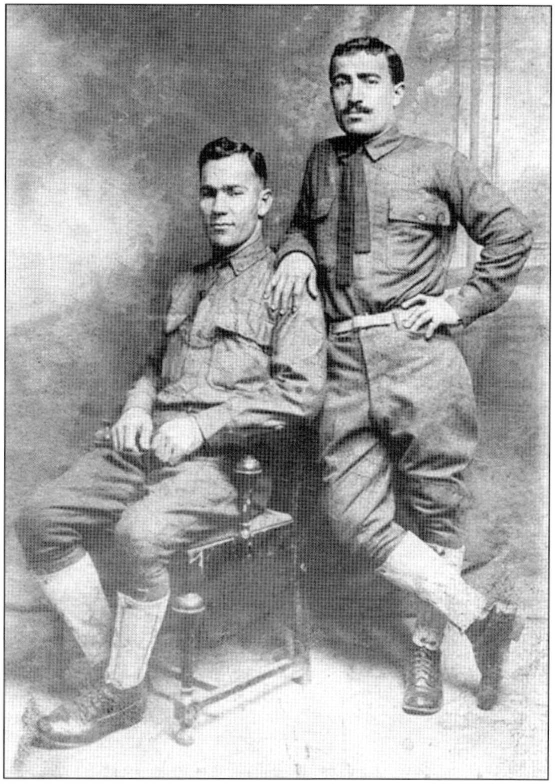

Seen here is the grave of Usta (master) Wasil Pera (1871–1939) from the Ardishai village in Urmia. He was a member of the Assyrian National Association and is buried at Elmwood Cemetery in River Grove, Illinois. (Author's collection.)

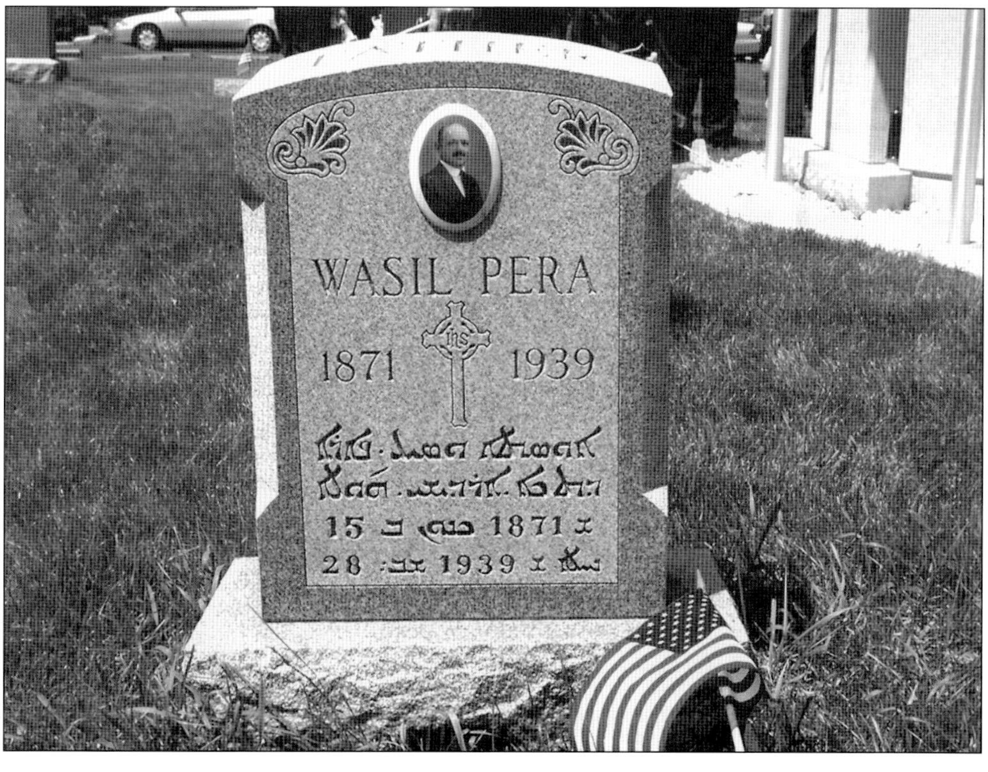

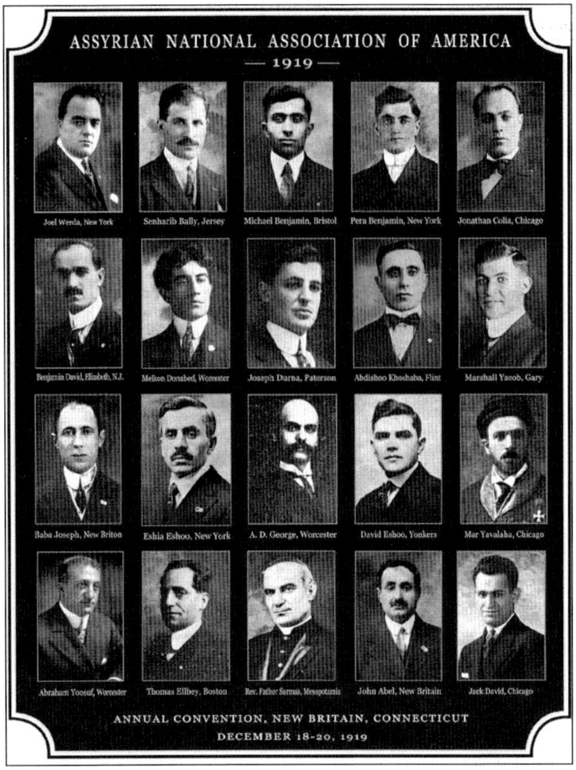

This is the program from the annual convention of the Assyrian National Association of America in Connecticut in 1919. (Courtesy of Ashurbanipal Library, AUAF.)

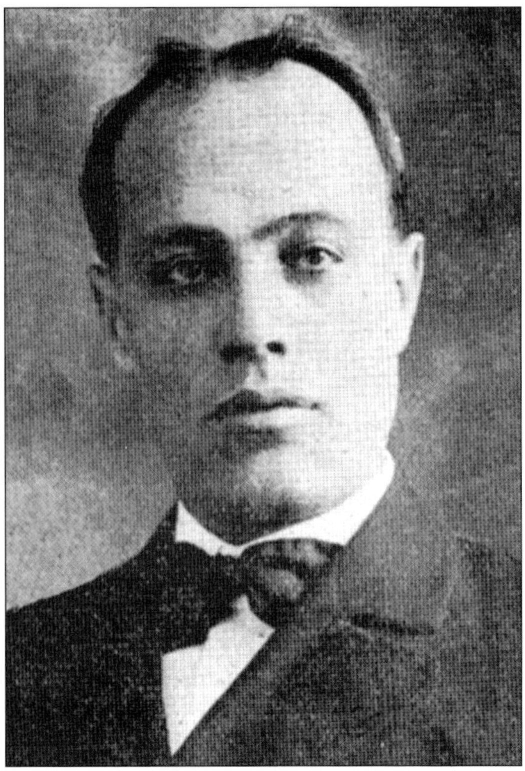

Jonathan Shimon Colia (1877–1940) was president of the Assyrian National Association of Chicago from 1919 to 1920. He was an official delegate from Chicago at the annual convention of the Assyrian National Association of America in New Britain, Connecticut, in 1919. He was appointed chairman of the convention in Chicago in 1920. In 1933, he was secretary of the Council of Assyrian Societies. He lived at 36 East Walton Place in Chicago and made his career as a cabinet maker, upholsterer, and window dresser. (Courtesy of Jack David Jr.)

Dr. Freydun Atouraya was president of the National Assyrian Council of Georgia Republic, a poet, and a politician in Tiflis in 1919. He sent several letters to the association; in one of them, he asked Joel Werda to be a representative of the Russian Assyrians in the Paris Peace Conference. (Courtesy of the Assyrian National Council of Illinois.)

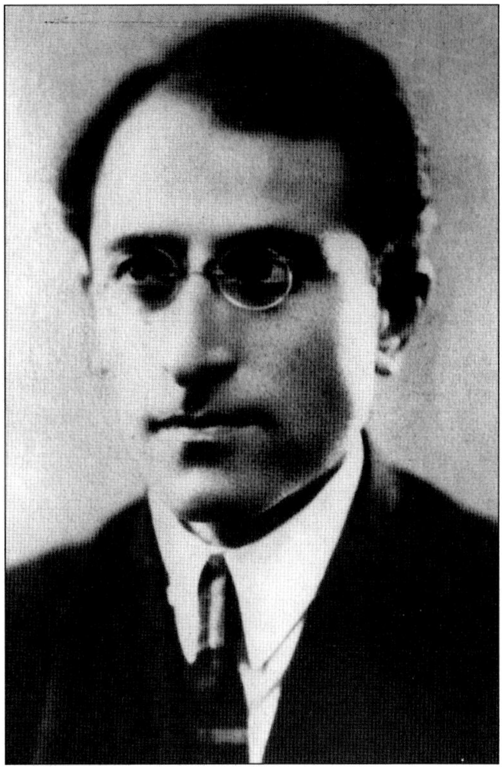

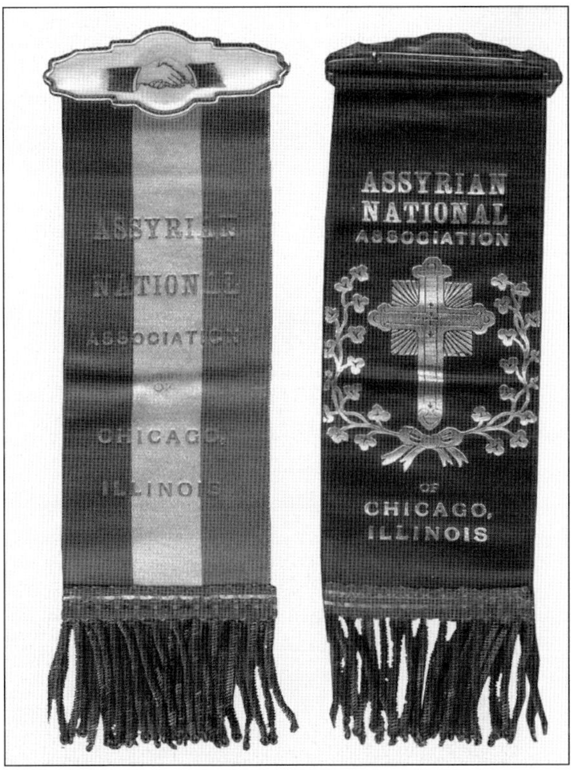

This silk ribbon was worn by members of the Assyrian National Association of Chicago. (Courtesy of Jack David Jr.)

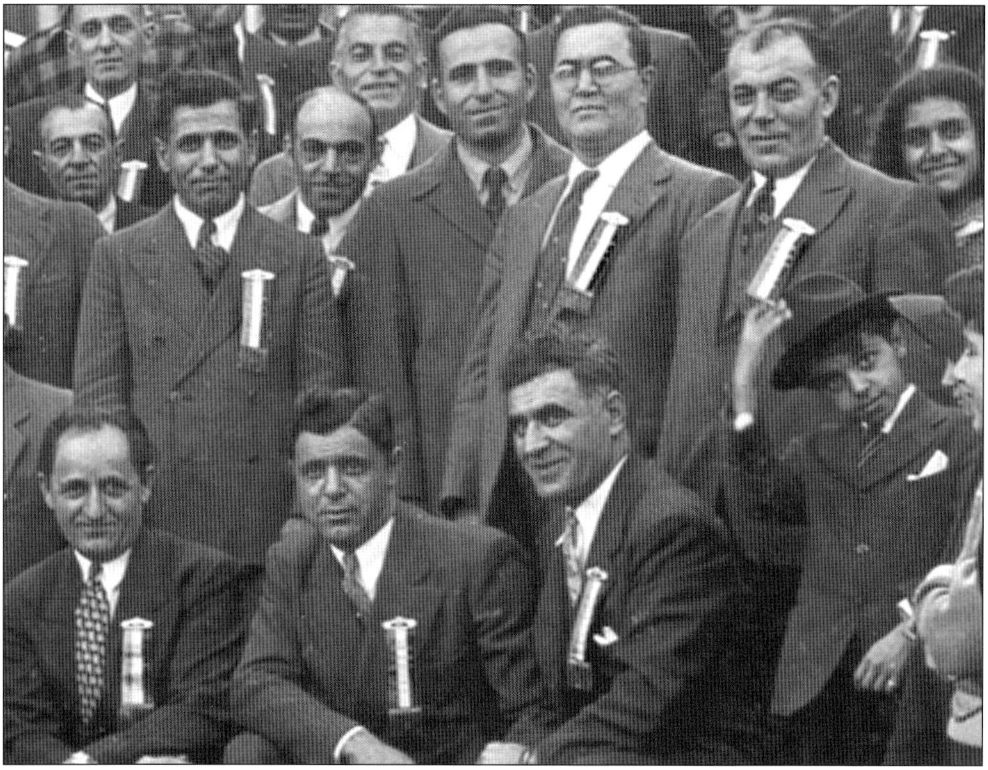

ANA members wear their ribbons pinned on their chests. This ribbon was made for the association members and was used for many public meetings. (Courtesy of Jack David Jr.)

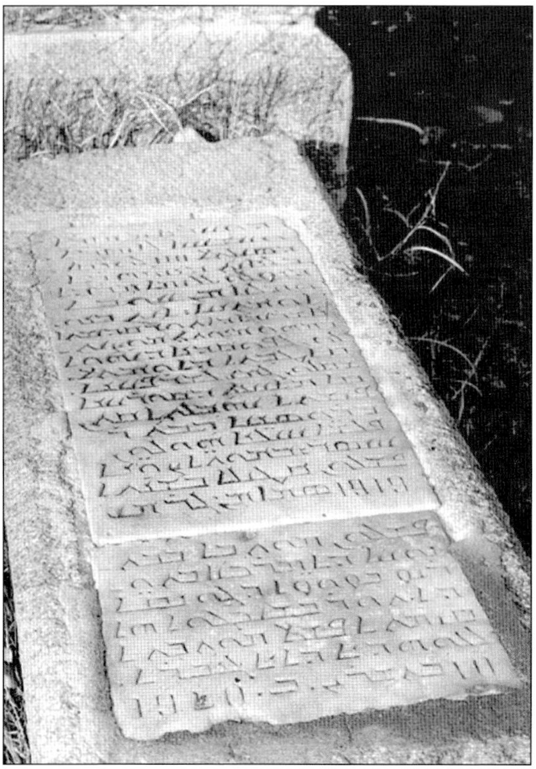

This is a picture of a monument erected in honor of Assyrians who were captured in Sharafkhaneh in Iran and mutilated by Islamic extremists in 1919. The fragments of their bones were gathered and buried in the Christian cemetery in Tabriz. The association members sent a note of protest to the Iranian government. Members of the ANA raised money for a monument dedicated to Assyrian martyrs and erected it in Tabriz, Iran, in 1920. (Courtesy of Dr. Norman Solhkhah.)

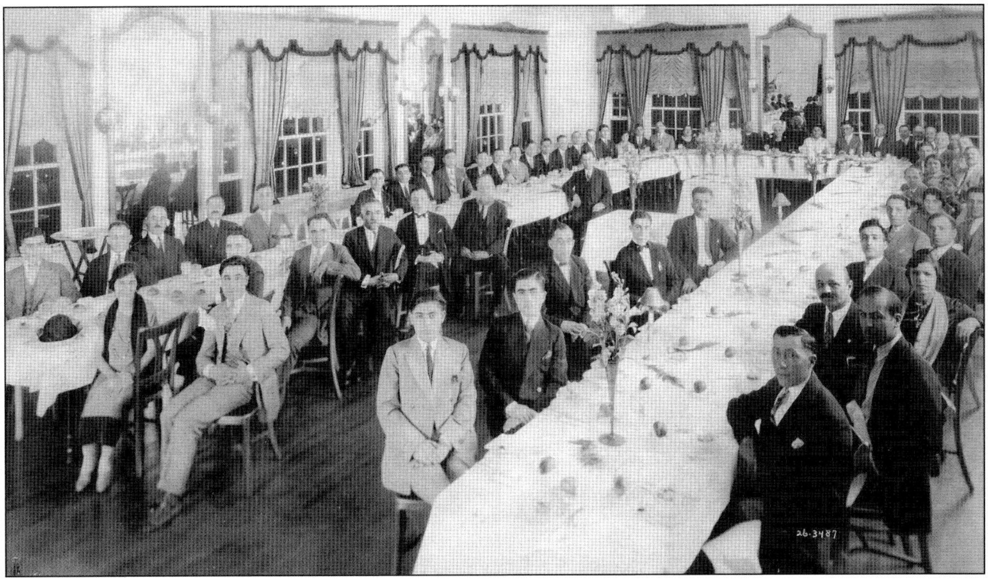

In 1926, Lady Surma Khanum, the sister of the Catholic patriarch of the Assyrian Church of the East, Mar Shimun Benyamin, came to the United States. She visited California and Illinois. Pictured here is a banquet in her honor organized by ANA members. (Courtesy of Jack David Jr.)

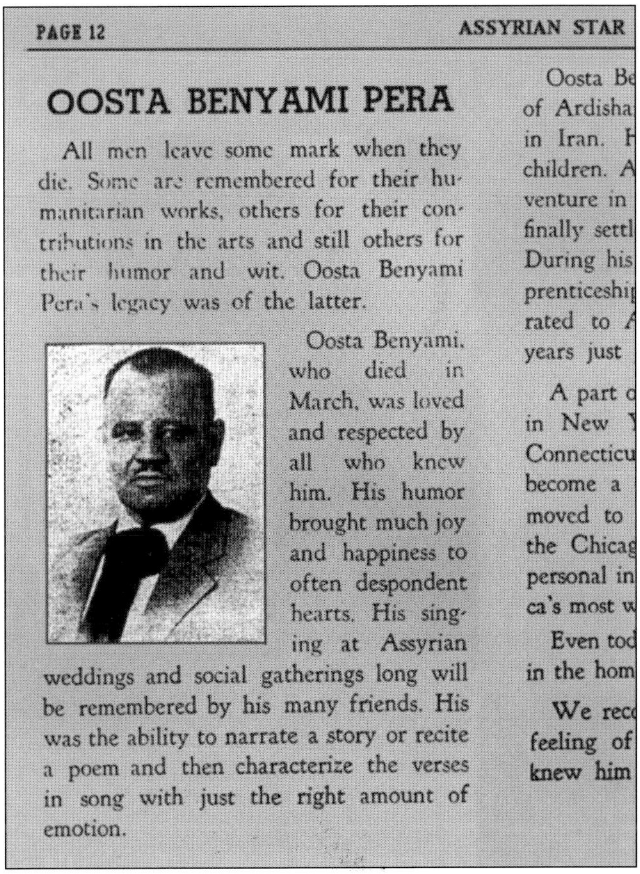

PAGE 12 ASSYRIAN STAR

OOSTA BENYAMI PERA

All men leave some mark when they die. Some are remembered for their humanitarian works, others for their contributions in the arts and still others for their humor and wit. Oosta Benyami Pera's legacy was of the latter.

Oosta Benyami, who died in March, was loved and respected by all who knew him. His humor brought much joy and happiness to often despondent hearts. His singing at Assyrian weddings and social gatherings long will be remembered by his many friends. His was the ability to narrate a story or recite a poem and then characterize the verses in song with just the right amount of emotion.

Oosta Be
of Ardisha
in Iran. H
children. A
venture in
finally settl
During his
prenticeshi
rated to A
years just

A part o
in New Y
Connecticu
become a
moved to
the Chicag
personal in
ca's most w

Even tod
in the hom

We rec
feeling of
knew him

This is the obituary of Benyami Pera in the *Assyrian Star*. Pera, called Oosta (Master) Benyami, was born in the village of Ardishai, Iran. He was a folklore narrator and singer at association events and many social gatherings. He studied painting at the Chicago Art Institute. One of his famous paintings was *Assyrian Levy Officer*. (Courtesy of Ashurbanipal Library, AUAF.)

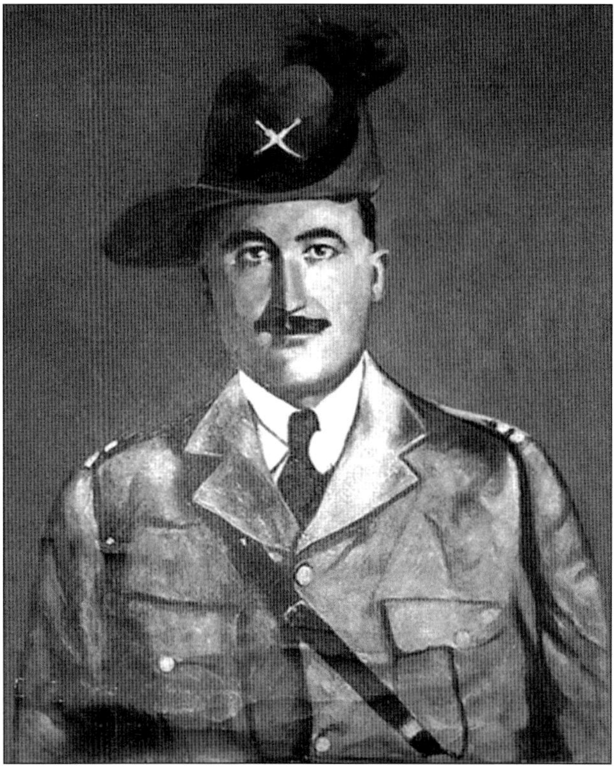

This is *Assyrian Levy Officer*, painted by Oosta Benyamin Pera. The picture hung for many years on the association's wall. This painting was missing for more than 60 years but was recently found by Younadam Youkhana, who presented it to AUAF in 2012. (Courtesy of Jack David Jr.)

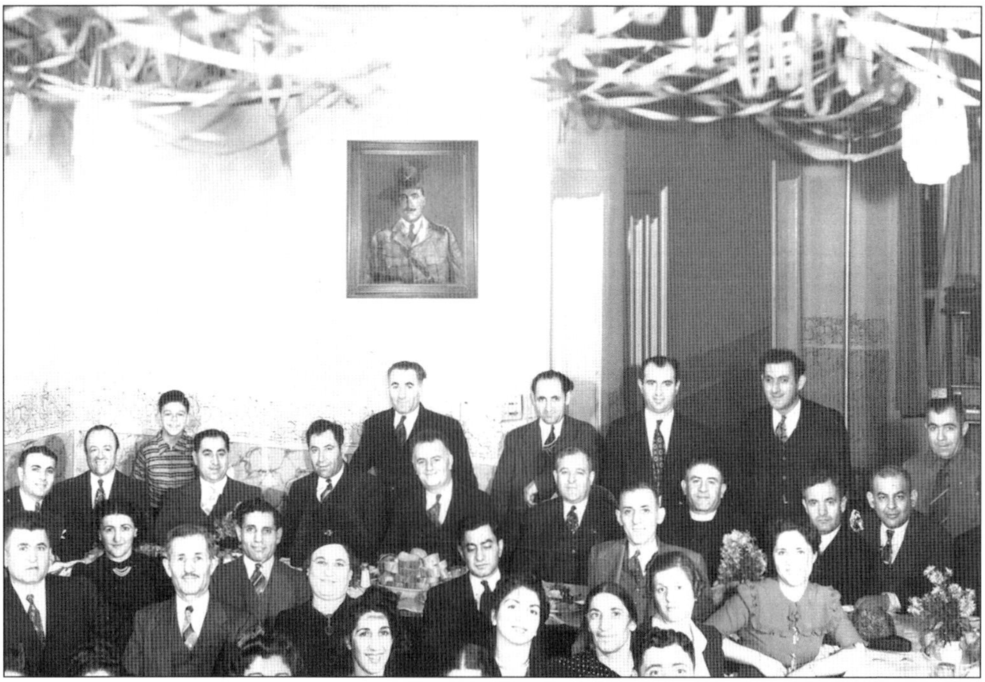

Pictured are association members at a meeting. The first meeting was held at 1805 Hammond Street in Chicago. On the wall is the painting *Assyrian Levy Officer* by Oosta Benyamin Pera. (Courtesy of Jack David Jr.)

This is a rare S.E. James vinyl record of Assyrian songs by Louise Joseph (soprano) and Sargis Khanbaba. Sargis played banjo (*tar*) and released three records. (Author's collection.)

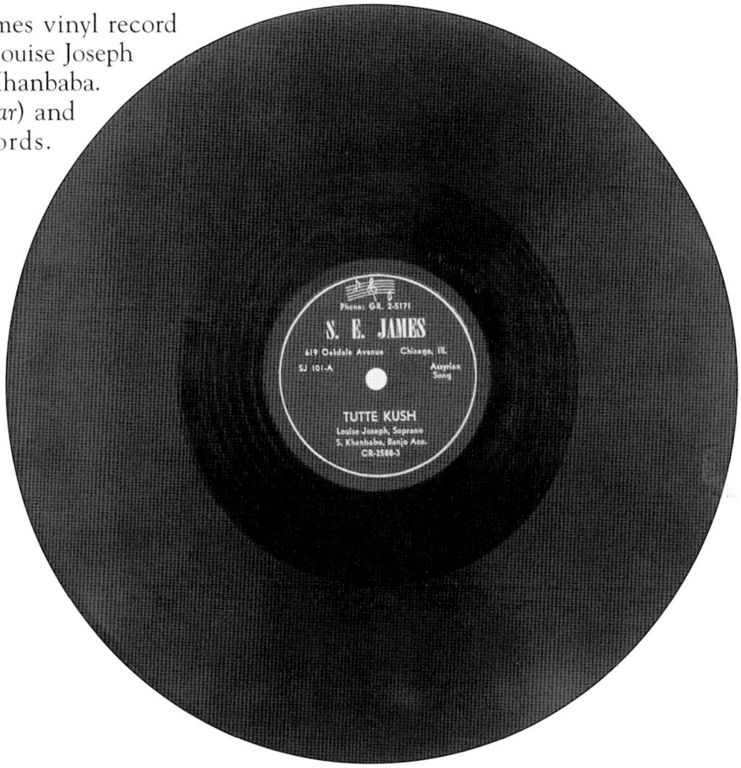

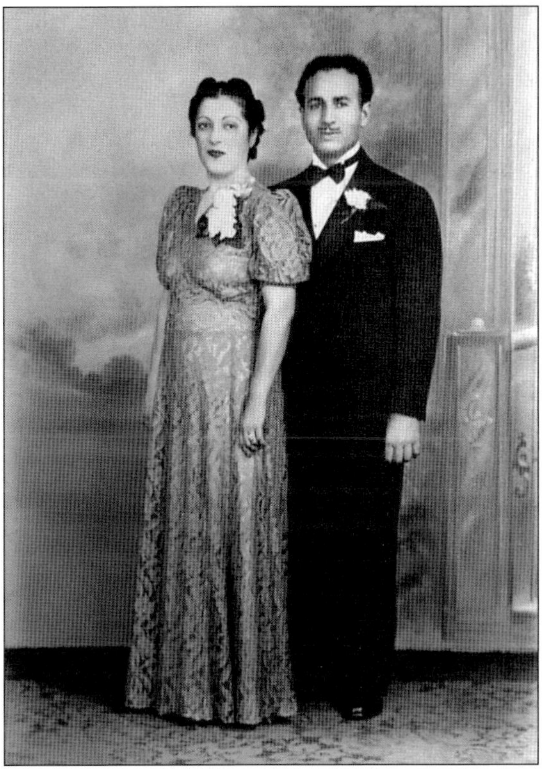

Pictured here are Mary and Joseph "Smiling Joe" Werda. Mary Werda was the first president of the Ladies Auxiliary in 1937. (Courtesy of Jack David Jr.)

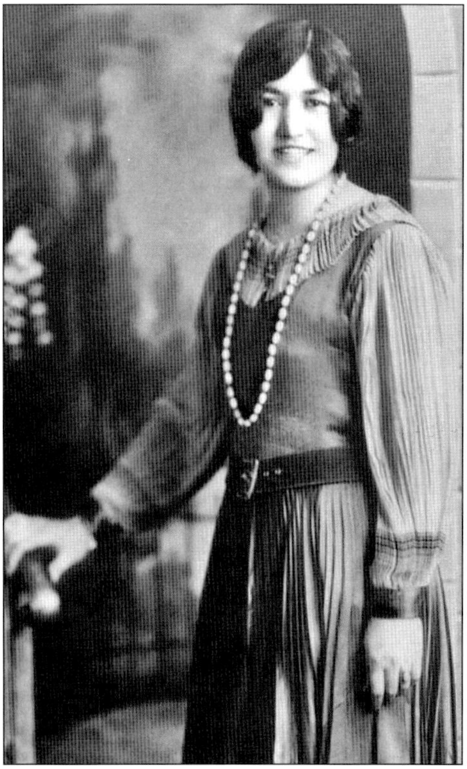

Murassa Georges (Urshan) was an Assyrian American Association activist. She was a famous soprano in the United States. In 1956, she became the Ladies Auxiliary president and served six terms. She signed a contract with Columbia Records to record 12 songs. (Courtesy of Abboud Zeitoune.)

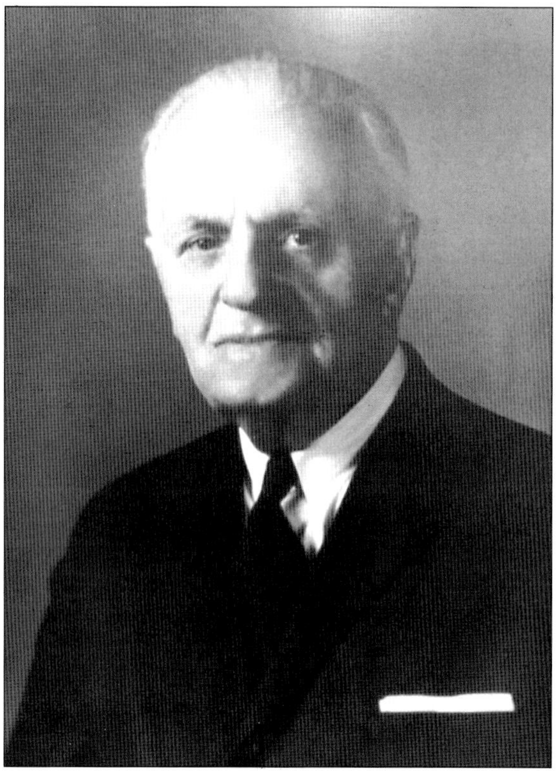

David Jacobs (1893–1971) was a founder of the Assyrian American Association in Yonkers, New York, in 1914 and one of the founders and the treasurer of the Assyrian American Federation. In 1970, he was named the Assyrian Man of the Year by the AAF. In 1971, he won $250,000 from the state lottery. (Courtesy of Fred Sarkiso.)

Paul Pera Georges was born in Gavilan, Iran, on August 15, 1905. At 12 years of age, he met and fell in love with the 11-year-old Murassa, a future famous singer, in the Baqubah refugee camp. They married on July 20, 1930, in Crown Point, Indiana. In 1975, he became president of the AAAC. (Courtesy of Gary E. Daniels.)

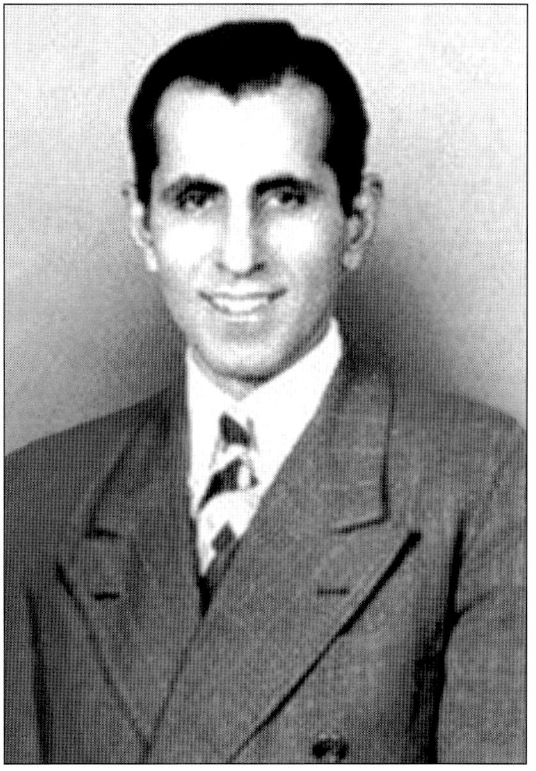

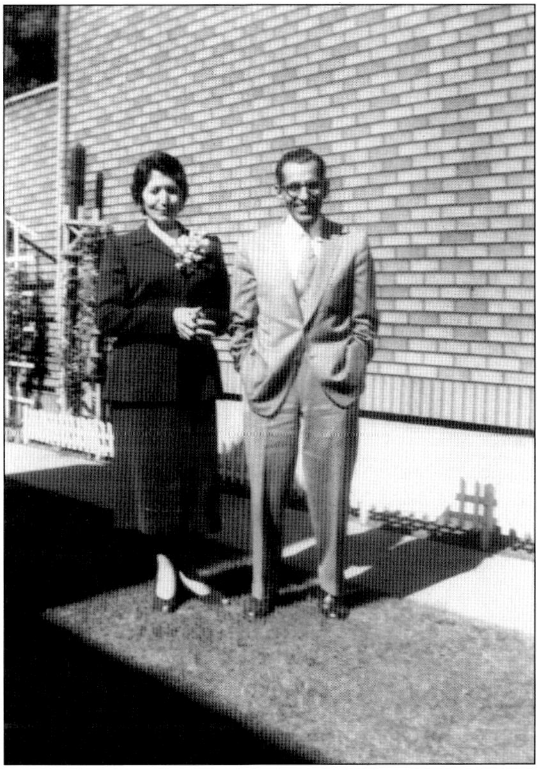

Pictured here are Paul and Murassa Georges together in their old age. For many years, they were leaders and active members of ANA. (Courtesy of Gary E. Daniels.)

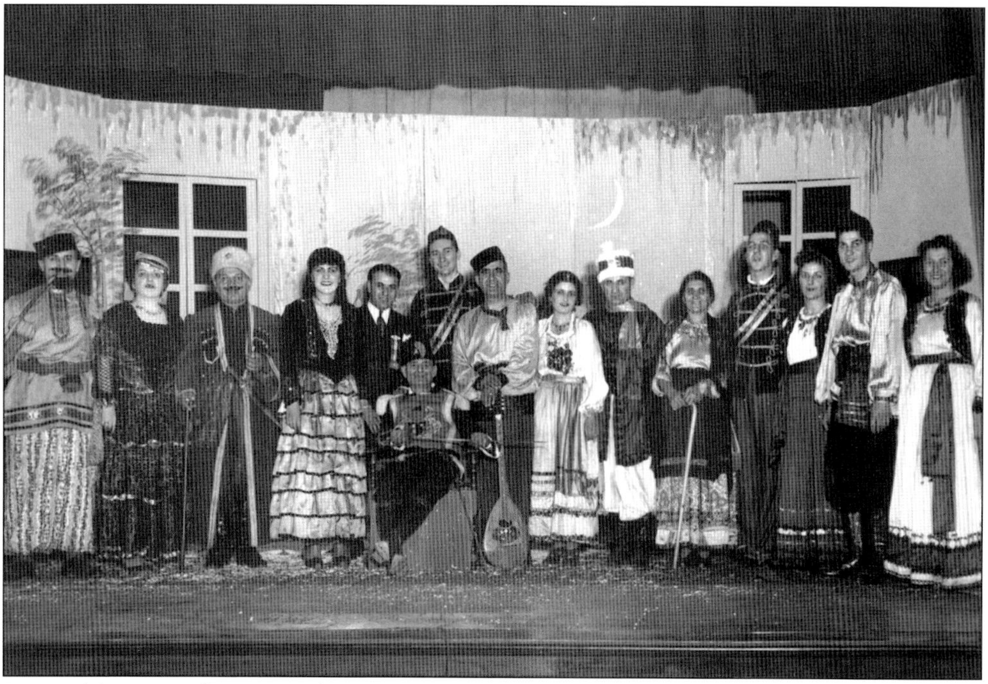

Pictured here is a theater production of the drama *Scheherazade d'Azerbaijan*. The association performed many dramas; many of them were written and directed by Lily Khanbaba and Sargis Khanbaba. (Courtesy of Sarah N. Benjamin.)

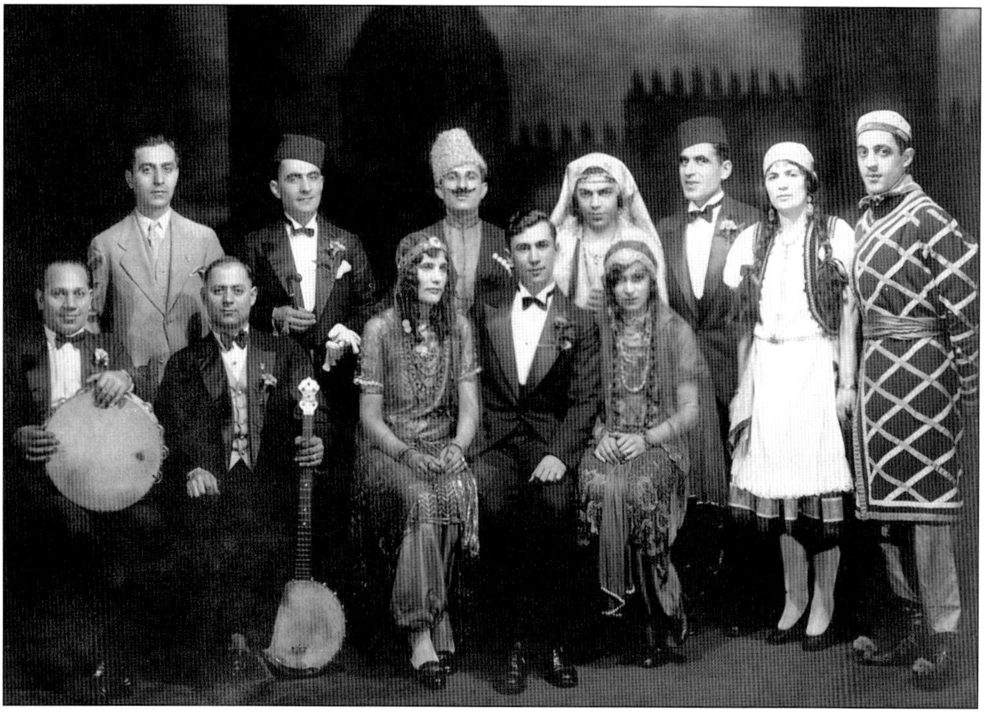

Pictured here is Sargis Khanbaba (standing third from right) with his theater group in 1935 during a production of the satirical drama *Molla Nasraddin*. (Courtesy of Jack David Jr.)

Bob and Sarah Benjamin were association leaders and actors. Those who attended their performances witnessed impressive scenes from the Benjamins. (Courtesy of Sarah N. Benjamin.)

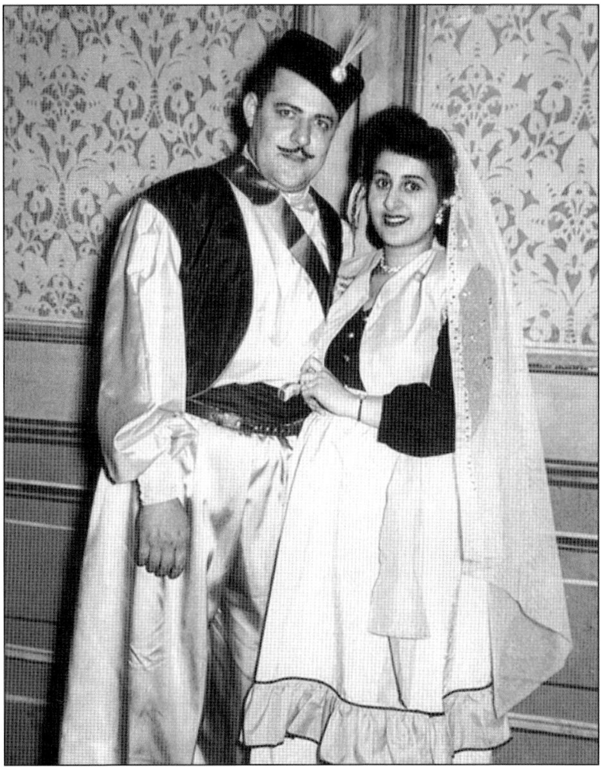

This is the wedding party at the marriage of Sarah and Bob Benjamin, two unforgettable members of Shotaputa. The couple always attended all organizational activities, including picnics, plays, dance performances, and meetings. (Courtesy of Sarah N. Benjamin.)

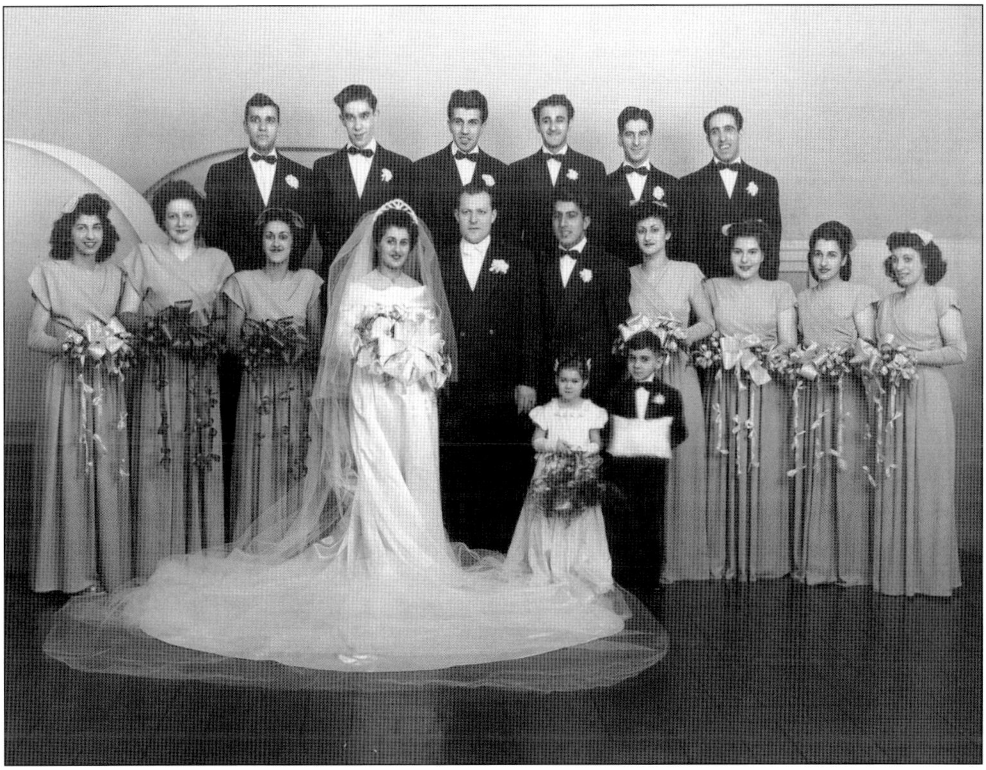

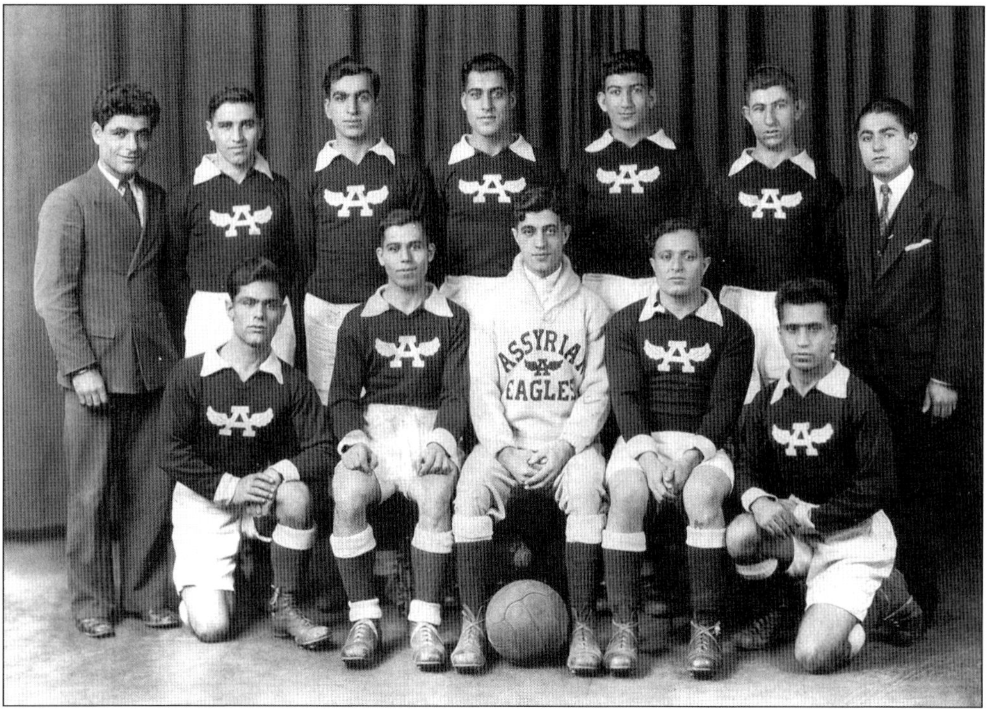

More new sports entered the Assyrian life—most notably, soccer. Pictured here is the Assyrian Eagles soccer team of 1931. (Courtesy of Jack David Jr.)

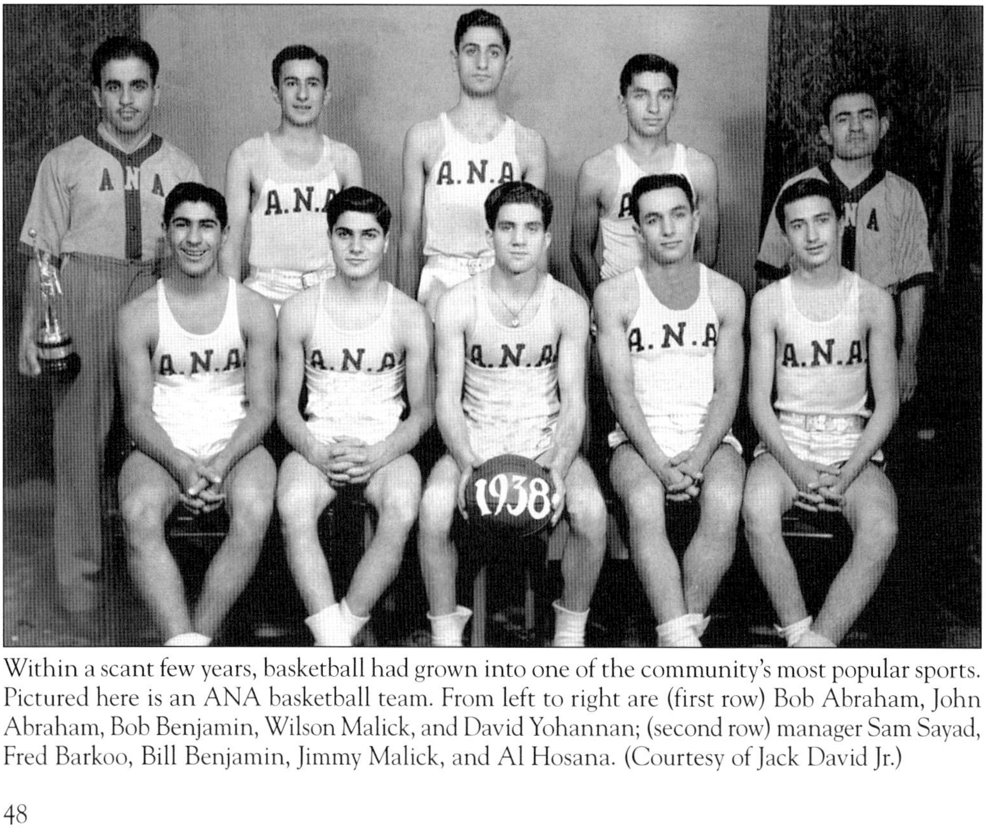

Within a scant few years, basketball had grown into one of the community's most popular sports. Pictured here is an ANA basketball team. From left to right are (first row) Bob Abraham, John Abraham, Bob Benjamin, Wilson Malick, and David Yohannan; (second row) manager Sam Sayad, Fred Barkoo, Bill Benjamin, Jimmy Malick, and Al Hosana. (Courtesy of Jack David Jr.)

Pictured here is Sen. John Nimrod (1922–2009) in his Chicago softball playing days. He was also a successful basketball player for the association. (Courtesy of Jack David Jr.)

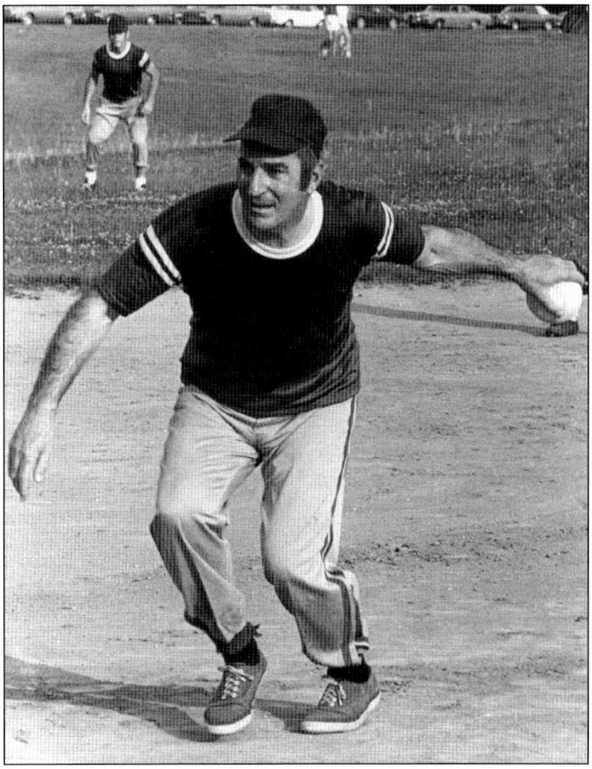

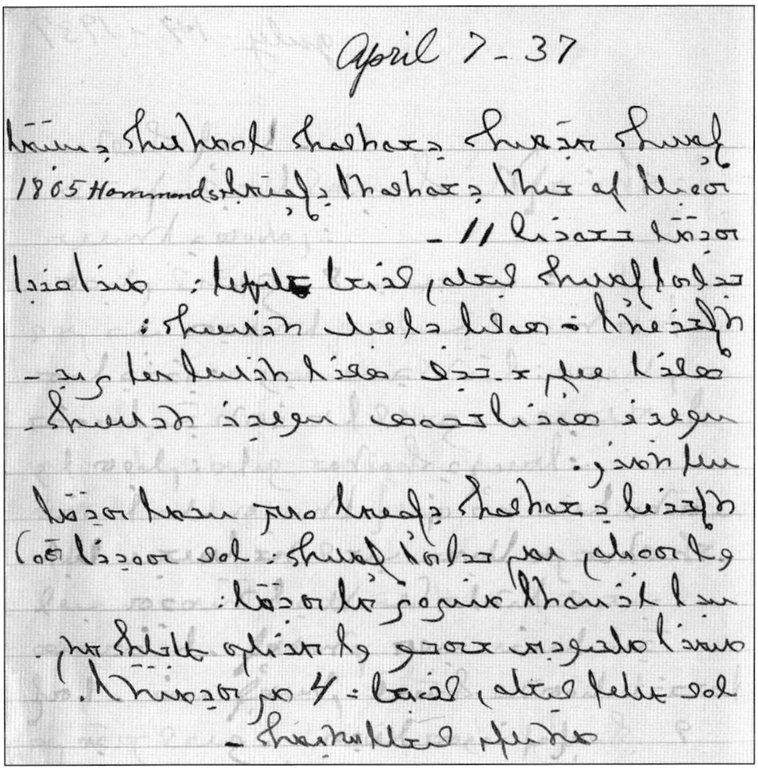
April 7-37

These are the minutes of a meeting of the Ladies Auxiliary on April 7, 1937. The newly elected staff included Mary Werda, president; Sophia Daniel, vice president; Nanjan Badal, first secretary; Anna Sayad, second secretary; and Soriya Bakos and Khanna Bakos, treasurers. (Courtesy of Ashurbanipal Library, AUAF.)

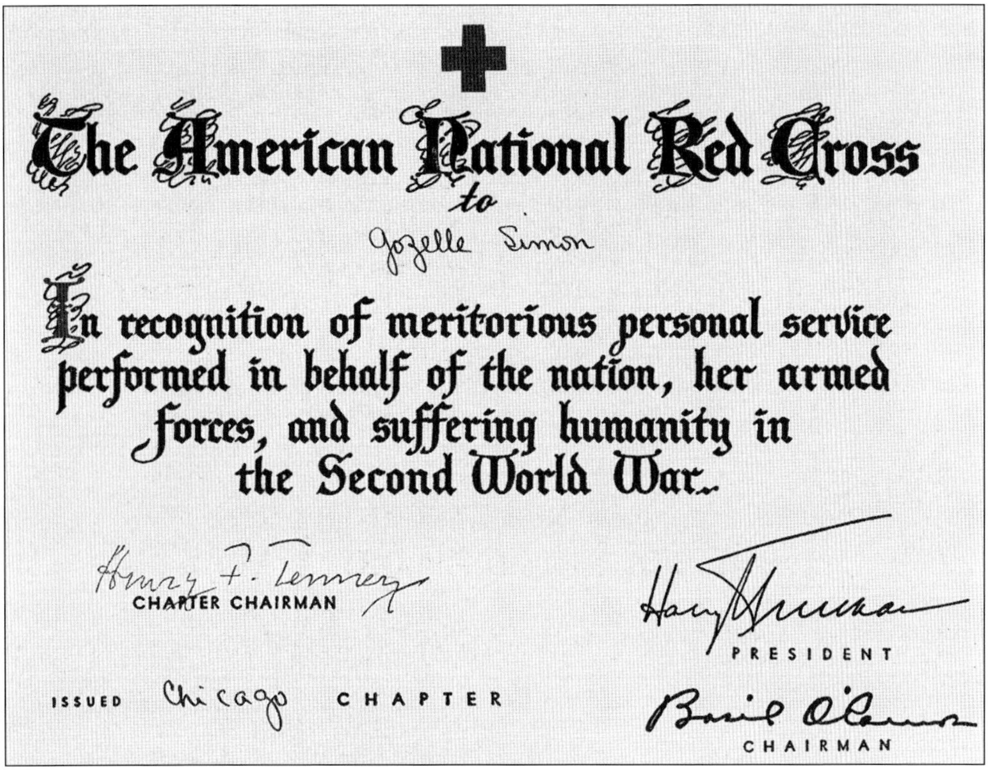

The American National Red Cross
to
Gozelle Simon
In recognition of meritorious personal service performed in behalf of the nation, her armed forces, and suffering humanity in the Second World War.

Henry F. Tenney
CHAPTER CHAIRMAN

Harry Truman
PRESIDENT

ISSUED Chicago CHAPTER

Basil O'Connor
CHAIRMAN

This is the certificate the American Red Cross issued to Gozelle Simon. She helped organize classes to train volunteers and carry out civil defense efforts. (Courtesy of Sarah N. Benjamin.)

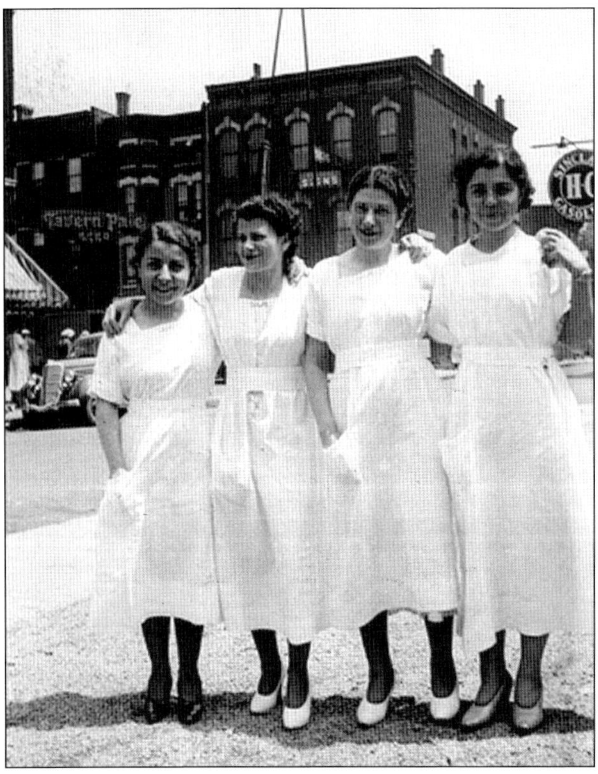

Pictured here is the Ladies Auxiliary at nurse's aide training in the 1940s. It was available for those who had graduated from high school. Courses in canteen management and nutrition were also offered. Another division, called home services, focused on helping servicemen and their families. (Courtesy of Jack David Jr.)

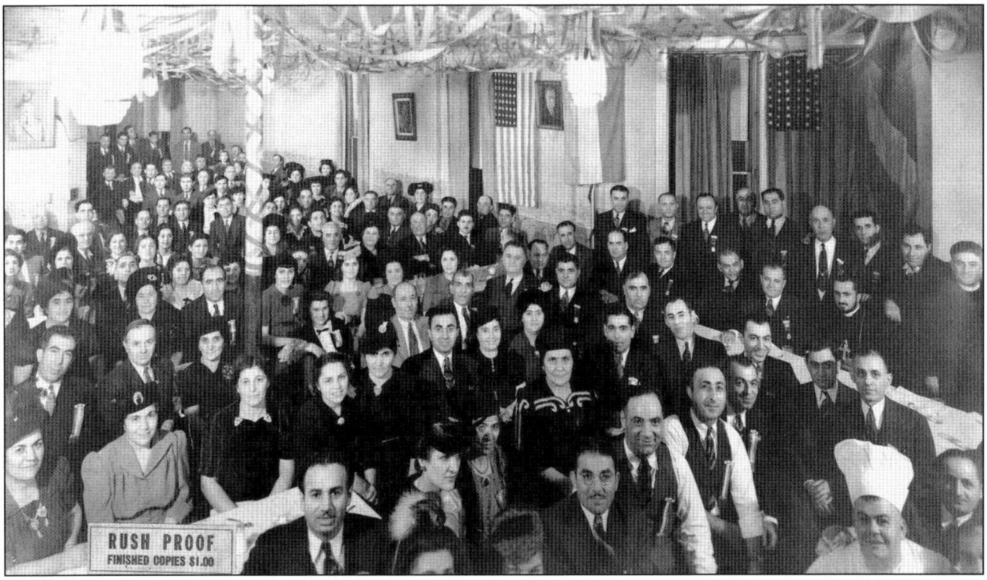

In October 1940, His Holiness Mar Eshai Shimun XXI, catholicos-patriarch of the Assyrian Church of the East, visited Chicago. A testimonial banquet was given by the association at 2108 North Halsted Street. (Courtesy of Sam Andrews.)

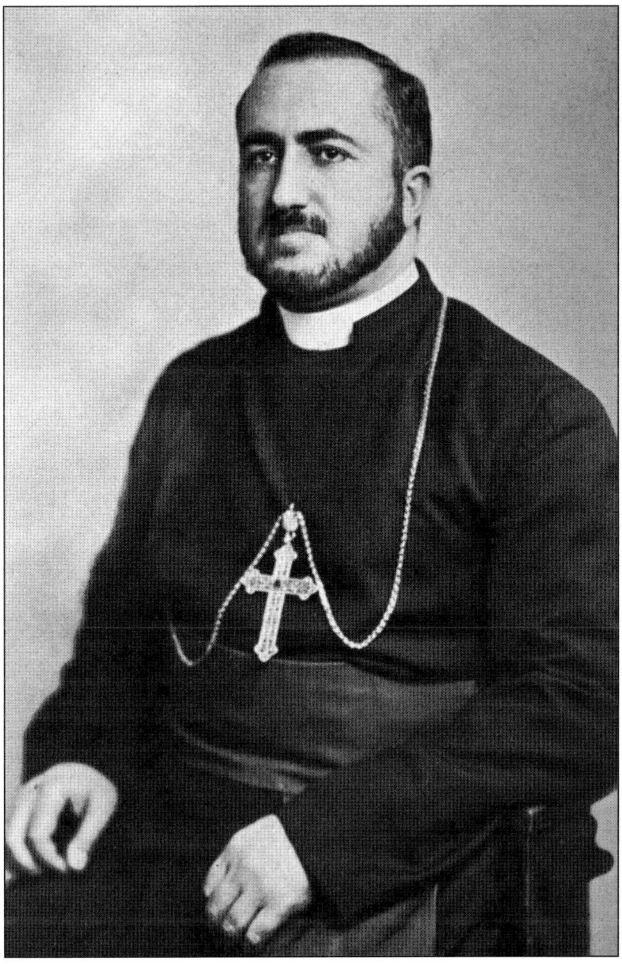

Mar Eshai Shimun XXI settled in Chicago in 1940 and lived at 6346 North Sheridan Road. (Courtesy of Rev. Charles Klutz.)

Mar Shimun's American Visit Committee
of
Assyrian Americans of Chicago

Officers:
Malcom Shabaz, *Chairman*
Joel Sargis, *Secretary*
Jonathan George, *Treasurer*

Entertainment Committee:
George Eshaya, *Chairman*
Costan Aslanoff, *Secretary*
Gabriel Sargis Simon Alawardy
Sal Odishoo Ezra Mitchil
Bob Shimmon

Committee:
David Adam Sam Badall
Jonathan Paul Jerry Bacus
Cyrus Morhad Pnuel Joseph
Simon Davajan Abeshalom Addi
Bob Eshoo Joel Sargis
Mano Oshana Malik Abraham
Sam Aziz Mrs. Jenny Joseph
Abraham Daniel William Pasha
Michael George

Banquet Chairman
Professor E. J. James, M. A., B. D., Ph. D.

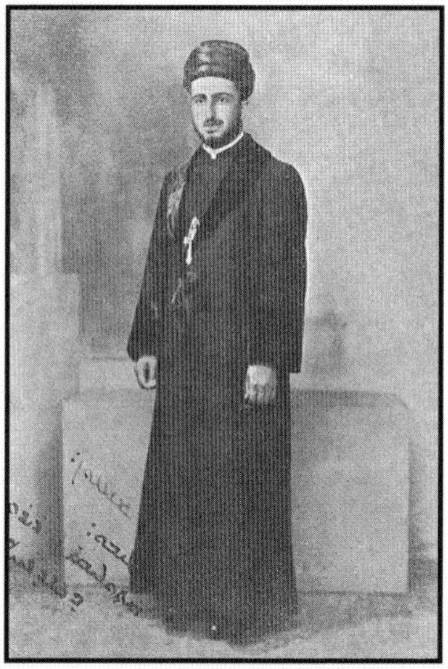

His Beatitude
Mar Eshai Shimun XXI
Catholicos Patriarch of the East

This is the cover of the program for the testimonial dinner of Mar Eshai Shimun XXI in Chicago in 1940. The banquet was conducted by Malcolm Shahbaz, ANA president. (Courtesy of Rev. Charles Klutz.)

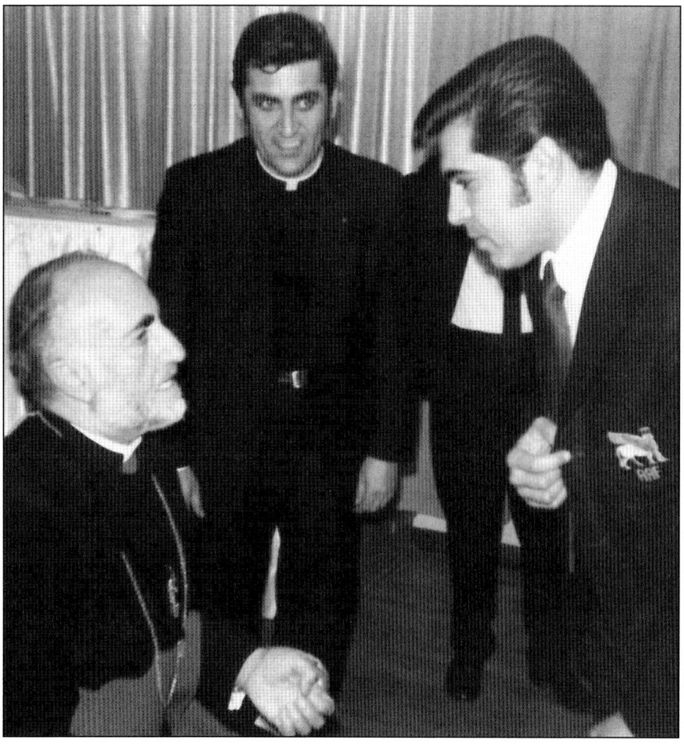

Edward Nadirsha shows Mar Eshai Shimun XXI the new Assyrian American Federation logo in the form of an ancient Assyrian winged bull. In 2003, Nadirsha was elected AAAC president. (Courtesy of Edward Nadirsha.)

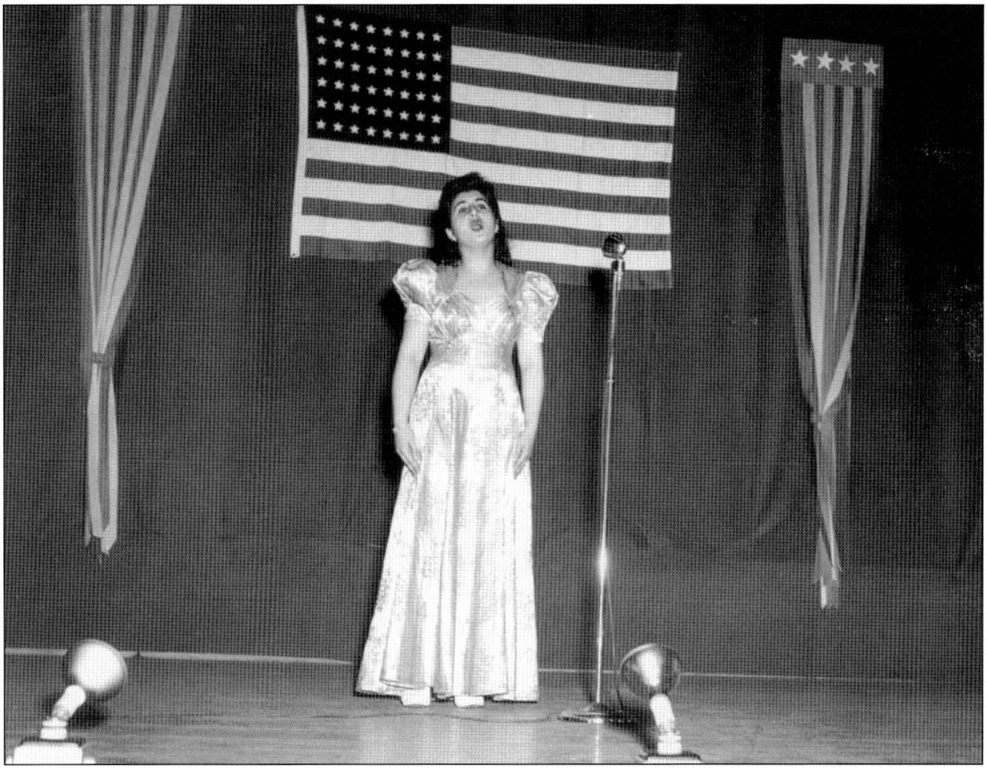

In the 1940s, the Red Cross determined that soldiers should not be deprived of culture. On June 2, 1942, Sarah Benjamin sings at a Red Cross troop variety show. (Courtesy of Sarah N. Benjamin.)

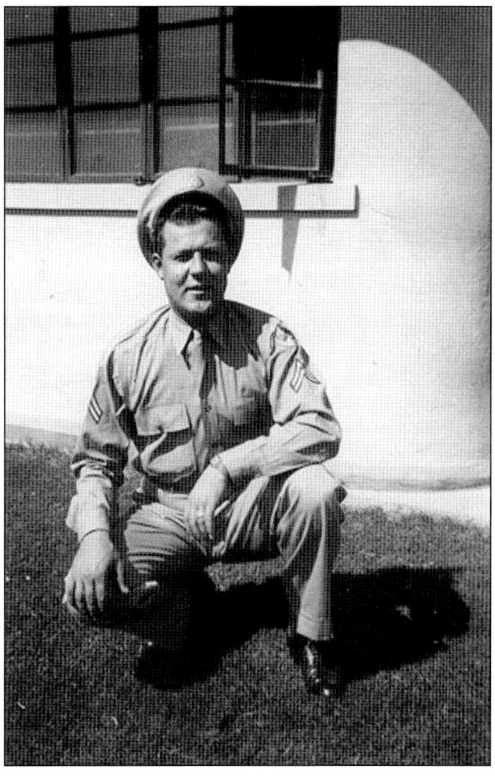

Bob Benjamin was a staff sergeant during World War II, stationed in New Guinea. The New Guinea campaign of the war lasted from January 1942 until the end of World War II in August 1945. (Courtesy of Sarah N. Benjamin.)

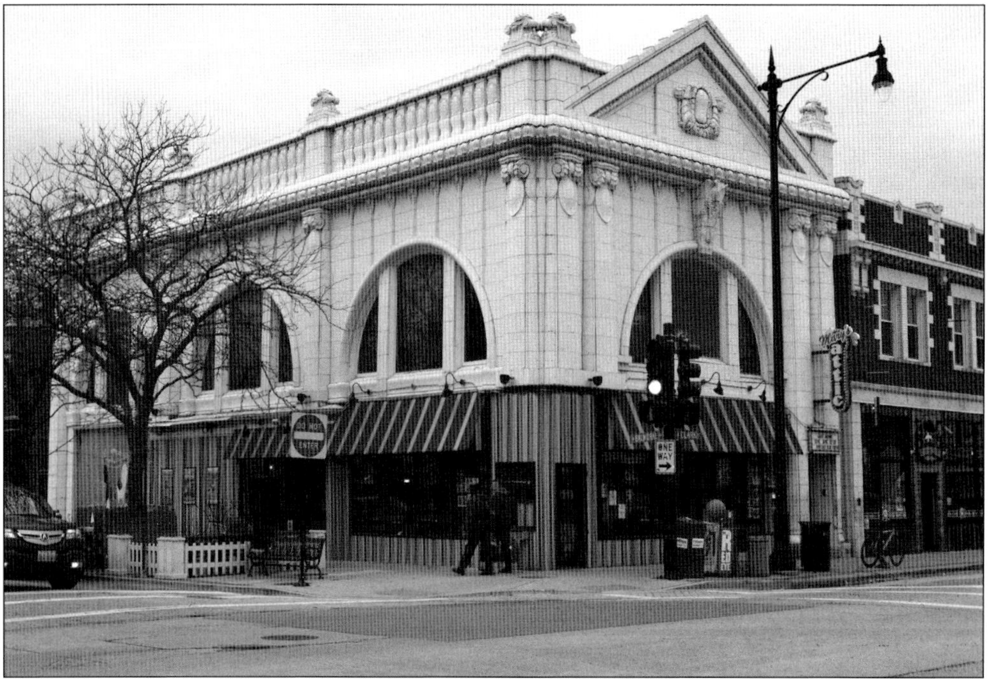

In the 1950s, the association moved to a new location at 5400 North Clark Street in Chicago. Shotaputa members rented the office on the second floor of the corner building. (Courtesy of Dr. Norman Solhkhah.)

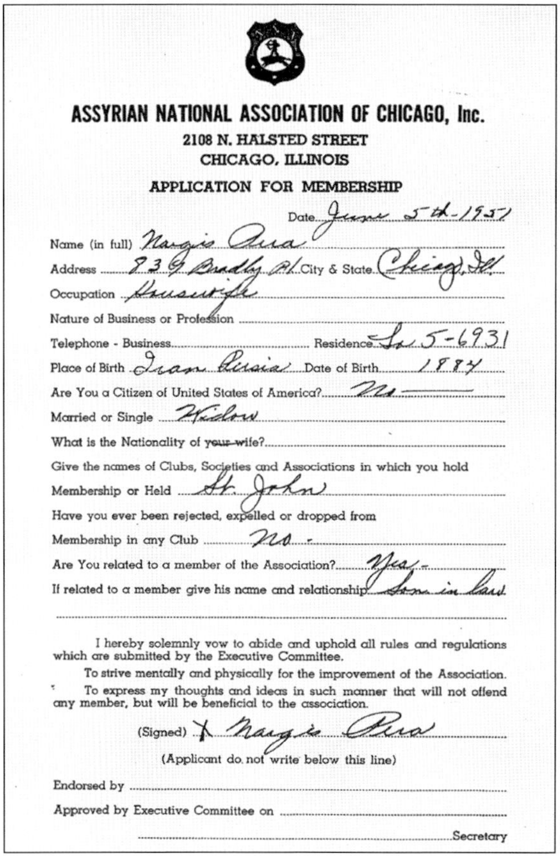

ASSYRIAN NATIONAL ASSOCIATION OF CHICAGO, Inc.
2108 N. HALSTED STREET
CHICAGO, ILLINOIS

APPLICATION FOR MEMBERSHIP

Date June 5th-1951

Name (in full) Nargis Pera
Address 939 Bradley Pl. City & State Chicago, Ill.
Occupation Housewife
Nature of Business or Profession
Telephone - Business Residence La 5-6931
Place of Birth Iran Persia Date of Birth 1884
Are You a Citizen of United States of America? No
Married or Single Widow
What is the Nationality of ~~your wife~~?
Give the names of Clubs, Societies and Associations in which you hold Membership or Held St. John
Have you ever been rejected, expelled or dropped from Membership in any Club no
Are You related to a member of the Association? Yes
If related to a member give his name and relationship Son in law

I hereby solemnly vow to abide and uphold all rules and regulations which are submitted by the Executive Committee.
To strive mentally and physically for the improvement of the Association.
To express my thoughts and ideas in such manner that will not offend any member, but will be beneficial to the association.

(Signed) X Nargis Pera

(Applicant do not write below this line)

Endorsed by
Approved by Executive Committee on
Secretary

This is the Assyrian National Association membership application of Nargis Pera in 1951. She was born in 1884 in Iran. (Courtesy of the AAAC archives.)

The bylaws of the Assyrian American Association of Chicago were revised on July 1, 1953, by Sol A. Odishoo (president), Robert Eramia (secretary and chairman), Joseph Davajon, and Sam Samuels. (Courtesy of the AAAC archives.)

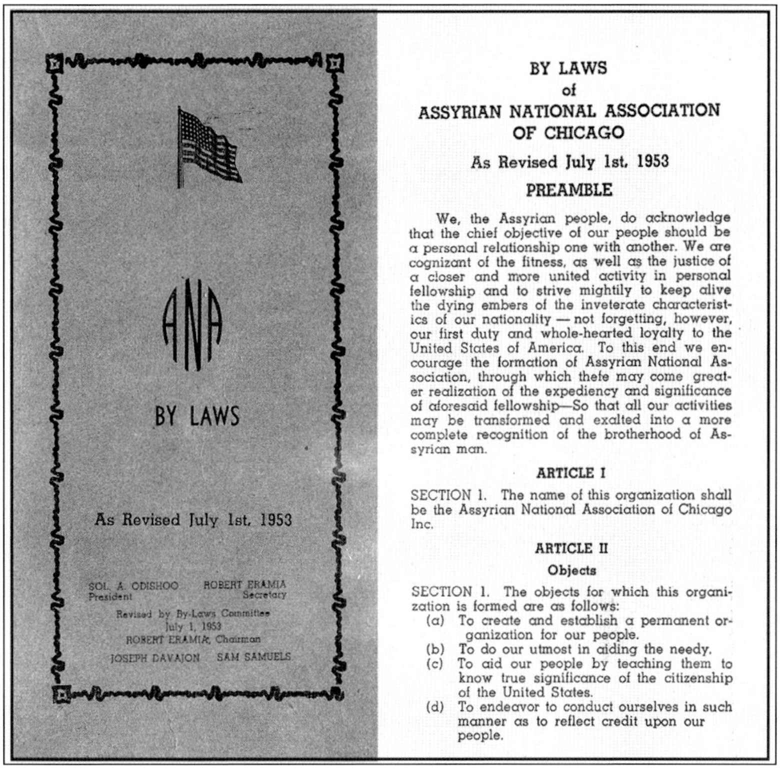

ANA

BY LAWS

As Revised July 1st, 1953

SOL. A. ODISHOO, President — ROBERT ERAMIA, Secretary

Revised by By-Laws Committee
July 1, 1953
ROBERT ERAMIA, Chairman
JOSEPH DAVAJON — SAM SAMUELS

BY LAWS
of
ASSYRIAN NATIONAL ASSOCIATION
OF CHICAGO

As Revised July 1st, 1953

PREAMBLE

We, the Assyrian people, do acknowledge that the chief objective of our people should be a personal relationship one with another. We are cognizant of the fitness, as well as the justice of a closer and more united activity in personal fellowship and to strive mightily to keep alive the dying embers of the inveterate characteristics of our nationality — not forgetting, however, our first duty and whole-hearted loyalty to the United States of America. To this end we encourage the formation of Assyrian National Association, through which thefe may come greater realization of the expediency and significance of aforesaid fellowship—So that all our activities may be transformed and exalted into a more complete recognition of the brotherhood of Assyrian man.

ARTICLE I

SECTION 1. The name of this organization shall be the Assyrian National Association of Chicago Inc.

ARTICLE II

Objects

SECTION 1. The objects for which this organization is formed are as follows:

(a) To create and establish a permanent organization for our people.
(b) To do our utmost in aiding the needy.
(c) To aid our people by teaching them to know true significance of the citizenship of the United States.
(d) To endeavor to conduct ourselves in such manner as to reflect credit upon our people.

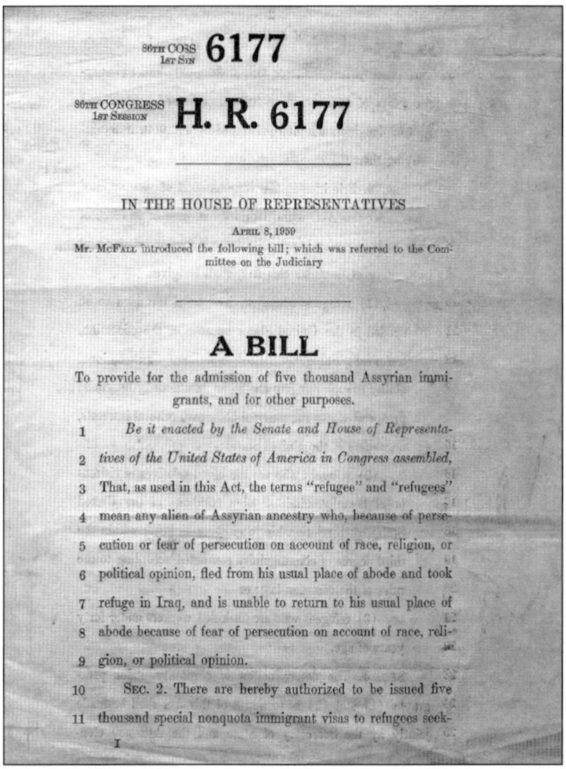

86TH CONG 1ST SESSION 6177

86TH CONGRESS 1ST SESSION H. R. 6177

IN THE HOUSE OF REPRESENTATIVES

APRIL 8, 1959

Mr. MCFALL introduced the following bill; which was referred to the Committee on the Judiciary

A BILL

To provide for the admission of five thousand Assyrian immigrants, and for other purposes.

Be it enacted by the Senate and House of Representatives of the United States of America in Congress assembled, That, as used in this Act, the terms "refugee" and "refugees" mean any alien of Assyrian ancestry who, because of persecution or fear of persecution on account of race, religion, or political opinion, fled from his usual place of abode and took refuge in Iraq, and is unable to return to his usual place of abode because of fear of persecution on account of race, religion, or political opinion.

SEC. 2. There are hereby authorized to be issued five thousand special nonquota immigrant visas to refugees seek-

I

This bill was enacted by the US Senate and House of Representatives in 1959. It provided 5,000 Assyrian immigrants admission to the United States as refugees. (Courtesy of ancestry.com.)

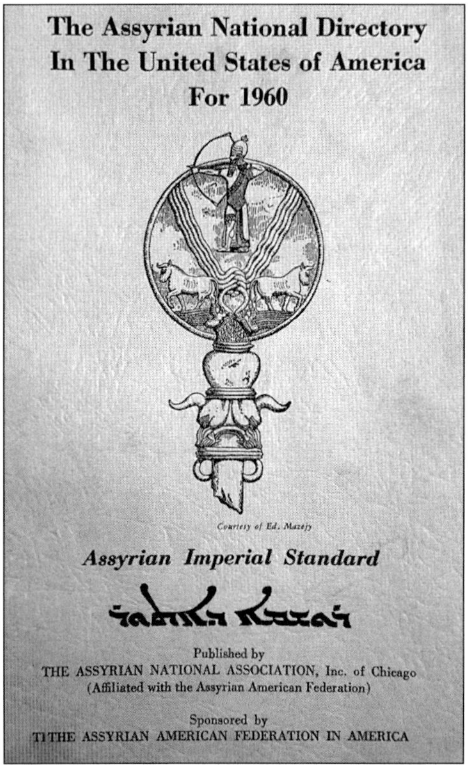

The Assyrian National Directory was published by AAAC in 1960. The ANA has affiliated with the AAF since 1933. (Courtesy of Ashurbanipal Library, AUAF.)

Pictured are Jacob David Sr. (right) and Bishop Raphael I Bidavid of Amadiya, Iraq. On March 21, 1989, Raphael I Bidawid was elected patriarch of Babylon and head of the Chaldean Catholic Church. (Courtesy of Jack David Jr.)

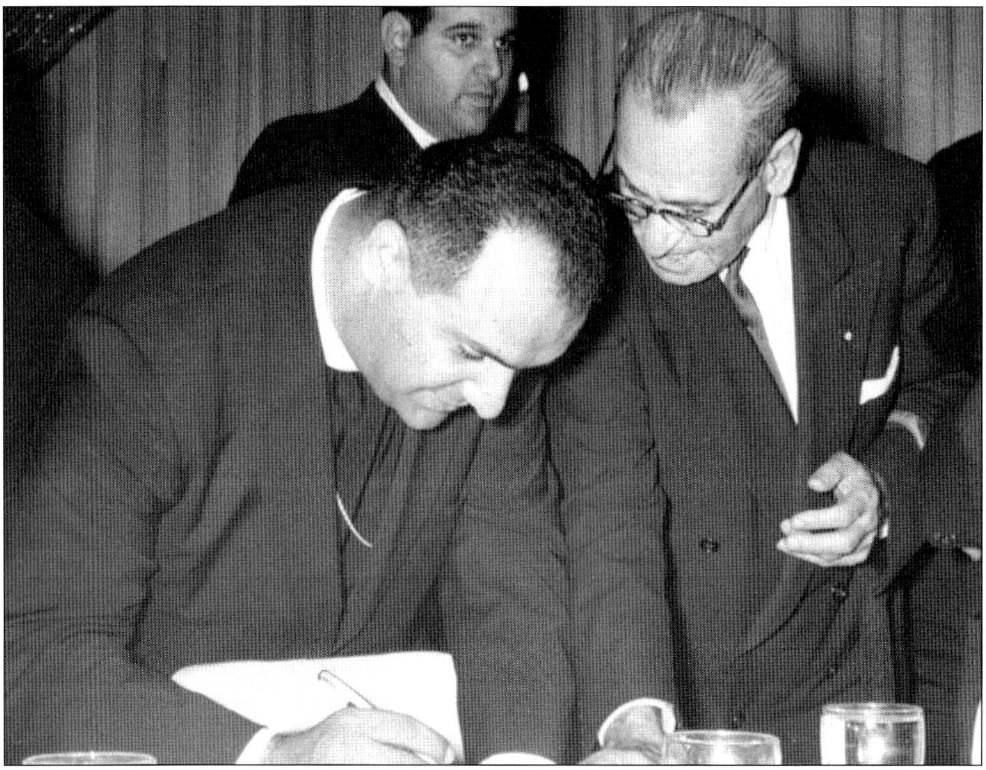

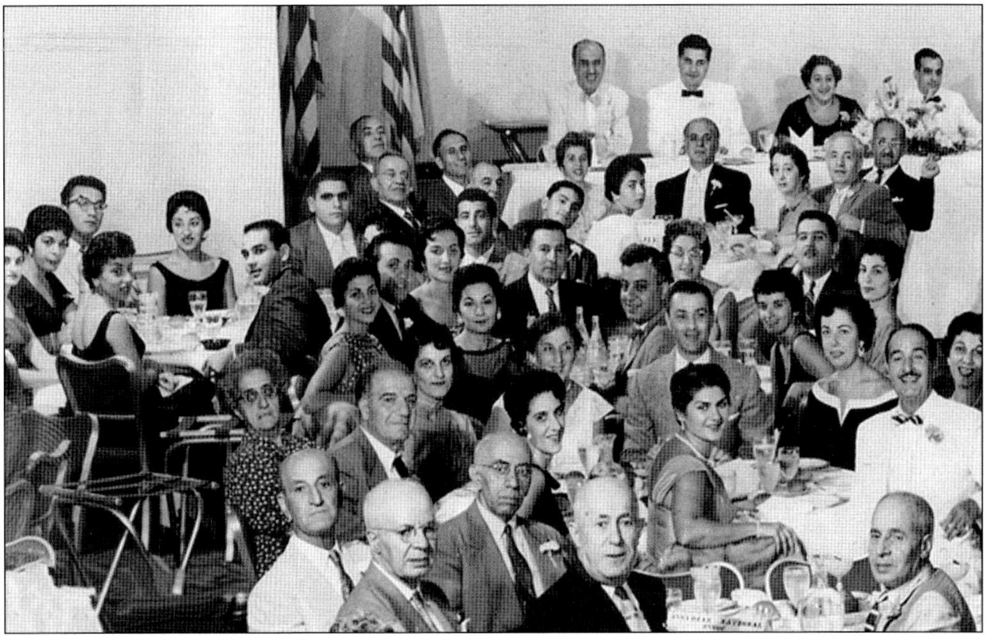

The AAAC delegation is pictured at a banquet of the Assyrian American National Federation convention in New York on September 1, 1957. Gabriel Sargis is seated in a black jacket. (Courtesy of Jack David Jr.)

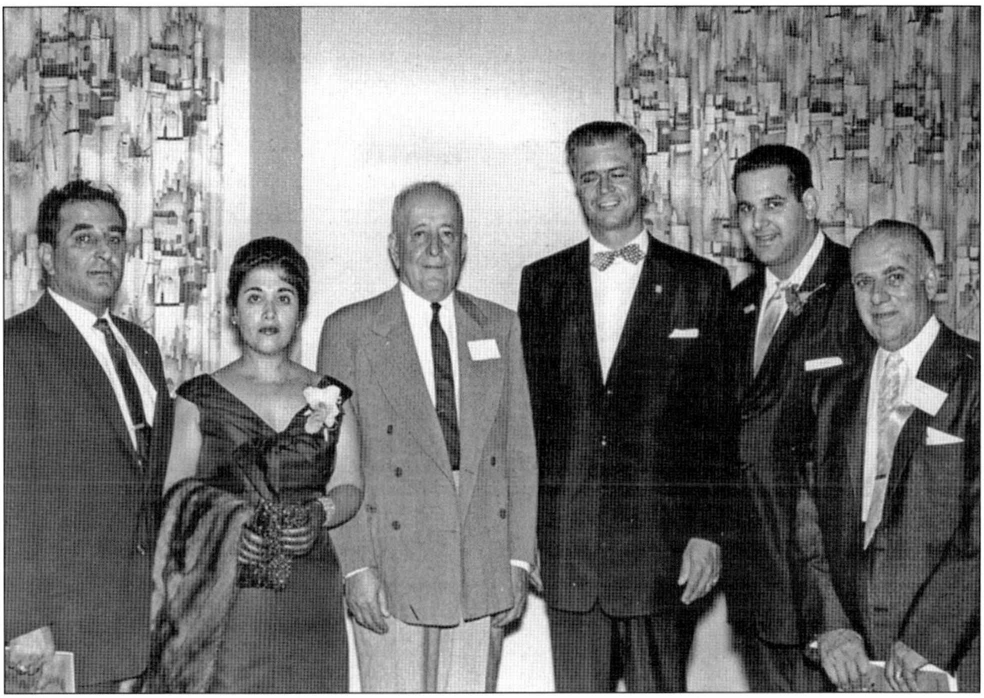

Pictured at the convention of the Assyrian American Federation in Detroit, Michigan, in 1958 are, from left to right, Karam Jacobs (AANF president, 1955–1956), Frances Jacobs, Dr. Khedro Khedro, Gov. Gerhard Mennen Williams of Michigan, Jacob David Jr., and Gabriel Sargis. (Courtesy of Jack David Jr.)

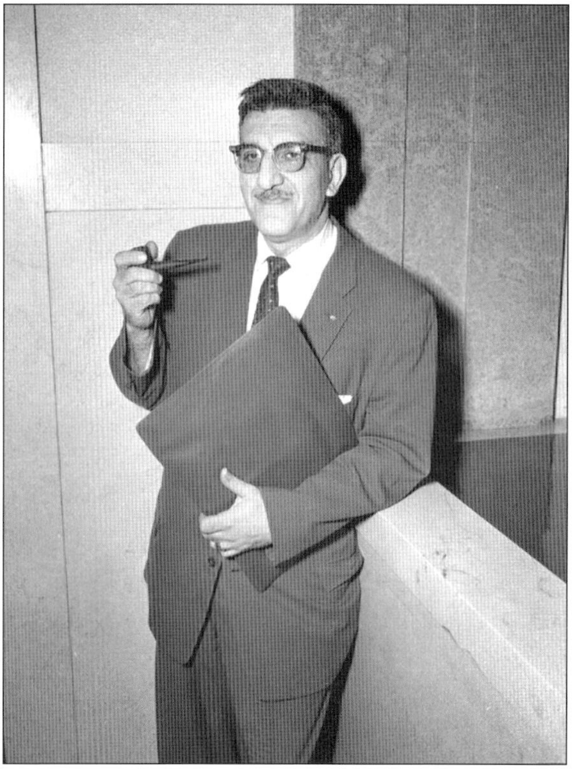

Paul Newey, an AAAC member, was the chief investigator of the Chicago Crime Commission and was recognized as a legendary crime fighter in the city from 1956 to 1960. (Courtesy of Sarah N. Benjamin.)

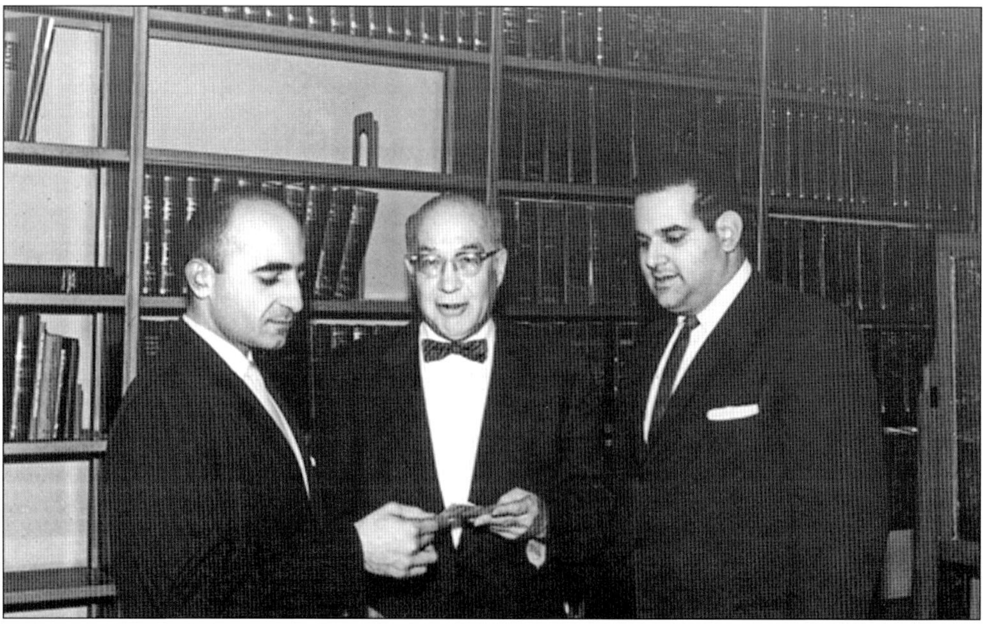

Jack David Jr. (right) receives the I. Ronald Yonan scholarship in 1961. It is presented by Dean Noble Lee (center) of the John Marshall Law School and Adam Benjamin Jr. (left) of Gary, Indiana, a member of the US House of Representatives from Indiana's 1st district (1977–1982). Jack David Jr., like his father, Jacob David, was an active member of the association. He was an *Assyrian Star* writer and columnist. (Courtesy of Jack David Jr.)

Three

The Development of the Organization

In 1963, the Assyrian American Association, under the leadership of Pres. John Israel, purchased a new building at 1618 West Devon Avenue in Chicago. It was built as New Devon Theater in 1912. In 1920, it became a Ford dealership. In the 1940s, it served as a meeting hall for the 50th Ward Republican Party, and then housed the Rogers Park chapter of America First, an antiwar group. By 1952, it appears to have been home to Devon-Clark Radio, which changed to Devon-Clark Television by 1954, an electronics store selling Westinghouse electronics and air conditioners.

On March 9, 1963, the association invited His Excellency Mar Zaya Dachtou, archbishop of Urmia and bishop of Salamas, Iran. An honorary banquet was held in the new building. On March 29, 1964, the Assyrian National Association was renamed the Assyrian American Association of Chicago (AAAC) under the presidency of Gabriel Sargis.

According to Emanuel Ishoo, current AAAC board of directors member and radio host, in July 1965, Shotaputa established *The Voice of the Assyrian American Association* (*Qala d'Shotaputa*) at WEAW 1330 AM. The program was broadcast on Saturday from 2:00 p.m. to 3:00 p.m. under the programming of Paul George, well known as Uncle Paul, and Clames Ganji. Later, this program was broadcast by many talented journalists and speakers, such as Tony Azzo, legendary poet Ninos Aho, Sargon Isaac, Ivan Giwargis, Alfred Daniel, Pnuel Hormizd, Shimon Khammo, Ben Daniel, Johnson Sargis, Maureen Moshe, Rumel Rasho, Nariman Rasho, Lida Hormizd, Rabi Werda Daniel Sliwo (Patriarch Mar Giwargis Sliwo), Emanuel Ishoo, Sarah N. Benjamin, and many others. In 1974, the program name was changed to *Voice of Truth* (*Qala d'Shrara*).

In 1967, the Assyrian American Welfare Council and the Assyrian American Association organized the first Assyrian Blood Bank, transferable in all hospitals in Chicago, and Shotaputa was the first organization to donate 25 pints of blood.

According to Giliana Younan, current AAAC president, a large wave of Assyrian immigrants came from Iraq in the 1970s as a result of the Kurdo-Iraq war and during the Iran-Iraq war of the 1980s. New immigrants easily joined the association and became very active members. They had an indoor gathering every Sunday. In 1971, the AAAC published its first literary publication, *Zahrera*, edited by Ben Daniel (editor in chief), Emmanuel Esho (managing editor), Deacon Shmoel Younan (Assyrian editor), and Piere Shamon (designer and Assyrian and Arabic editor).

According to Raman Oshana, current AAAC sports director, in the 1970s, many famous singers performed at AAAC, such as Ashur Sargis, Garmen Tamraz, Sargon Gabriel, George Chaharbakhshi, Linda George, Sargon Yukhanna, and many others. In 1971, Hanny Talya, Roman Oushana, Edwin Talya, Fred Deeiel, and Tony Ibrahimi formed a band, East Bird. In 1971, Ashur Sargis sang his legendary song "Bet-Nahrain" for the first time. Also in 1971, a new soccer team, Lioness, was established by Raman Oshana, Steve Yonan, Fredy Deil, and Hanny Baba. Two years later, they renamed it Winged Bull. The team became a member of the National Soccer League of Chicago. In 1976, Winged Bull won a National Soccer League championship. The Winged Bull committee members of 1977 were Gilbet Eshaya (head coach), Albert Rasho (manager and AAAC president in 1977), Hormis Gewargis, Ewan Gewargis, Ninos Yokhanis, Raman Oshana, Sargon Gabriel, and Slivo S. Yonan.

AAAC has been a center for the Assyrian music industry since the early 1930s. The list of famous singers who started on the association's stage includes Morassa Georges, Shamiram Urshan (Oshana), Jarmen Tamraz, George Margalof, Esha Zaia, Ashur Bet Sargis, Sargon Gabriel, Alexzender David (Zander), George Chaharbakhshi, Juliana Jando, Linda George, Lida Lawando, Summer Lawando, John Eddy, Shabe Lawando, Elezabet Oshana, Shawel Malko, Janan Sawa, Lazer Malko, Joan David, Odi Simon, David Simon, Albert Oskar Baba, Enweya Shimoun, Charles Toma, Luther Eshoo, Jack Ishak, George Jando, Salem Sefo, Freddy Gabrail, Sargon Rasho, Male Merza, Olin Rihana, Nagham Mousa, Ogin Bet Shmoel, and many others.

Many AAAC members became famous and successful, such as Henri Charr, a graduate in film from Columbia College who was honored by the American Film Institute in 1974. He began his career with award-winning educational films and documentaries and turned to mainstream Hollywood cinema in genres including thriller, drama, action-adventure, family, and comedy. His docudrama *A Man Before His Time: The Unsung Story of Poet Freydun Atouraya* was nominated at the Golden Apricot Armenian Film Festival in 2015.

In 1993, the AAAC published a book, *Assyrian Americans Who Served in the Armed Forces of the United States*.

In the 2000s, many Assyrians of the association worked for the US military as interpreters in the Middle East; among them were Edward Nadirsha, Eddie Zomayah, Farhad Moshe, Edward Barcham, Dinkha Gabriel, and many others.

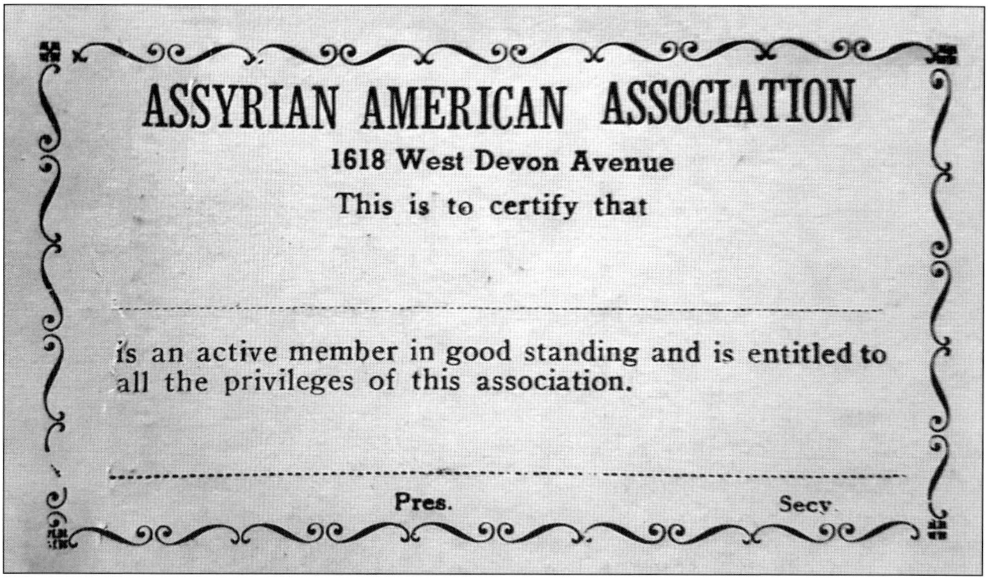

ASSYRIAN AMERICAN ASSOCIATION

1618 West Devon Avenue

This is to certify that

is an active member in good standing and is entitled to all the privileges of this association.

Pres. Secy.

This is a membership card of the Assyrian American Association from 1963. It was issued by John Israel (president), John Abraham (secretary), and Sam Samuels (manager). (Courtesy of the AAAC archives.)

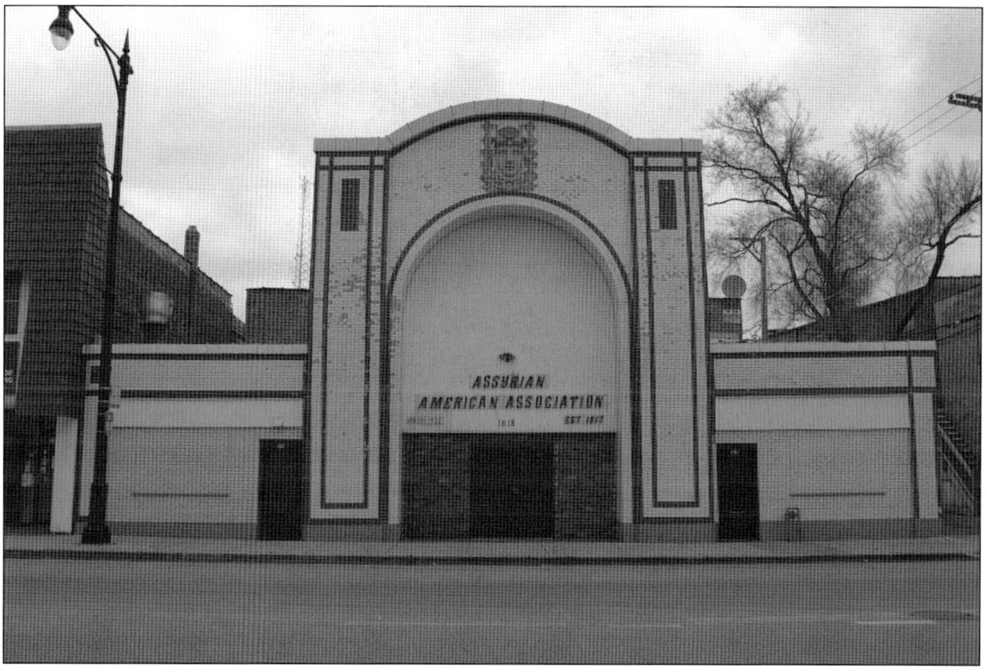

Pictured here is the Assyrian American Association building. It was constructed as the New Devon Theater in 1912. In 1963, it became the home of the AAAC. (Author's collection.)

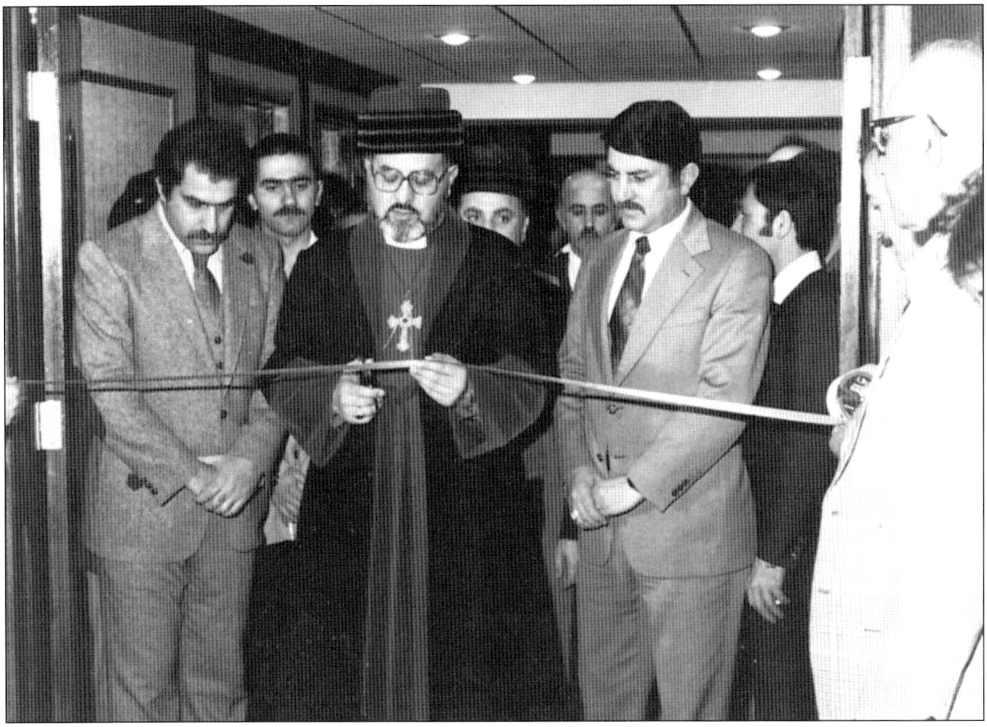

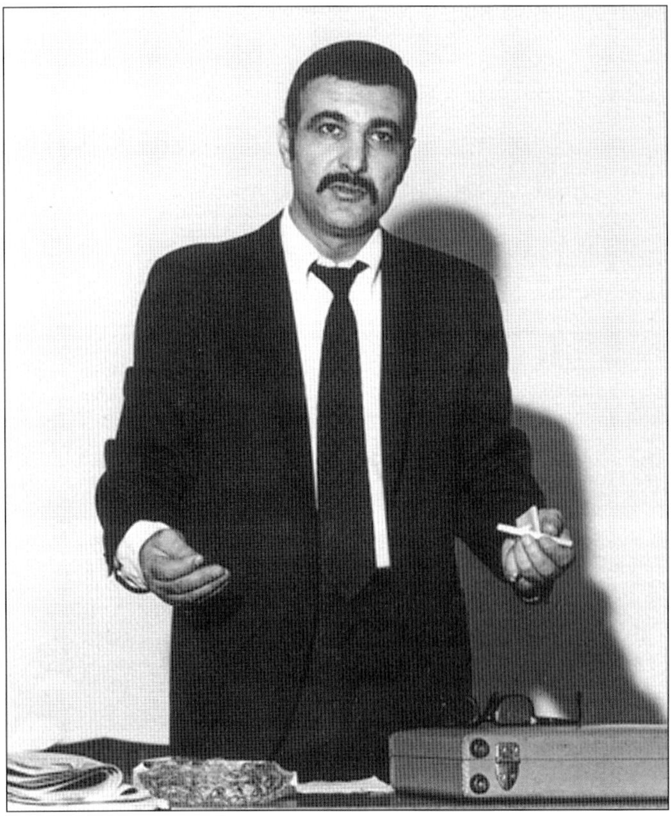

Mar Dinkha IV, the catholicos-patriarch of the Assyrian Church of the East (center), is pictured with Johny Odisho (left) and Ben Benjamin (right), cutting the ribbon at the grand reopening ceremony of the AAAC in 1981. (Courtesy of Emanuel Esho.)

Sam Andrews was the president of the Assyrian National Association of Chicago in 1969. He was born in Iran, and his father was Rabi Andrews Awdisho, a head (*mukhtar*) of the Gilani camp in 1924 in Iraq. Sam was a Korean War veteran. In 1970, he became secretary general of the Assyrian Universal Alliance. (Courtesy of Sam Andrews.)

Germaine Malik is pictured at the ANF convention in Chicago in 1969. Malik was born in Kermanshah, Iran. In 1944, she became a member of the Women's Union of Kermanshah. In 1979 and again in 2001, she was the Assyrian American Ladies Auxiliary president. (Courtesy of Germaine Malik.)

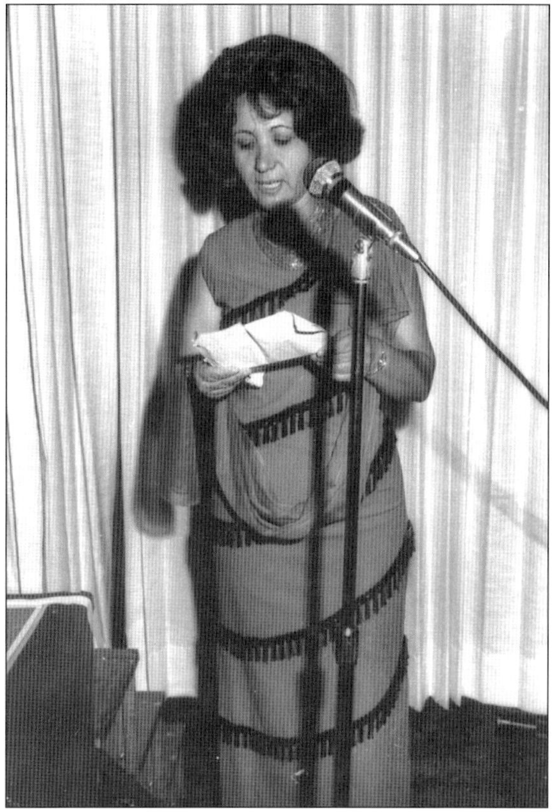

Assyrian American Association members are pictured here in 1970. From left to right are (first row) Shlimon Youkhana, Bob Mirza, Abe David, and David Nadir; (second row) Bejan Rasho (past president), Alber Rasho (past president), Jack Adams, Mike Rasho, Edward Nadirsha (past president), Danny Solomon, and John ?. (Courtesy of Edward Nadisha.)

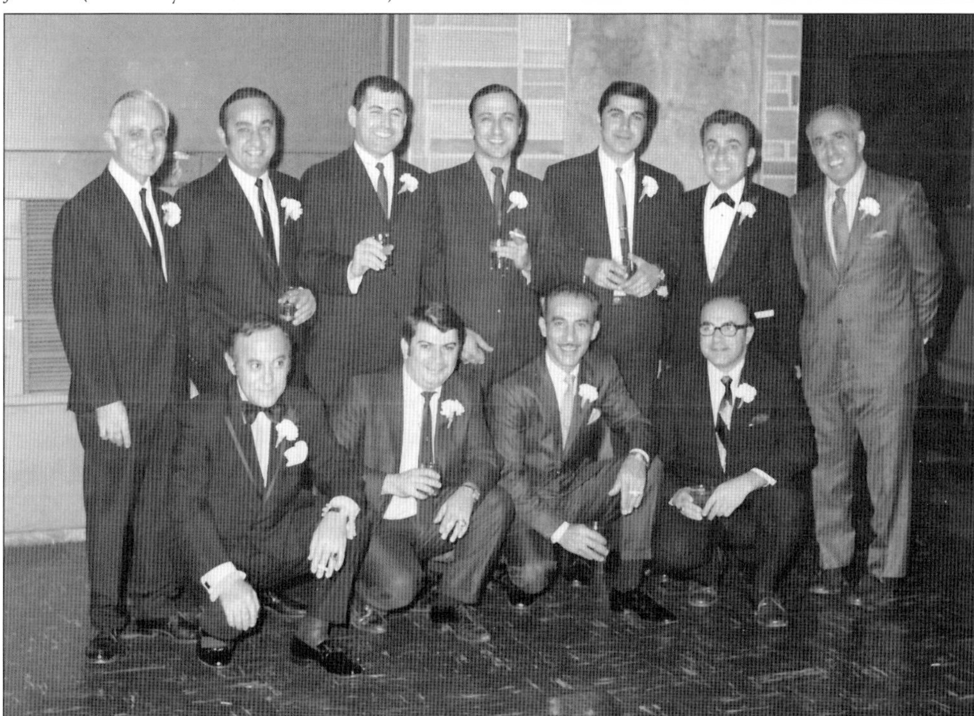

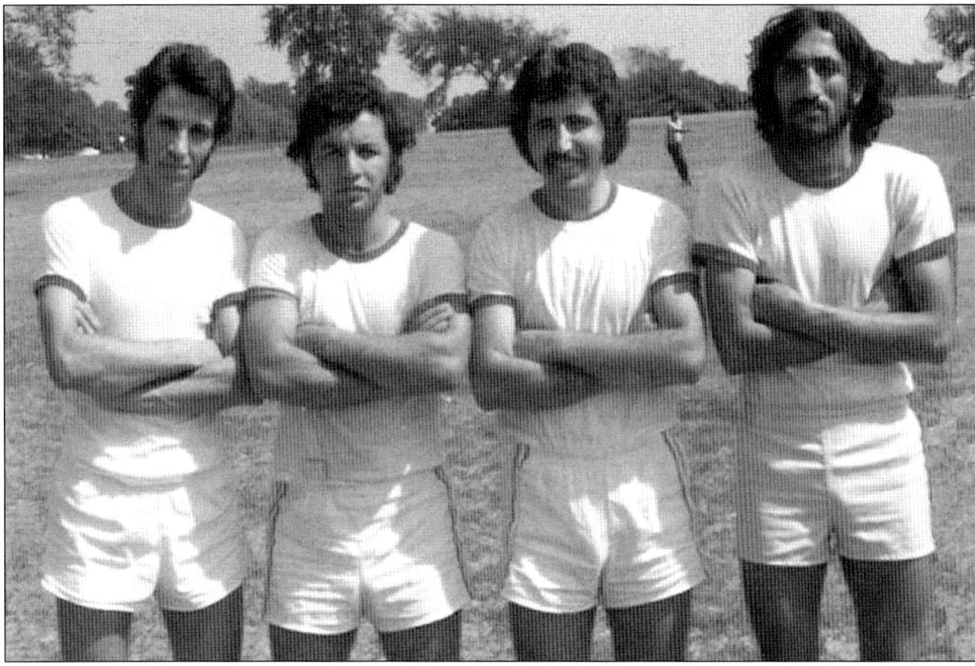

These were the first Winged Bull players in 1974. From left to right are Sargon Gabriel, Raman Oshana, Fred Deeiel, and Simon Khoshaba. (Courtesy of Raman Oshana.)

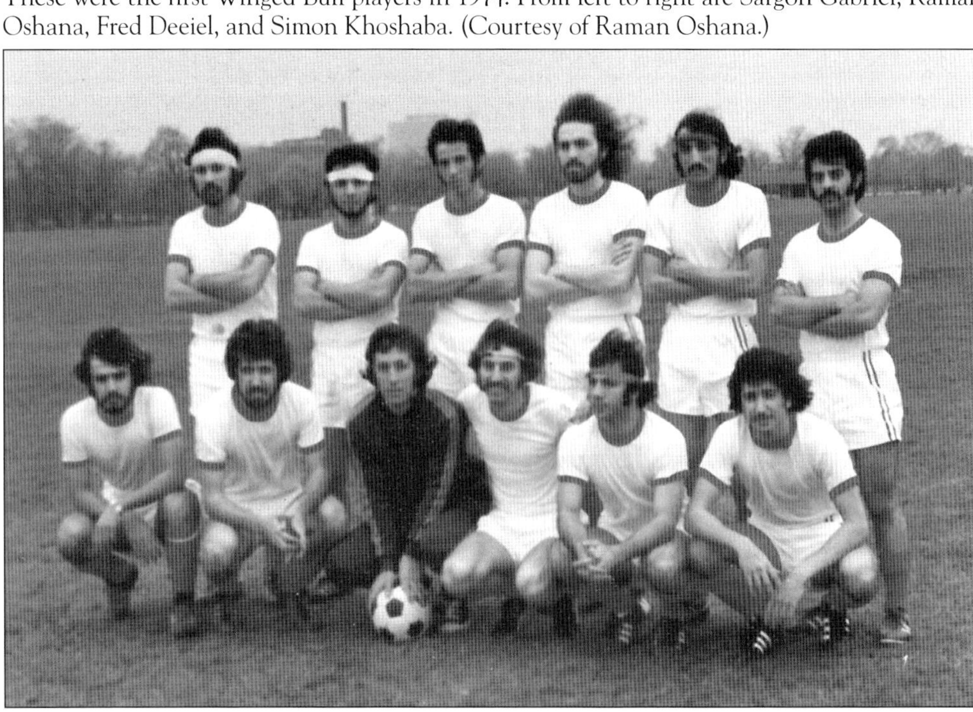

Pictured here is the Winged Bull team of 1977, managed by Gilbert Sami and George George. The team members are, from left to right, (first row) Robert Tamraz, Yuash Polus, Rani Lazar, Ninus Lazar, Freddy Diel, and Ninus Oshana; (second row) Ashur Gabriel, Raymon Oshana, Sargon Gabrial, George Charbahshi, Simon Khoshaba, and George Badalpur. (Courtesy of Raman Oshana.)

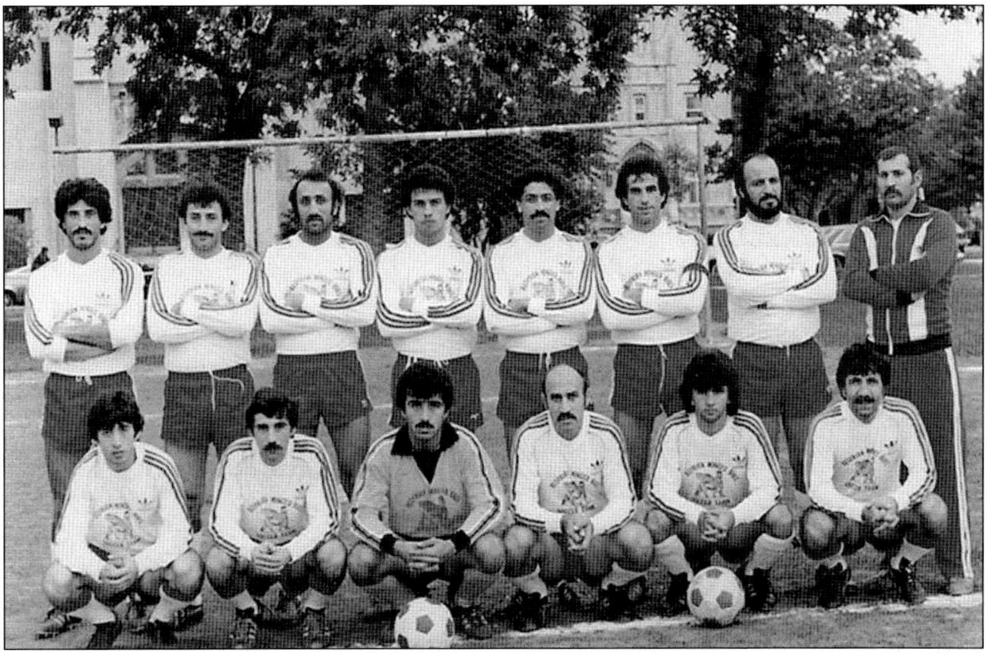

This is the 1975 Winged Bull soccer team that won the Third Division championship. Coach Ashur Gabriel is standing in the second row at far right. The team won the Second Division championship in 1976 and the Major Division championship and Illinois State Cup in 1980. (Courtesy of Ashur Gabriel.)

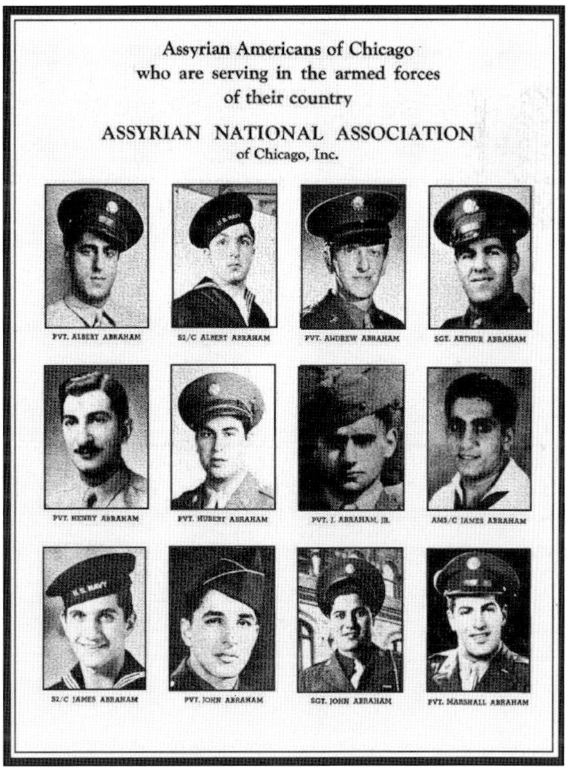

Assyrian Americans of Chicago
who are serving in the armed forces
of their country

ASSYRIAN NATIONAL ASSOCIATION
of Chicago, Inc.

PVT. ALBERT ABRAHAM	S2/C ALBERT ABRAHAM	PVT. ANDREW ABRAHAM	SGT. ARTHUR ABRAHAM
PVT. HENRY ABRAHAM	PVT. HUBERT ABRAHAM	PVT. J. ABRAHAM, JR.	AMS/C JAMES ABRAHAM
S2/C JAMES ABRAHAM	PVT. JOHN ABRAHAM	SGT. JOHN ABRAHAM	PVT. MARSHALL ABRAHAM

The association published some magazines and newspapers. In 1993, it published this book detailing Assyrian Americans who served in the military. (Courtesy of the AAAC archives.)

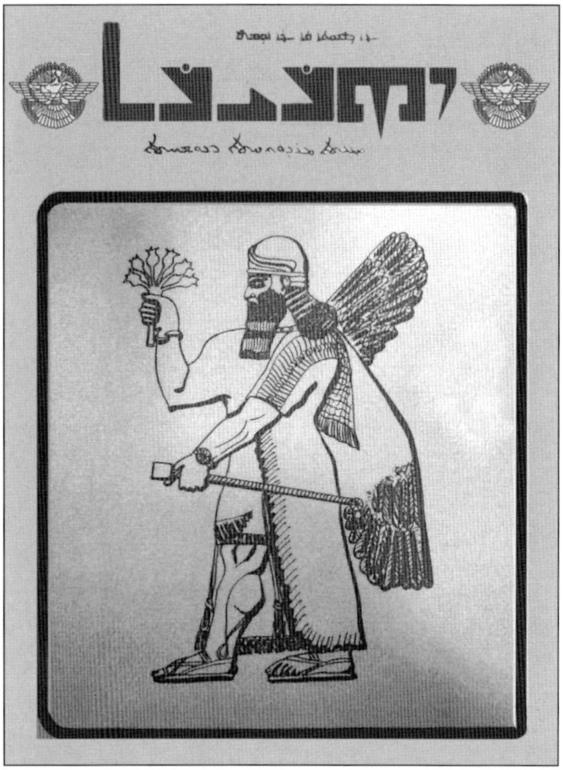

Zahrera magazine has been published by the AAA since 1971. The staff at the time of this issue included Ben Daniel (editor in chief), Emmanuel Esho (managing editor), Deacon Shmoel Younan (Assyrian editor), and Piere Shamon (designer and Assyrian and Arabic editor). (Courtesy of the AAAC archives.)

Dr. Norman Solhkhah is pictured at the Museum of the Oriental Institute of the University of Chicago. Dr. Norman served as vice president of the AAAC in 1974 and owned the Mesopotamian Museum. He was a sponsor of the Assyrian Empire Gallery at the Museum of the Oriental Institute, director of the Assyrian Genocide Institute, and founder of the Assyrian Memorial Park at Montrose Cemetery. He has published dozens of books on Assyrian history, art, and linguistics. (Courtesy of Dr. Norman Solhkhah.)

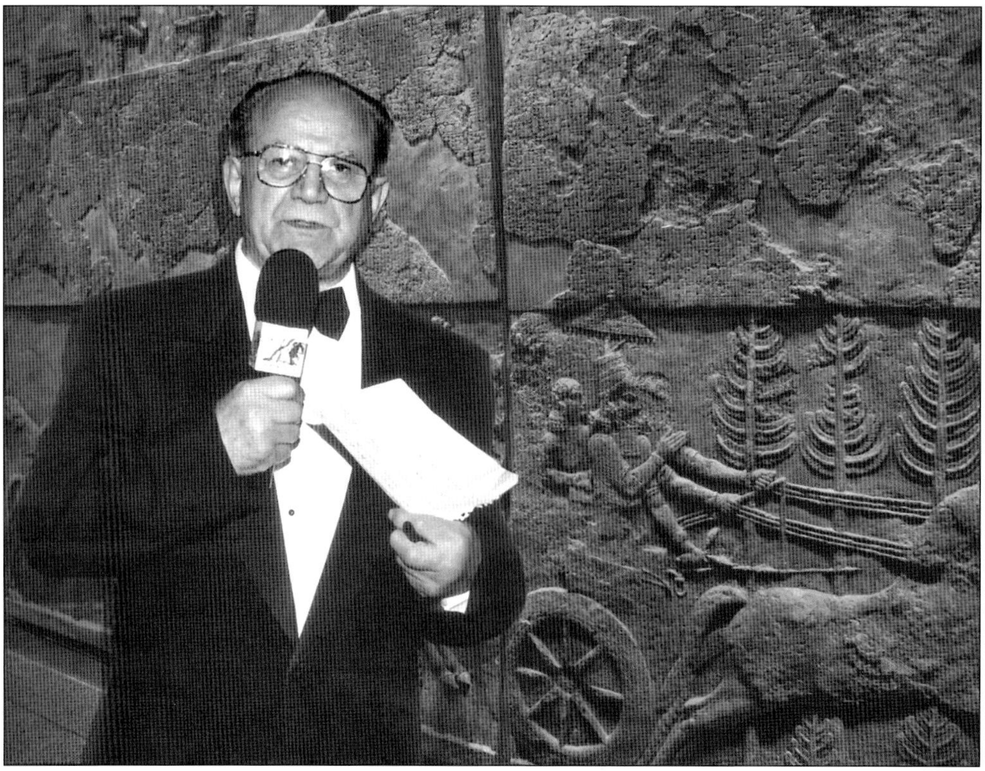

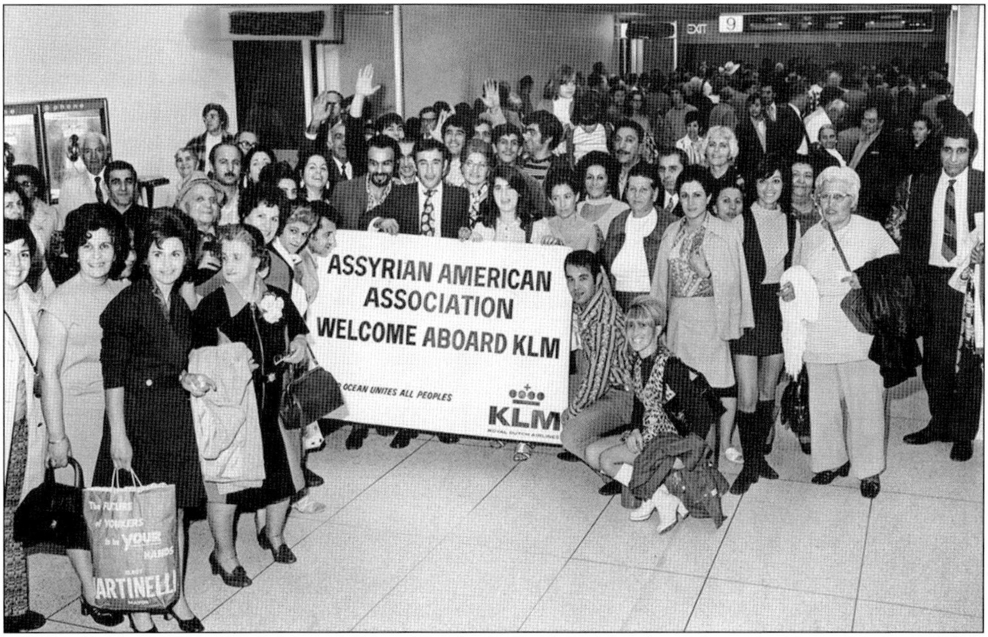

A group of Assyrian American Association members meet guests from Iran. The foreign delegation came to Chicago to attend a convention of the Assyrian American National Federation in 1974. (Courtesy of Raman Oshana.)

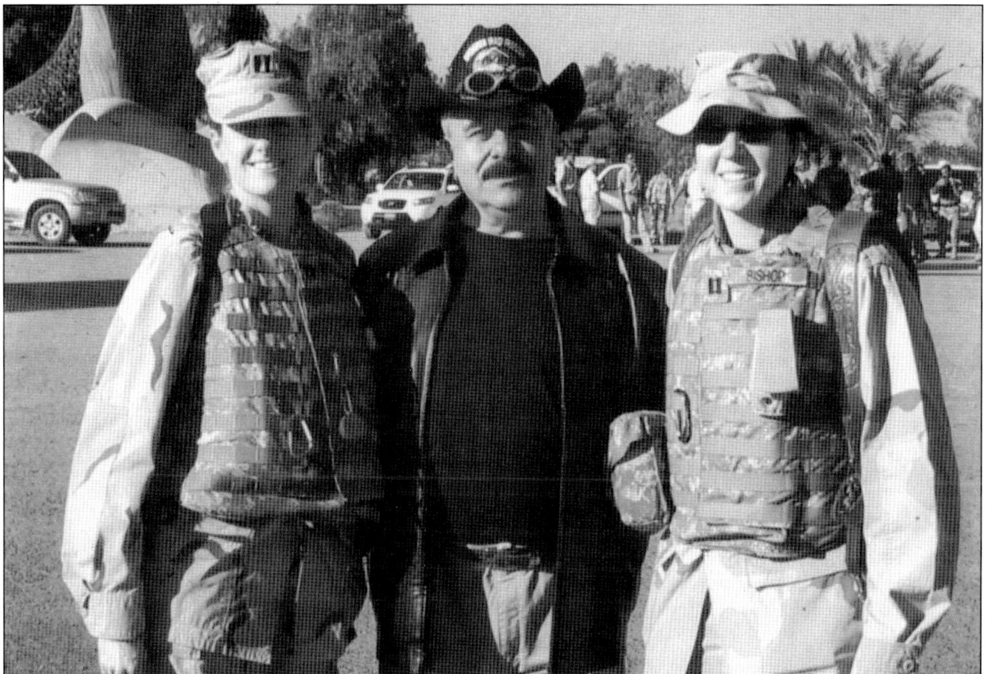

In March 2003, US forces invaded Iraq, vowing to destroy Iraqi weapons of mass destruction and end the dictatorial rule of Saddam Hussein. Many Assyrians worked for the US military as interpreters. Pictured here in 2007 is Edward Nadirsha (center) with his military colleagues in Baghdad. (Courtesy of Edward Nadirsha.)

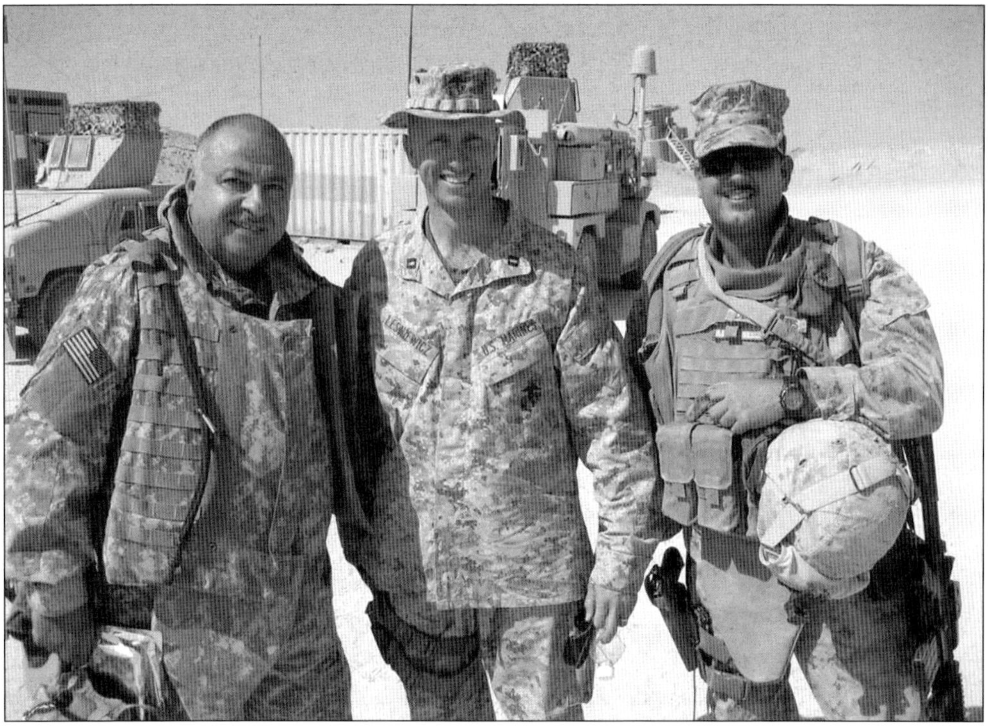

Pictured here from left to right are Eddie Zomayah, Captain Lesniewicz, and S.Sgt Danny L. Boitel at Alubadi Air Base in Iraq in 2008. Zomayah is a Middle Eastern languages specialist and a member of the AAAC executive committee. (Courtesy of Eddie Zomayah.)

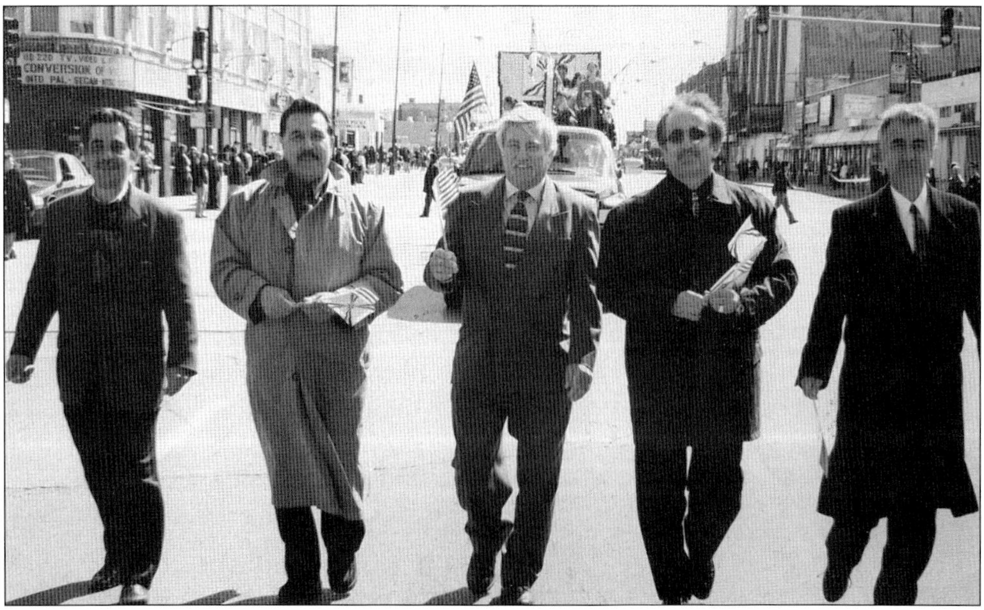

Pictured here are the AAAC leaders at the Assyrian New Year Parade on April 1, 2000. The Assyrian New Year Parade starts on the corner of Western and Granville Avenues and proceeds north on Western to Pratt Avenue. Pictured from left to right are Edward Nadirsha, William Badal, David Youkhanna, and George Shino. (Courtesy of Edward Nadirsha.)

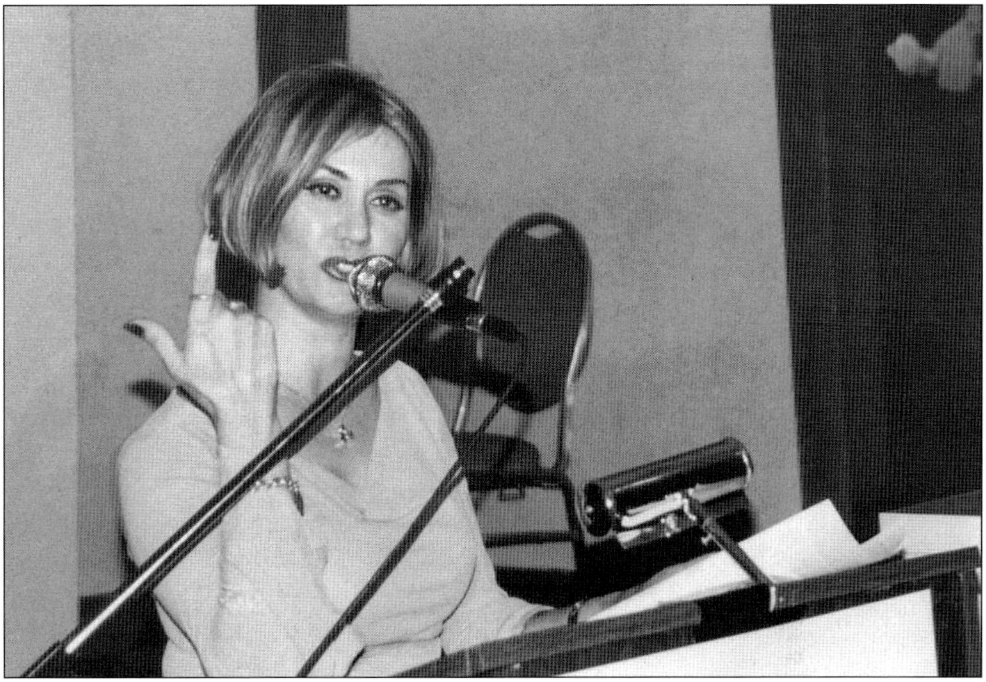

Marina Benjamin, one of the more famous contemporary Assyrian poets, reads her work at the AAAC Poetry Night in 2002. Her poetry is dedicated to love, humanity, and the beloved nation. (Courtesy of Marina Benjamin.)

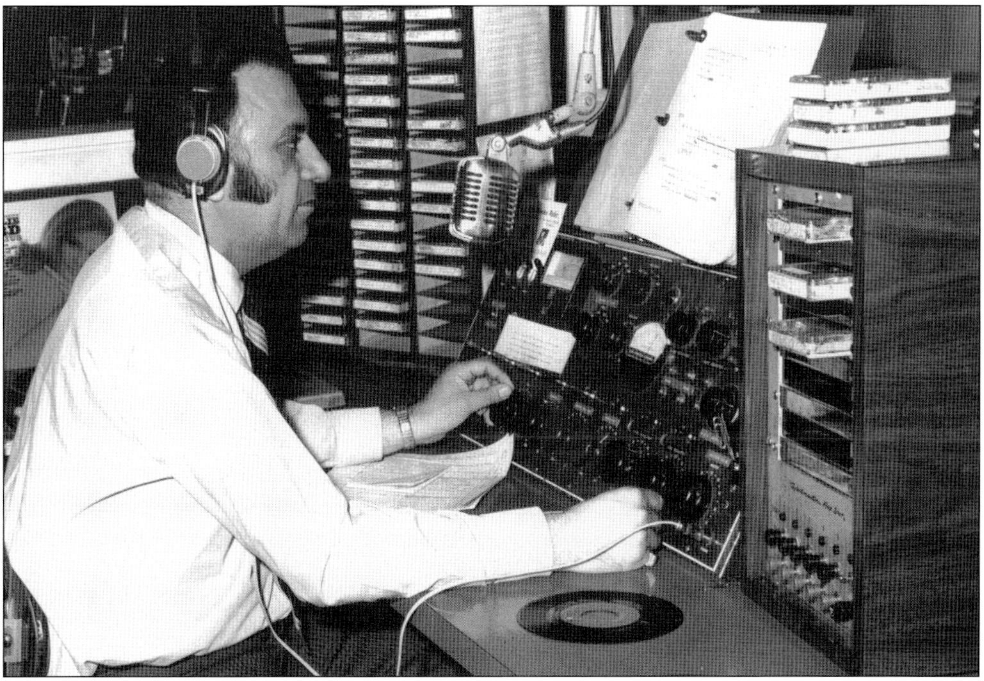

Klames Ganji, one of the first radio moderators of the association radio programs, is pictured in the 1960s. Later, he established his own radio program called *The Voice of the Assyrians*. (Courtesy of Minas Gorguis.)

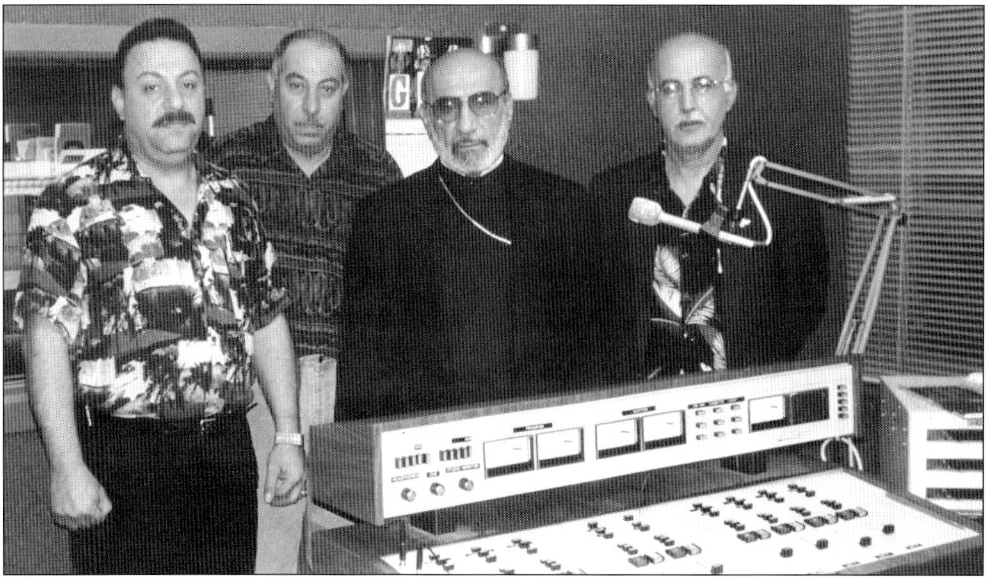

Pictured is the staff of the *Voice of Truth* (*Qala d'Shrara*) radio program of the AAAC. From left to right are Yosip Rasho, Sargon Stefan, Rev. Mar Warda Sliwa (current patriarch of the Assyrian Church of the East), and Ivan Giwargis. (Courtesy of Emanuel Isho.)

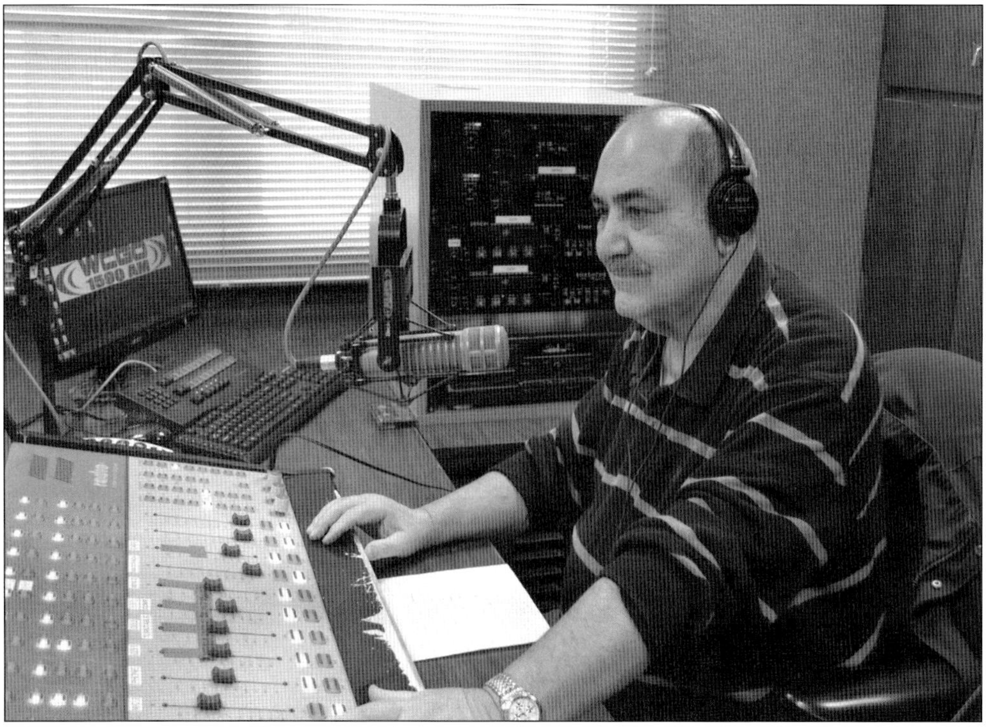

This is a 2015 photograph of Emanuel Isho (AAAC past president), radio chairman of *Voice of Truth* (*Qala d'Shrara*), which broadcasts on 1590 WCGO. He started his radio career as a volunteer in the 1980s. Isho is also the current cultural director of the AAAC. (Author's collection.)

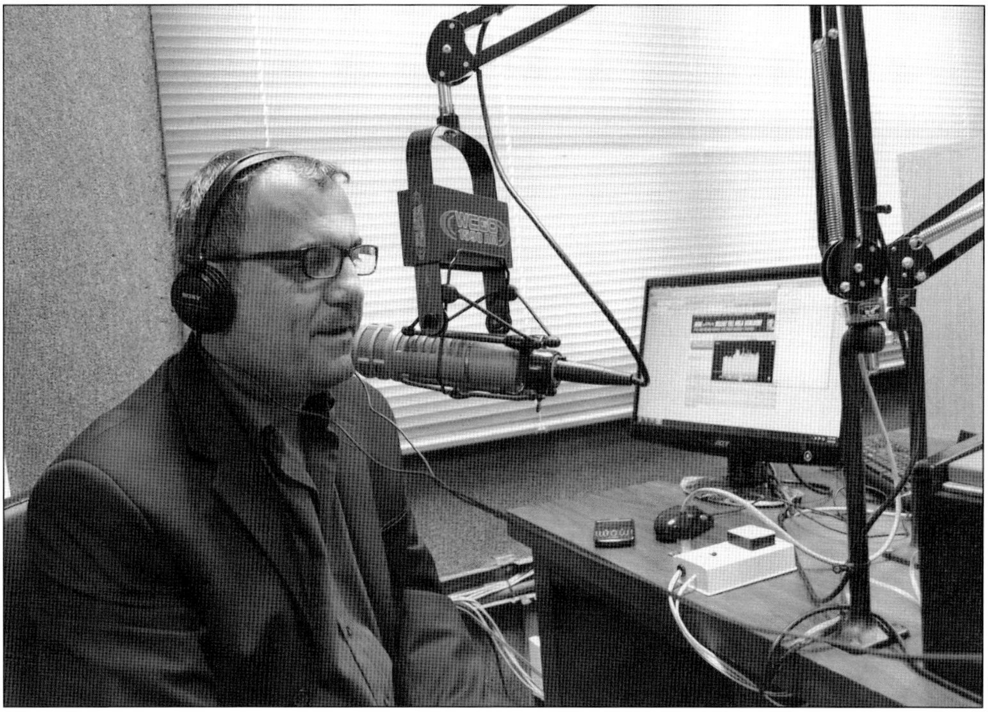

Johnson Sargis, a lifelong radio man, is seen on the air on the AAAC radio program. His broadcast is one of the few independent-minded radio shows in Chicago. (Author's collection.)

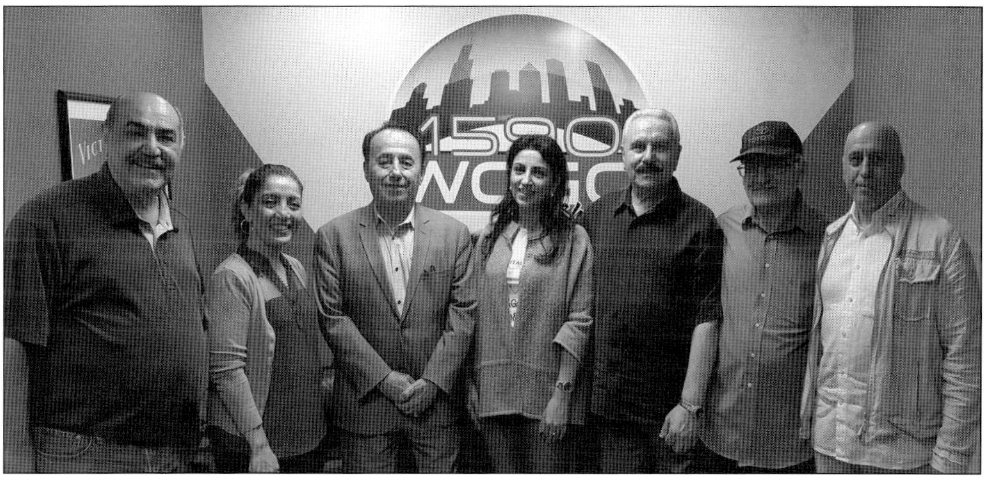

Pictured here is the Shotaputa radio team during an interview with Madlen Ishoeva, an Assyrian singer from Russia, in 2017. From left to right are Emanuel Isho, Teena Khaee, Glen Younan, Madlen Ishoeva, Edward Nadirsha, Edmond Hasso, and Vasili Shoumanov. (Author's collection.)

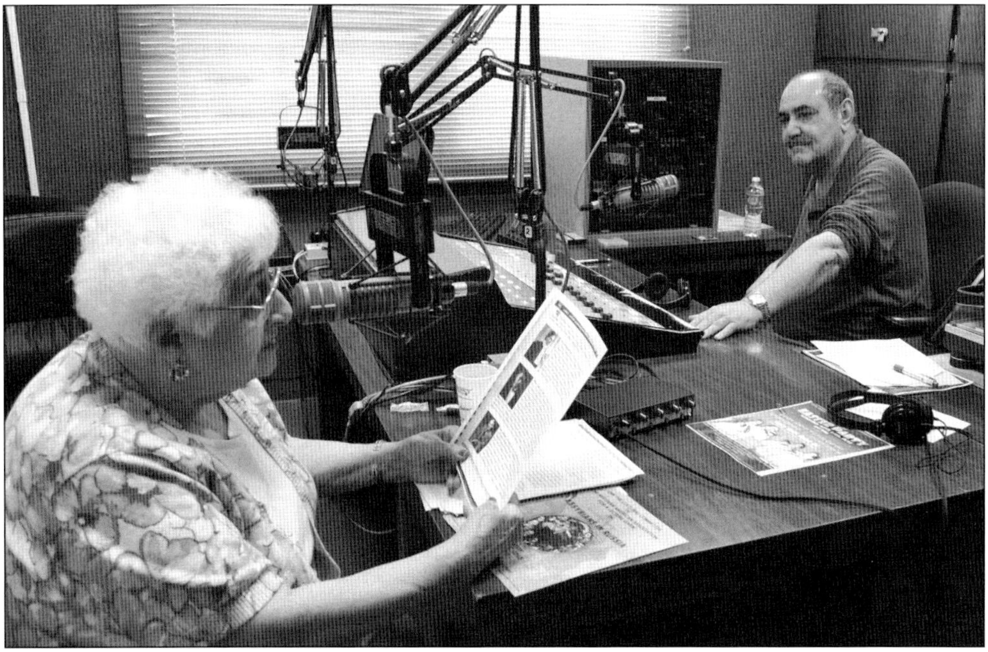

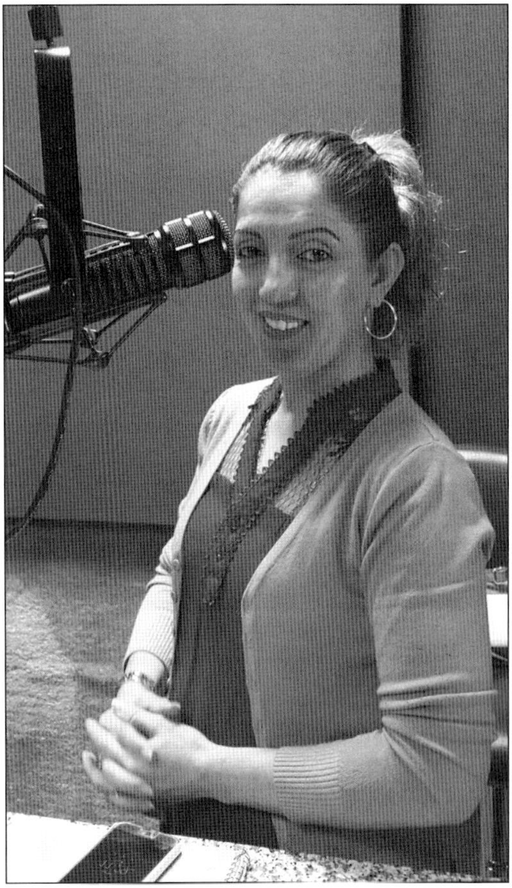

Sarah N. Benjamin passed away on April 25, 2018. She was born in Chicago on October 18, 1922, to Ezra and Katherine Newey and graduated from Waller High School and Wright Junior College. She was a professional opera singer and was active in the Assyrian community and the Women's Auxiliary of the Chicago chapter. Benjamin became a popular co-host on an Assyrian-American radio program heard Saturday mornings throughout Chicagoland on 1590 WCGO. (Author's collection.)

Teena Khaee is pictured behind a microphone in the Assyrian American Association's radio studio. Every Saturday, Khaee is the host on *Voice of Truth* on 1590 WCGO. (Author's collection.)

Voice of Truth brings a mix of new guests and a range of experts to the microphone to discuss what is happening in the Assyrian community. Linda Dekelaita is an AAAC and Assyrian church radio host. (Author's collection.)

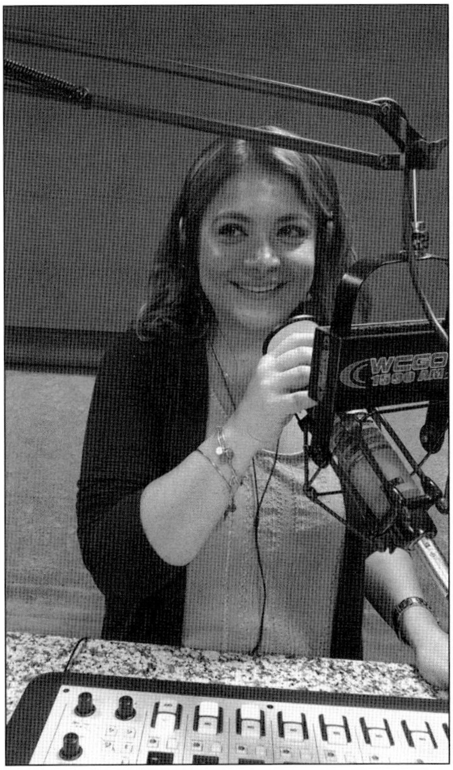

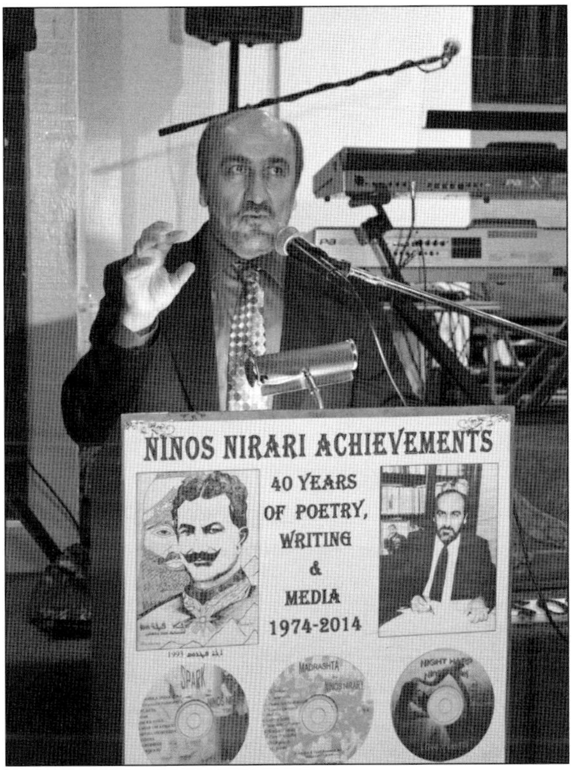

Ninos Nirari, a renowned Assyrian poet and writer, is pictured on the AAAC stage celebrating his 40 years of accomplishments on September 1, 2014. (Author's collection.)

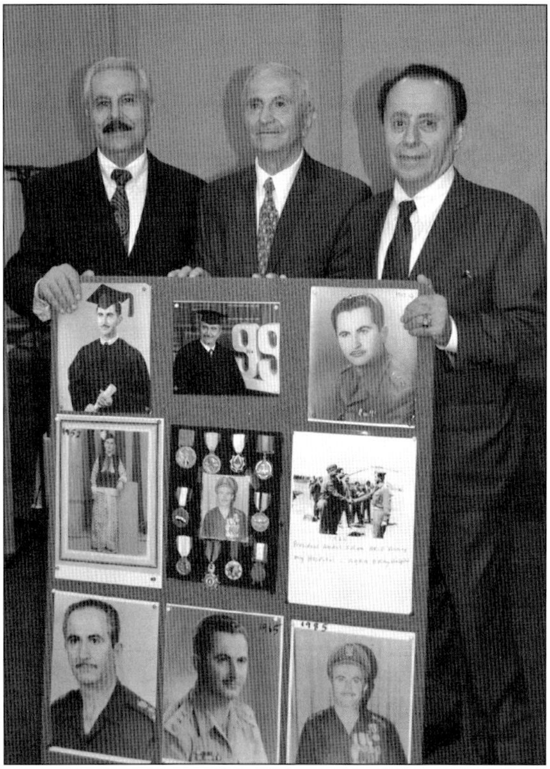

The AAAC honored Dr. Rouel Georgis for his lifetime of achievement in medical service for the Chicago Assyrian community on August 1, 2015. Dr. Georgis is a major general who served as a physician in the Iraqi army. From left to right are Edward Nadirsha, Dr. Georgis, and Glen Younan. (Author's collection.)

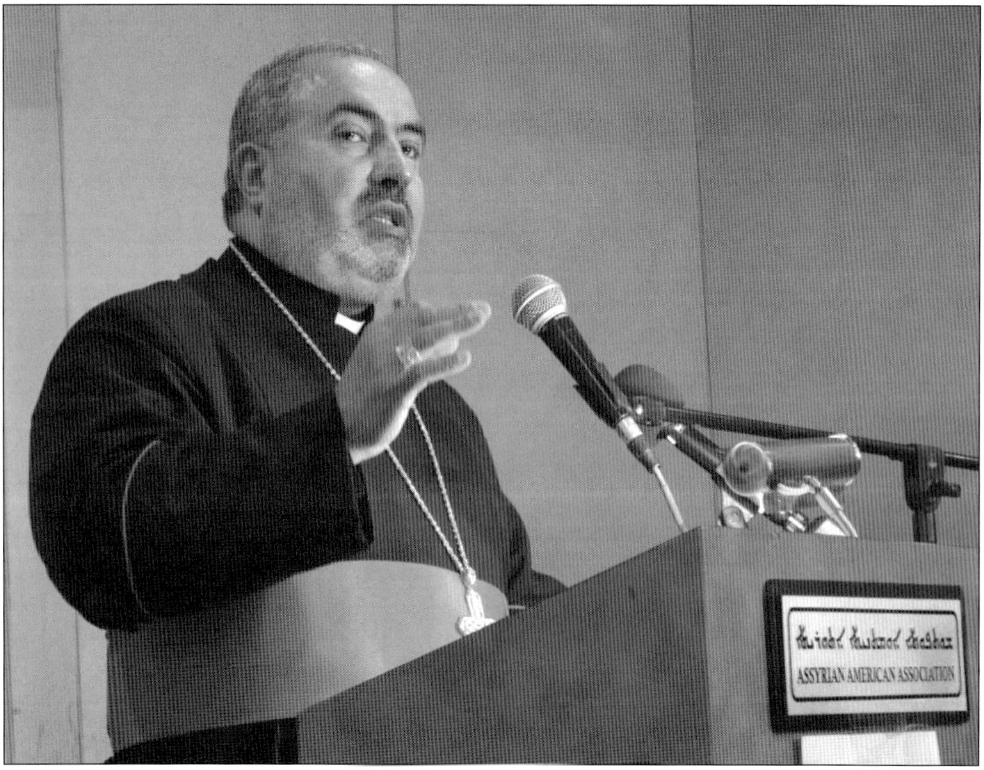

Mar Paulus Benjamin speaks at the Assyrian American Association of Chicago on September 16, 2016. Benjamin was born in the village of Qala, Urmia, in Iran. He served the military from 1993 to 1995 and came to the United States in July 2007. In 2012, Benjamin was elected bishop for the Diocese of the Eastern United States. (Author's collection.)

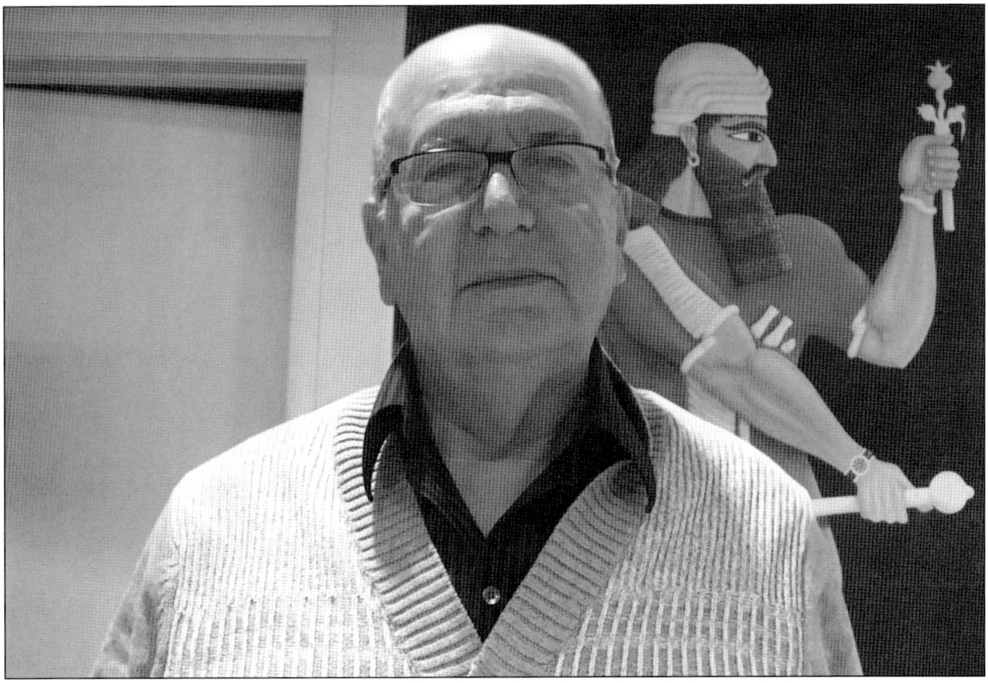

Sargon Isaac served as the AAAC president in 1976. His family was related to the famous and noble Mar Yukhannan family from Iran and Russia. (Courtesy of Edward Nadirsha.)

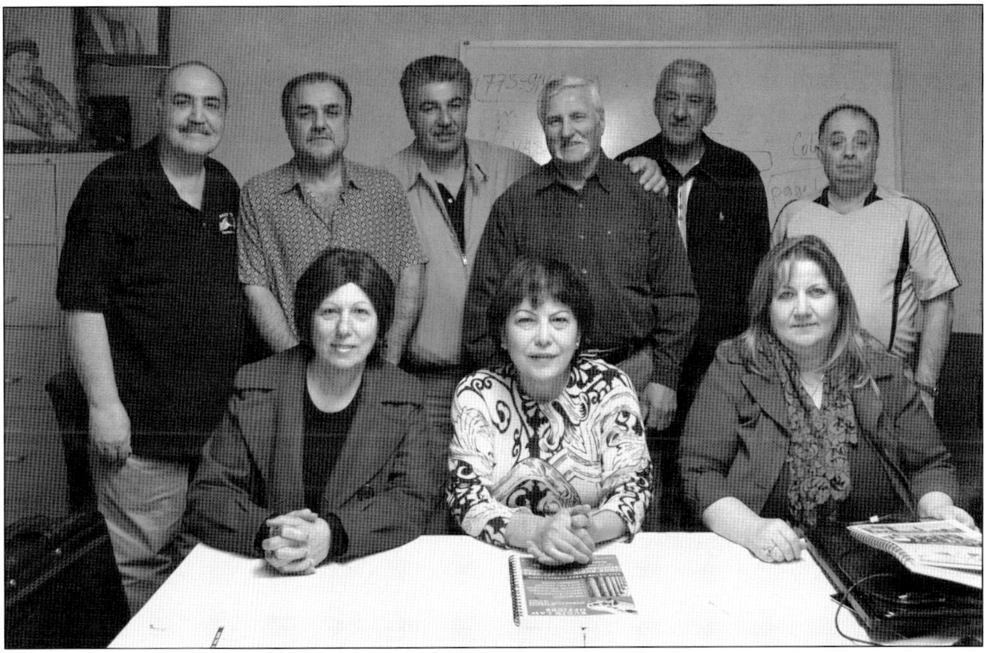

Pictured here are students of the AAAC computer course instructed by Vasili Shoumanov in 2013. From left to right are (first row) Dorin Narsay, Shamiram Grossman, and Janet Talya; (second row) Emanuel Isho, Wilson Narsay, Tony Yousif, William Badal, Albert Basliel, and Farid Talya. (Author's collection.)

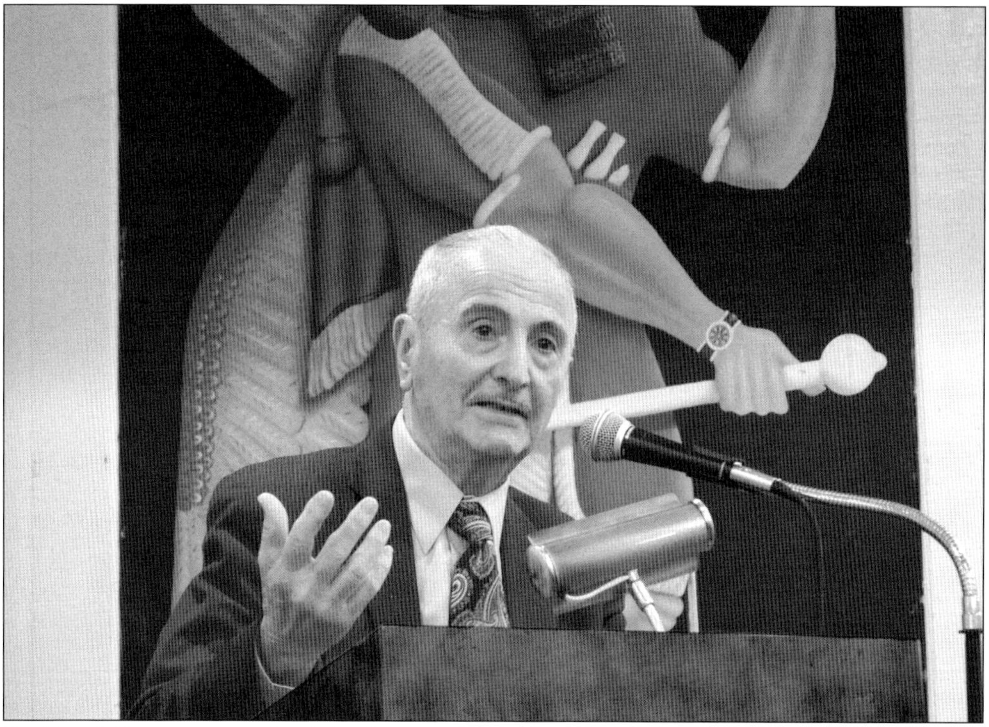

Dr. Rouel Georgis is on the AAAC stage presenting the lecture "Treatments for Cancer and Diabetes through the Natural Medicine," on January 26, 2014. (Author's collection.)

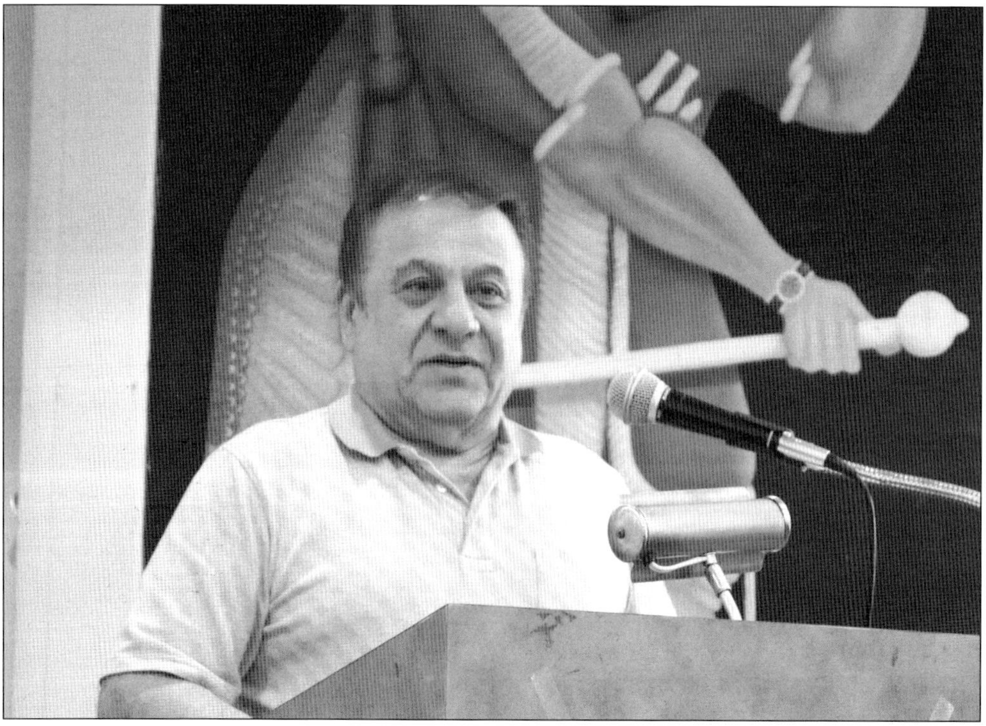

Kenneth Kocho delivers a lecture on alternative medicine in 2014. (Author's collection.)

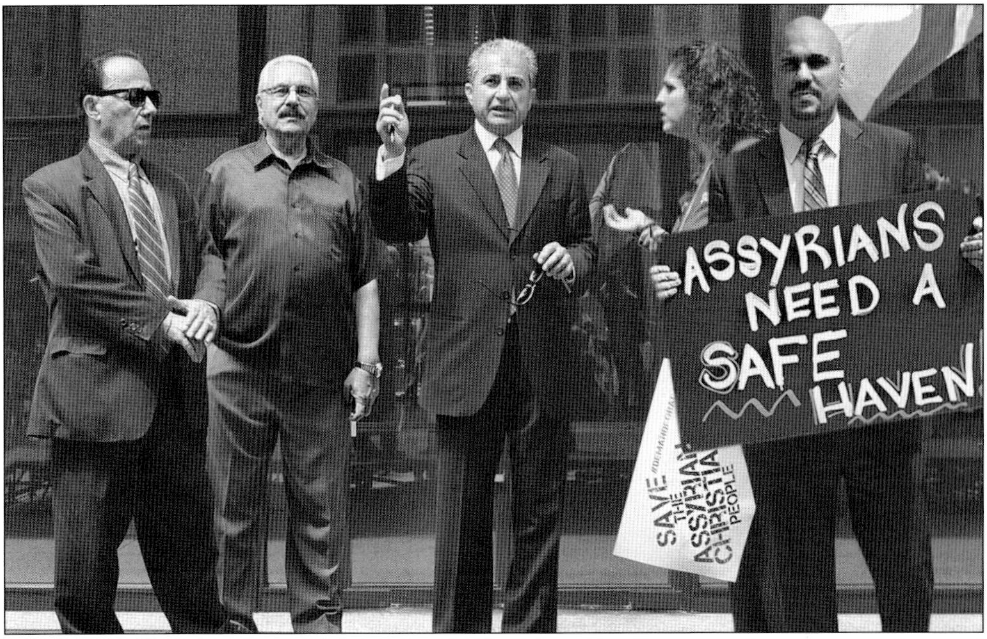

Assyrians staged a protest in downtown Chicago against persecution and massacres in Iraq and Syria. From left to right are Glen Younan, president of the Assyrian American Association; Edward Nadirsha, AAAC vice president; William Youmaran, president of the Assyrian American Federation; and attorney Tony Kalogerakos in 2013. (Author's collection.)

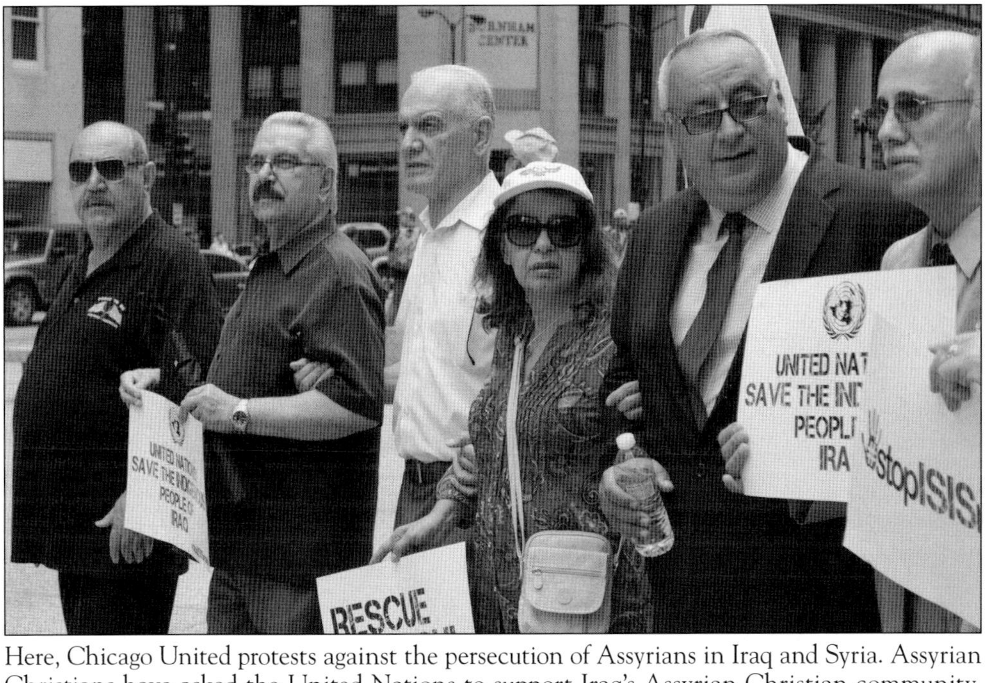

Here, Chicago United protests against the persecution of Assyrians in Iraq and Syria. Assyrian Christians have asked the United Nations to support Iraq's Assyrian Christian community. From left to right are Emanuel Isho, Edward Nadirsha (of the AAAC), Hermiz Tiro, Agnes Merza (Zowaa), Emanuel Khoshaba (Assyrian Patriotic Party), and Baito Chikko (AUA) in 2014. (Author's collection.)

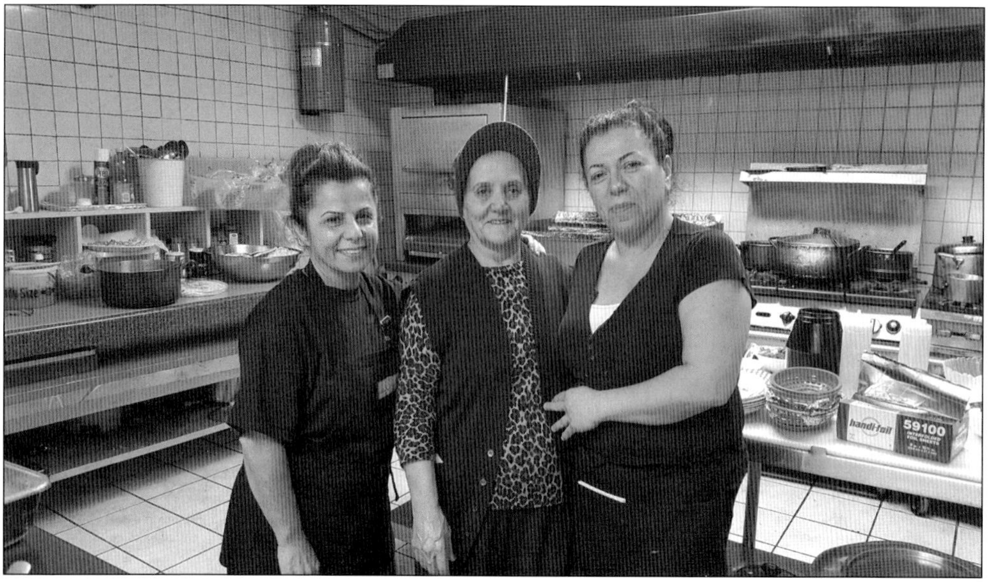

The AAAC is the best place to test traditional Assyrian food. Pictured here is a team of professional chefs preparing and cooking food. From left to right are Violet Kina, Laya Oudisho, and Juliet Yukhanna. (Author's collection.)

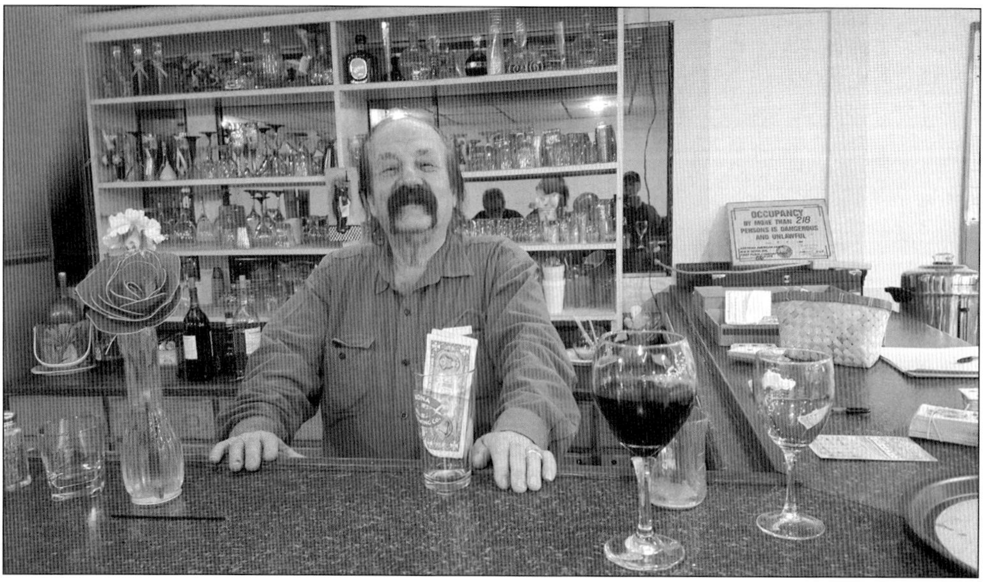

A smiling Yousip Younan is pictured behind the bar. He plans on giving the AAAC bar a "new look" with new features and promotions. (Author's collection.)

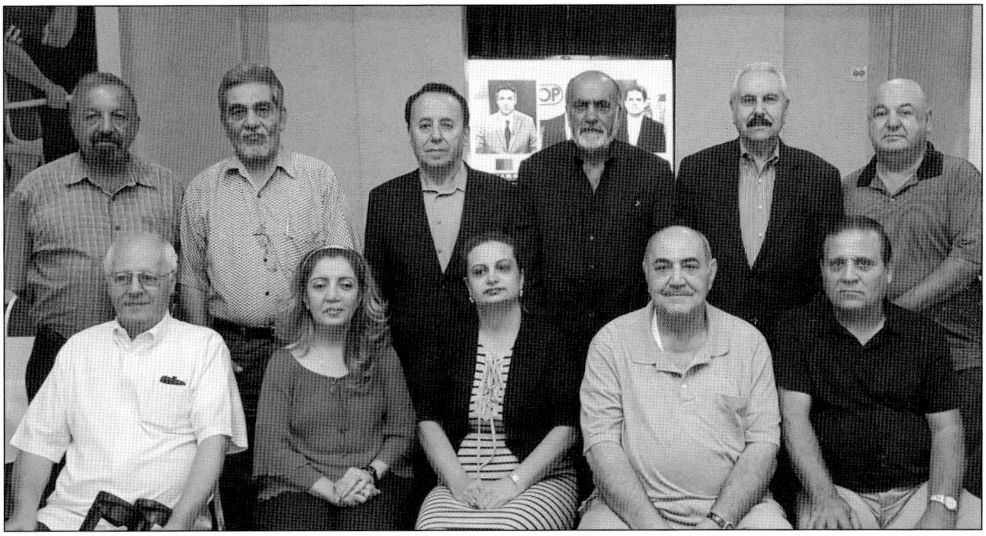

Seen here are Dr. Anahit Khosroeva and AAAC members in 2013. Khosroeva has a PhD in genocide study and works at the Institute of History, National Academy of Sciences of Armenia. From left to right are (first row) John Khoury, Teena Khaee, Dr. Khosroeva, Emanuel Isho, and Albert Malkonian; (second row) Raman Oshana, Joseph Gabrial, Glen Younan, Razmik Khosroev (national artist of Armenia), Edward Nadirsha, and Fransis Yousif. (Author's collection.)

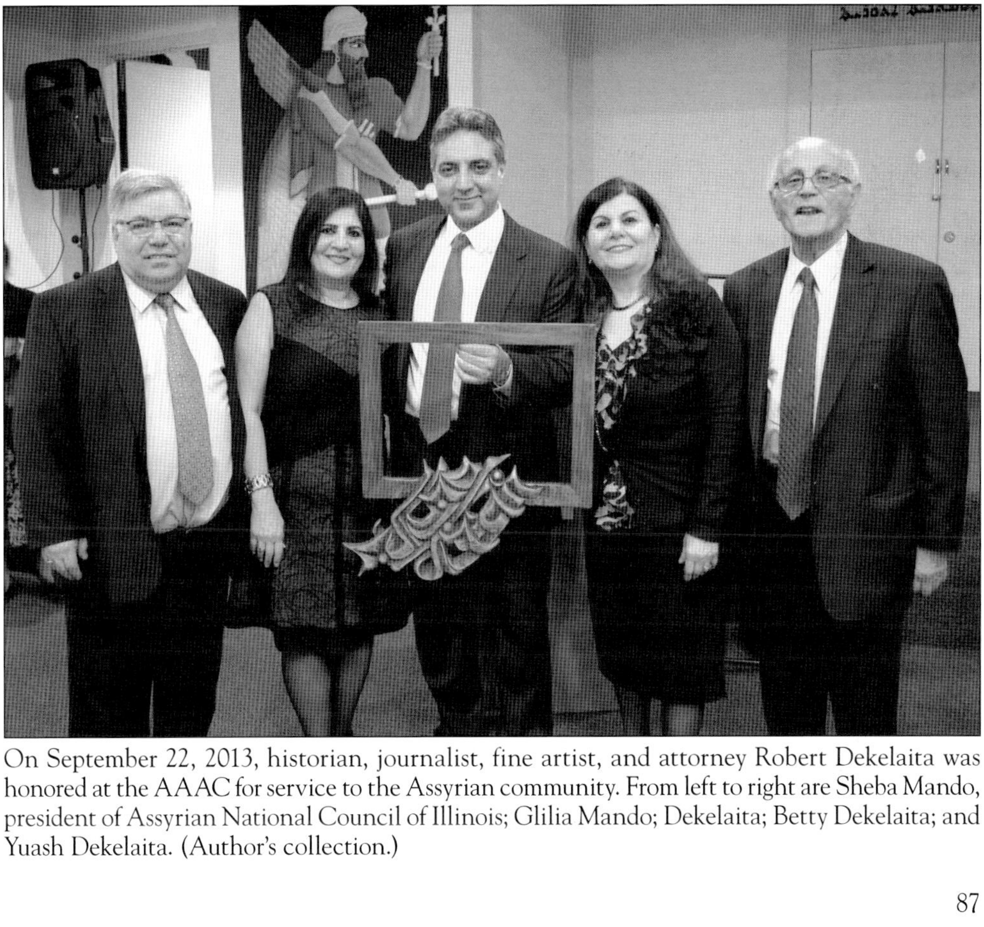

On September 22, 2013, historian, journalist, fine artist, and attorney Robert Dekelaita was honored at the AAAC for service to the Assyrian community. From left to right are Sheba Mando, president of Assyrian National Council of Illinois; Glilia Mando; Dekelaita; Betty Dekelaita; and Yuash Dekelaita. (Author's collection.)

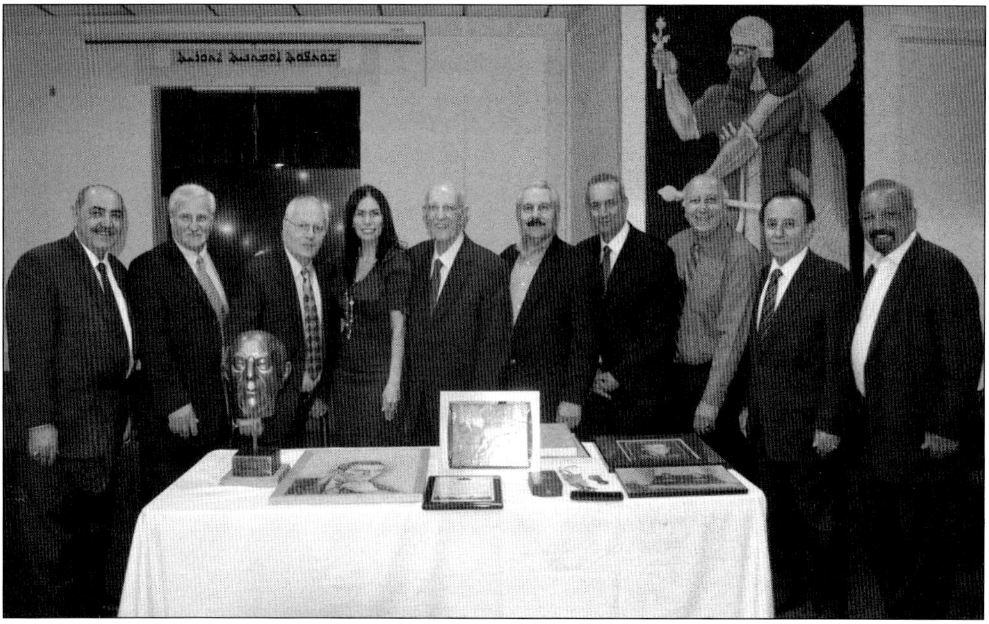

In this 2015 photograph, the AAAC honors Homer Ashurian, formerly an Iranian congressman. He was a popular lecturer on history and linguistics for many years at the AAAC. From left to right are Emanuel Isho, William Badal, John Khoury, Linda George, Ashurian, Edward Nadirsha, Sam Oushana, Emanuel Bet Somo, Glen Younan, and Raman Oshana. (Author's collection.)

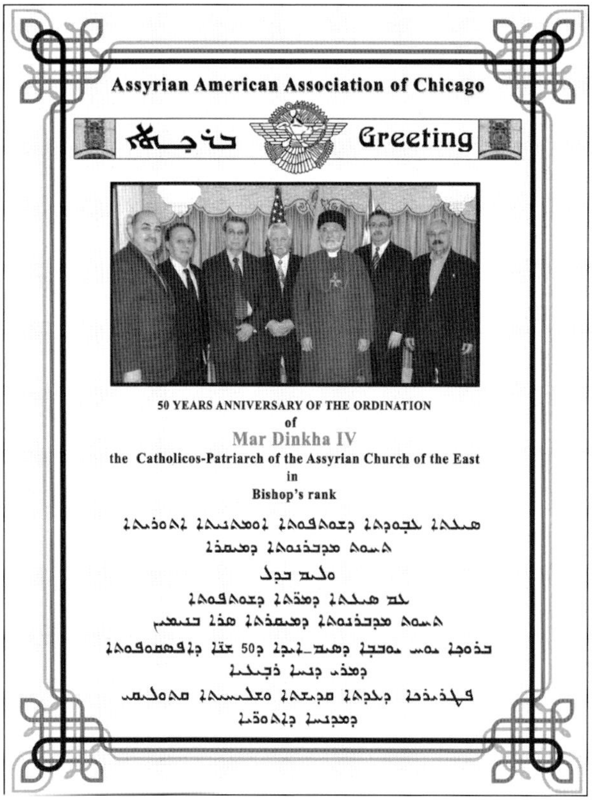

This greeting card was issued by the AAAC for Patriarch Mar Dinkha IV, the catholicos-patriarch of the Assyrian Church of the East. He served as a priest since July 15, 1957, and later was made a consecrated bishop in Iran on February 12, 1962, by Mar Eshai Shimun XXI, catholicos-patriarch. Dinkha served as bishop for 14 years, until his election as catholicos-patriarch on October 17, 1976. (Author's collection.)

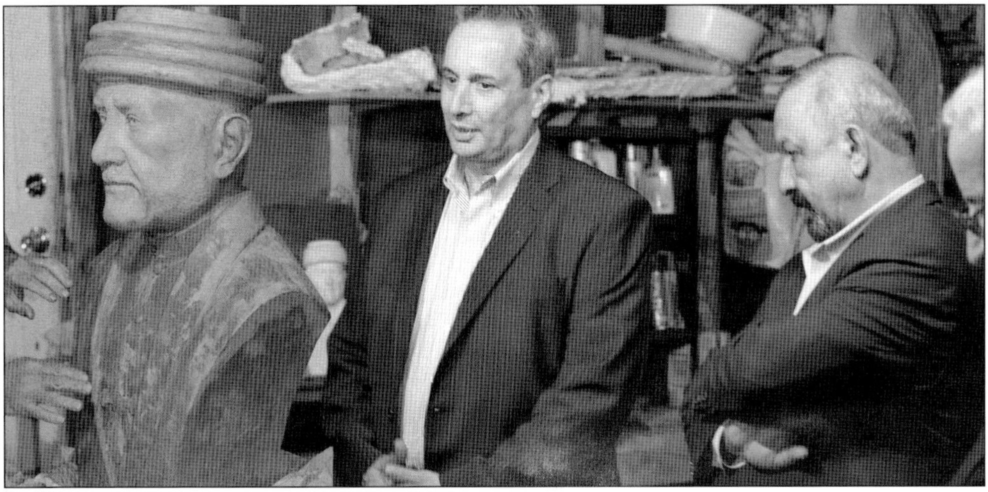

Sam Oushana (left) and his brother Raman Oshana examine a raw clay bust of Patriarch Mar Dinkha on October 24, 2015, before it was cast in bronze. Sam and Raman are successful businessmen and active members of the AAAC. (Author's collection.)

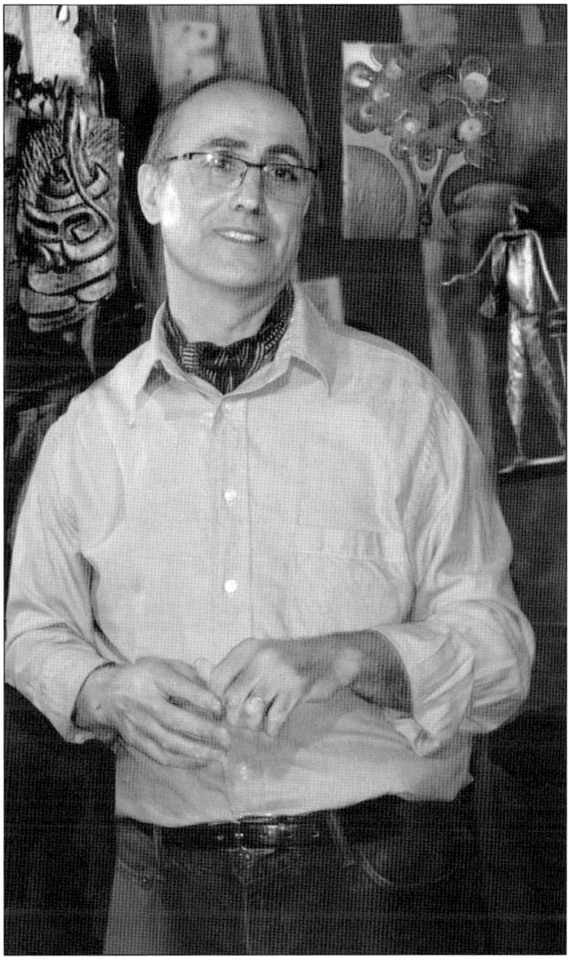

Dankha Zomaya is a painter and sculptor, with more than 35 solo and joint exhibitions in the Middle East, Europe, and the United States. His artwork is currently displayed at the New Art Gallery in the National Museum of Damascus, Syria. He is the sculptor of the bust dedicated to Patriarch Mar Dinkha IV. (Author's collection.)

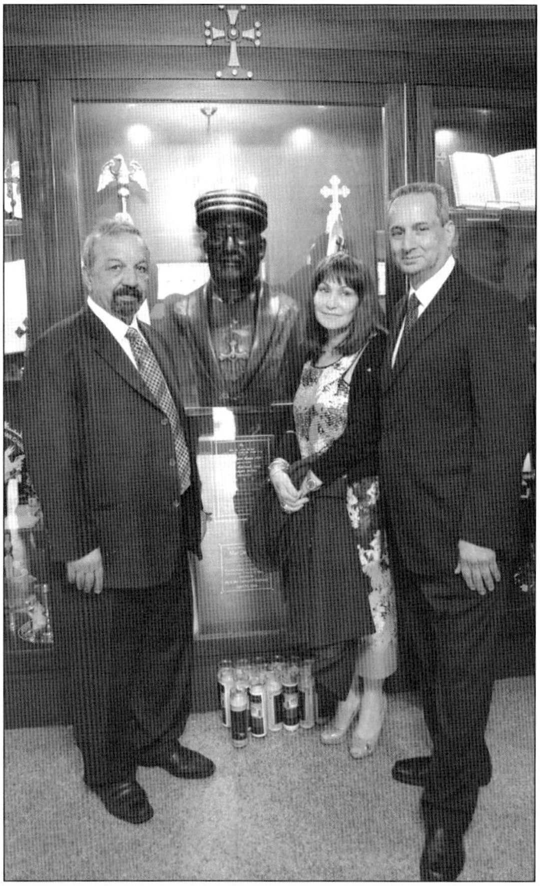

Pictured here is Sam Oushana's family standing by the Mar Dinkha IV monument at the opening of a new museum dedicated to the patriarch at St. George Church in Chicago on April 10, 2016. From left to right are Raman, Bernadette, and Sam Oushana. (Author's collection.)

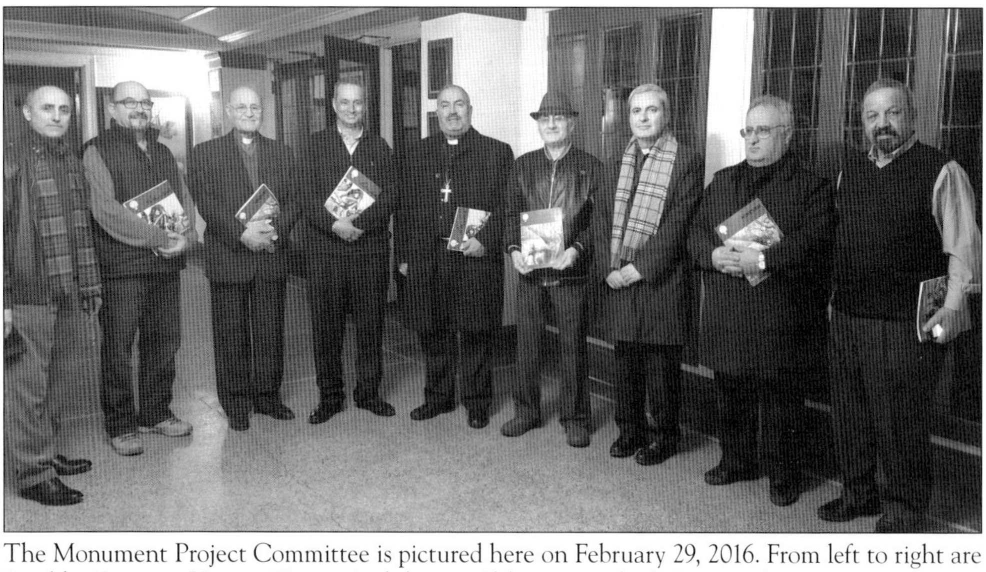

The Monument Project Committee is pictured here on February 29, 2016. From left to right are Dankha Zomaya, Hermiz Hasso, Archdeacon Shlemon Hezkiel, Sam Oushana, His Grace Mar Paulus Benjamin, Edward Hasso, Rev. Archdeacon Dr. William Toma, Deacon Tony Khoury, and Raman Oshana. (Author's collection.)

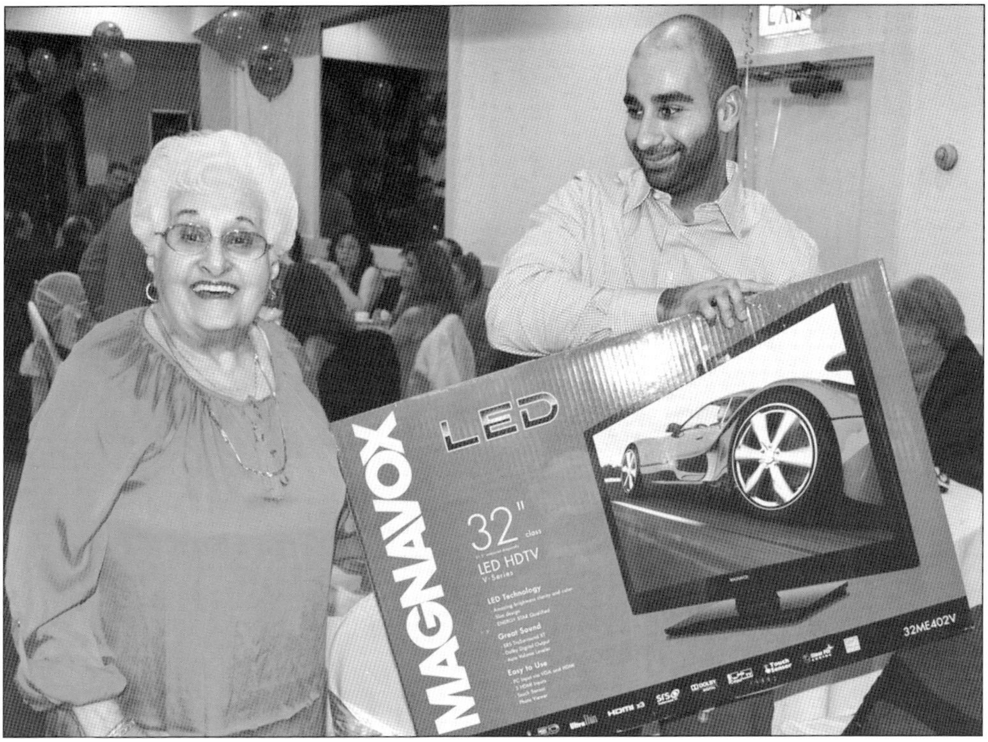

Sarah Benjamin receives the Woman of the Year award for her exemplary volunteer service at the AAAC in 2013. Benjamin has more than 60 years experience working with Assyrian organizations in the United States. (Author's collection.)

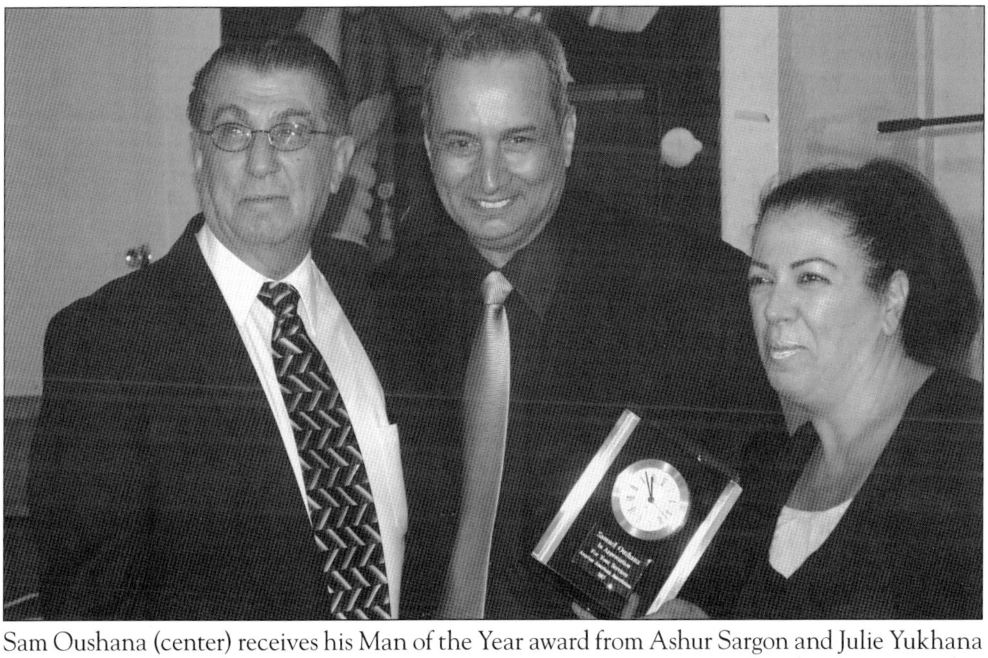

Sam Oushana (center) receives his Man of the Year award from Ashur Sargon and Julie Yukhana in 2015. Oushana has been working in the automotive industry for 40 years, and now owns Ogden Automotive Center in Chicago. (Author's collection.)

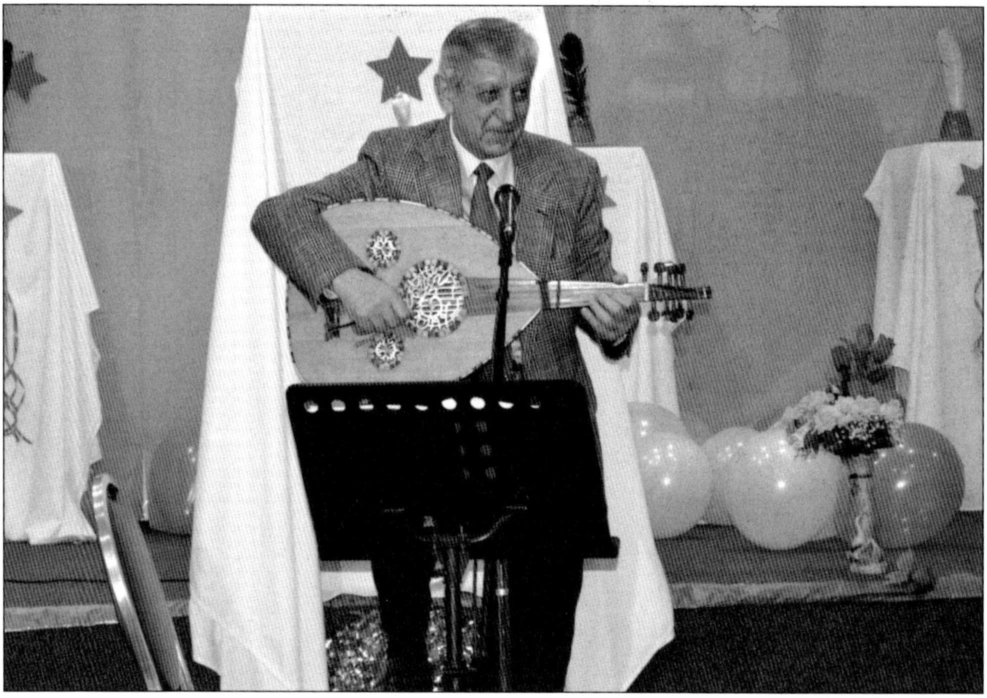

Journalist, poet, and musician Fidor Albazy is pictured playing the *oud* (a short-neck lute-type, pear-shaped stringed instrument) during a Valentine's Day performance at the AAAC in 2013. He began his career writing in both Arabic and Assyrian. (Author's collection.)

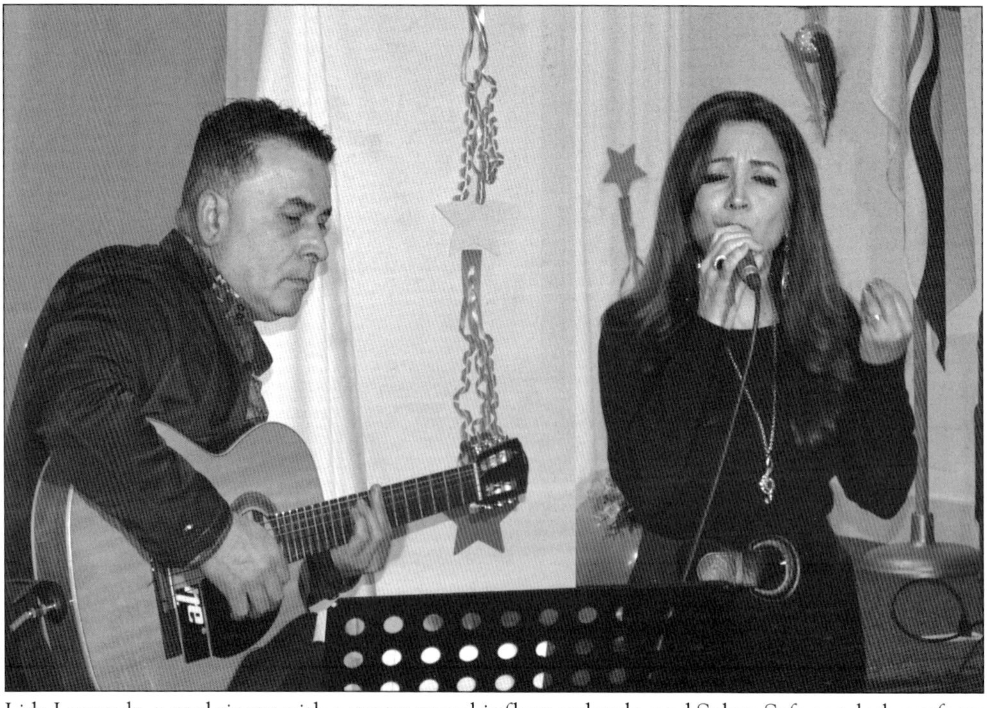

Lida Lawando, a soul singer with a strong gospel-influenced style, and Salem Sefo regularly perform on the AAAC stage. (Author's collection.)

Pierre Chamoun is a famous teacher and journalist. He was an editor of dozens of publications, including the *Assyrian Star*, *Voice of the East*, *Spar-Tibba*, and *Zahrira* (Ray). He writes poetry in modern and classical Assyrian. (Author's collection.)

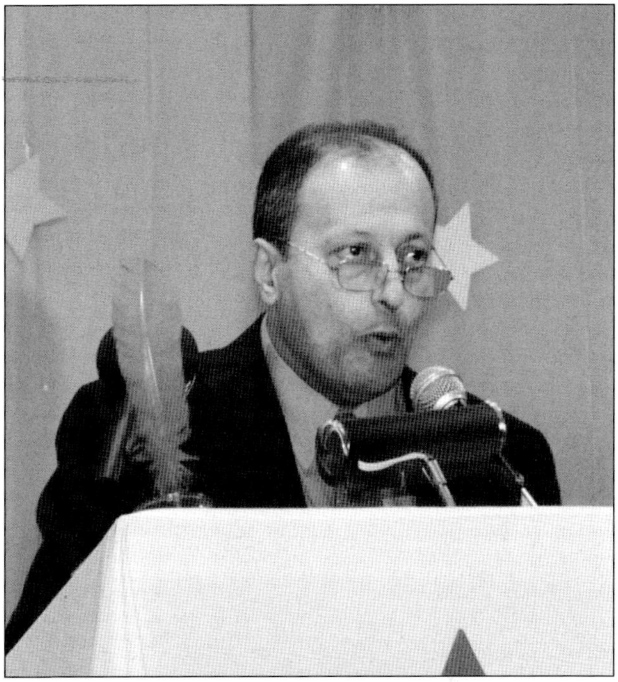

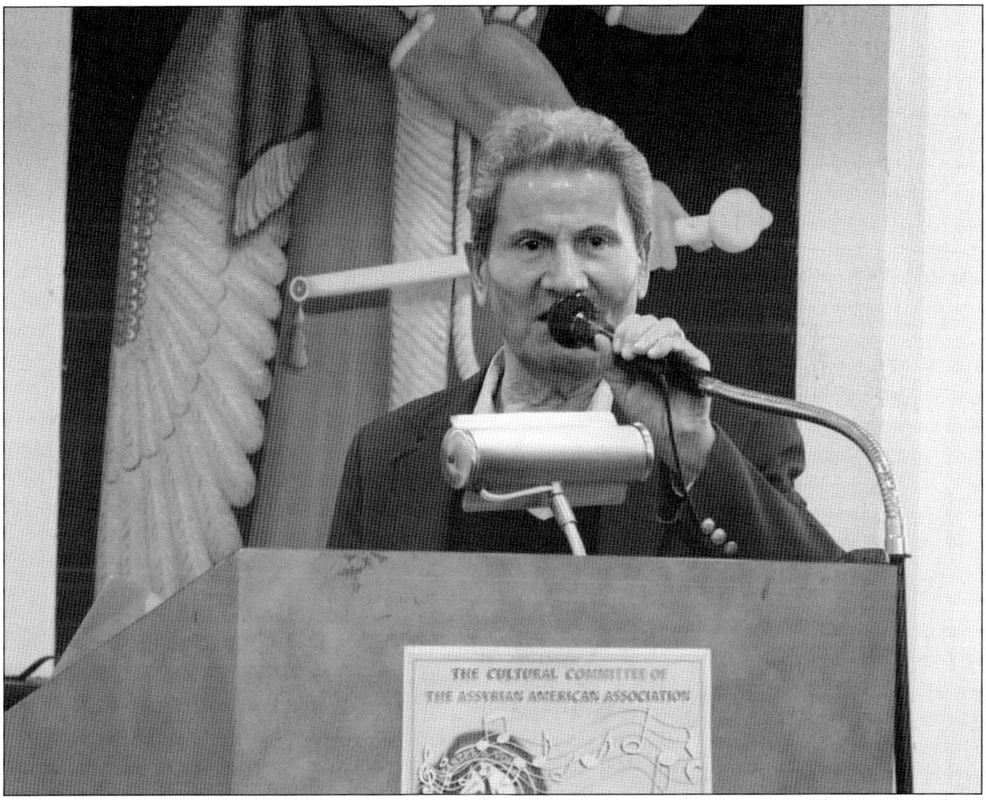

Ashur Solomon (Bet-Shlimon) is a linguist and journalist. He is pictured in 2013 presenting the lecture "The History of the Assyrian Language." (Author's collection.)

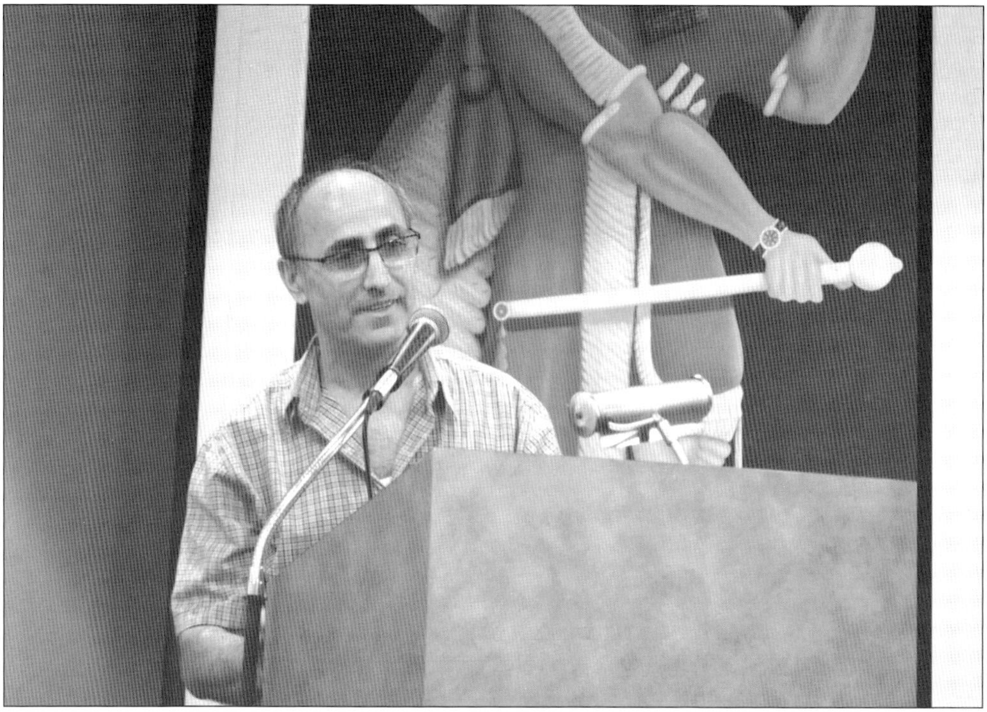

Artist Dankha Zomaya delivers a lecture entitled "Succession in Culture: Assyrian Roots in World Art" in 2014. (Author's collection.)

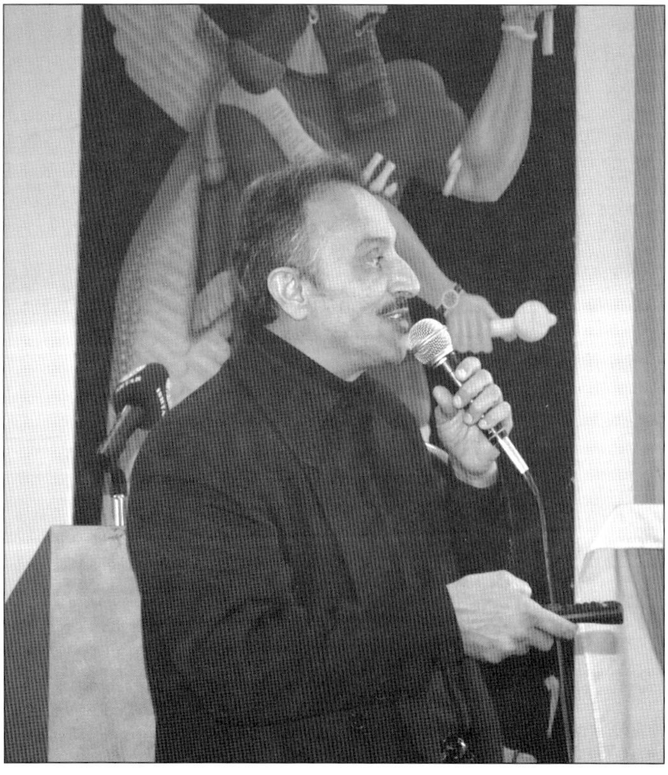

Jesse Avakian is delivering his lecture "The Lingual Connection between Ancient and Modern Assyrians" in 2012. (Author's collection.)

The lecture "Akkadian Words in Modern Assyrian" is being presented by Homer Ashurian in 2011. Ashurian is an archeologist and former Iranian congressman. He is a founder of the Cultural Center of the Assyrian Universal Alliance Foundation. (Author's collection.)

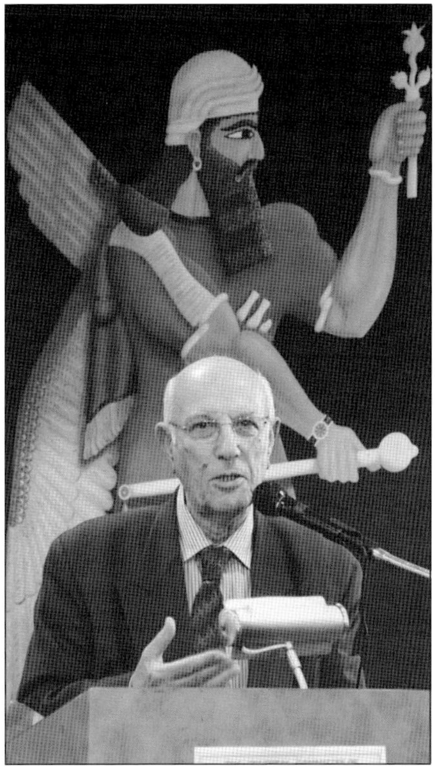

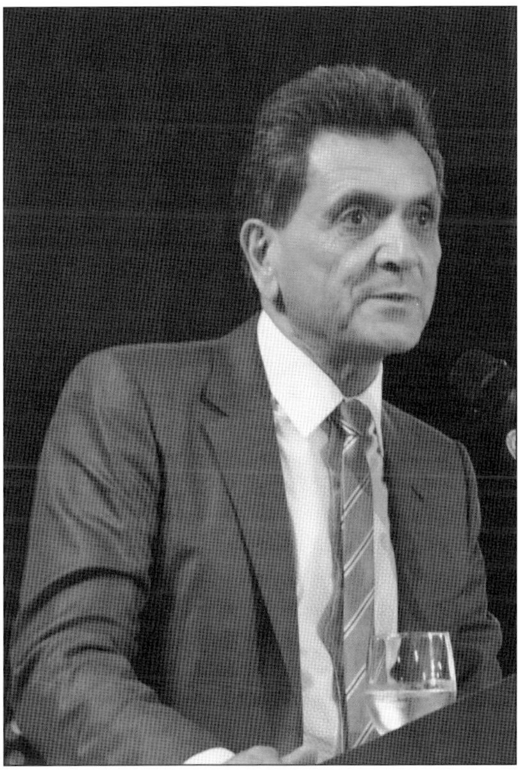

Radio legend and journalist Wilson Younan talked about recent conflicts in the Middle East. (Author's collection.)

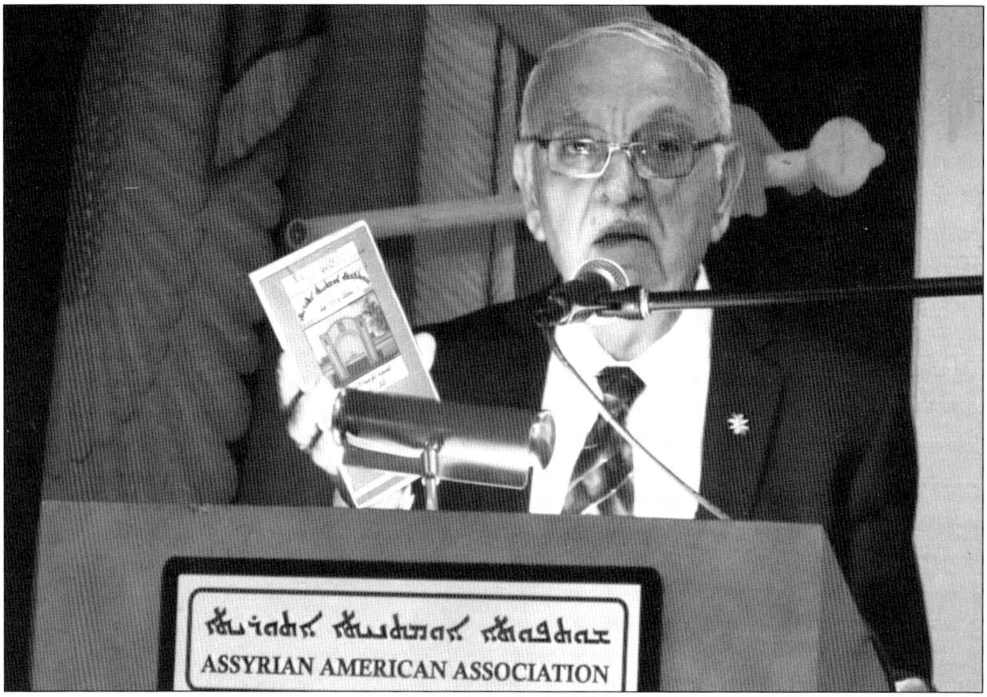

Michael Mammo, a journalist and teacher from Sweden, presented his lecture "Assyrian Language Today" in 2015. He is the author of dozens of books on poetry and language. (Author's collection.)

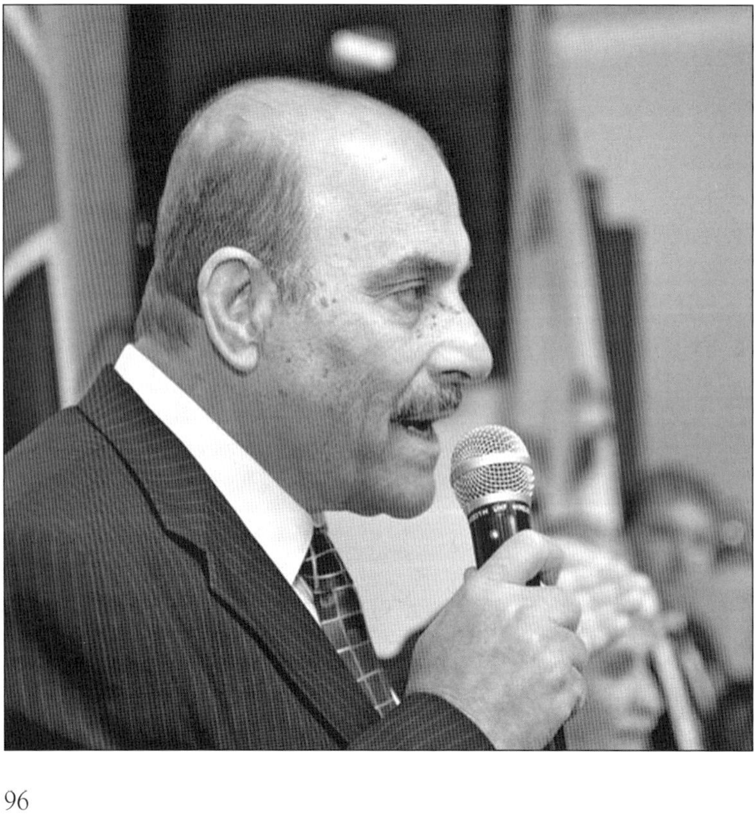

Ninos Aho is a world-renowned Assyrian poet and activist and an AAAC member. His poems have a romantic and patriotic style and tone, focusing on themes of love and homeland, past and future. (Courtesy of Sabri Atman.)

William David served as the AAAC president in 1974. He initiated a new publication program with the Assyrian Association in Toronto, Canada. (Author's collection.)

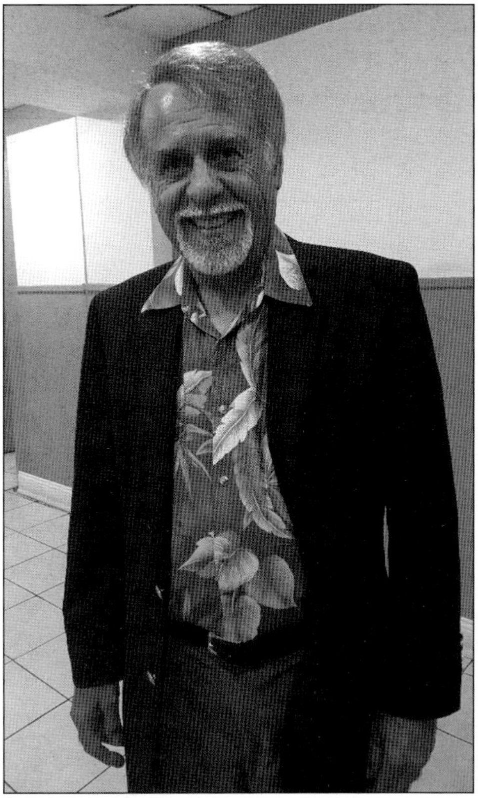

Shlimon Bet-Shmuel, a musician, singer, and author of *Musical Instruments of Ancient Mesopotamia* and *A Step into the Unknown*, is delivering the lecture "Early Recording of the Assyrian Songs" in 2014. (Author's collection.)

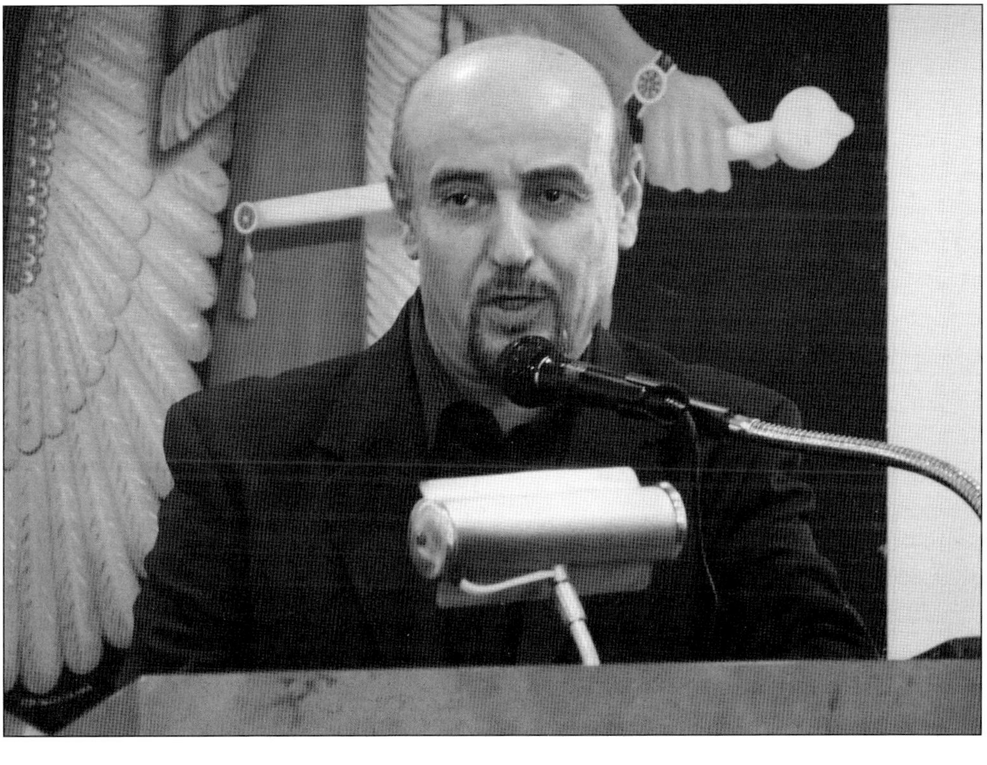

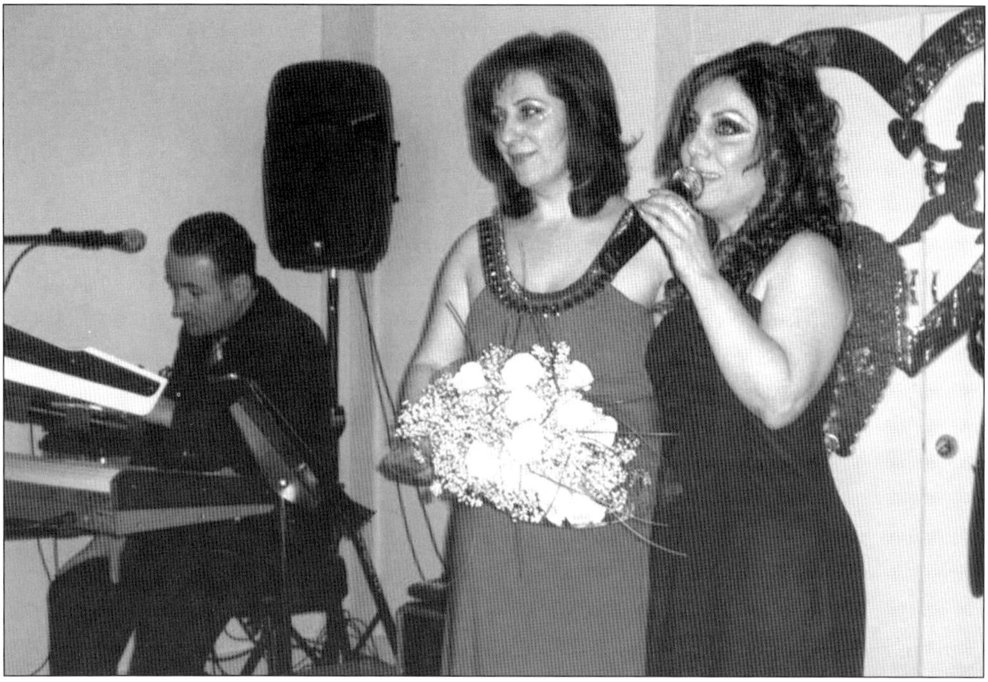

The AAAC invites artists from across the United States and other countries. Pictured here are Stella Rezgo (left), an Assyrian-Russian-Canadian singer, and Elizabeth Oushana, a songwriter and singer from Chicago, performing on Valentine's Day 2012. (Author's collection.)

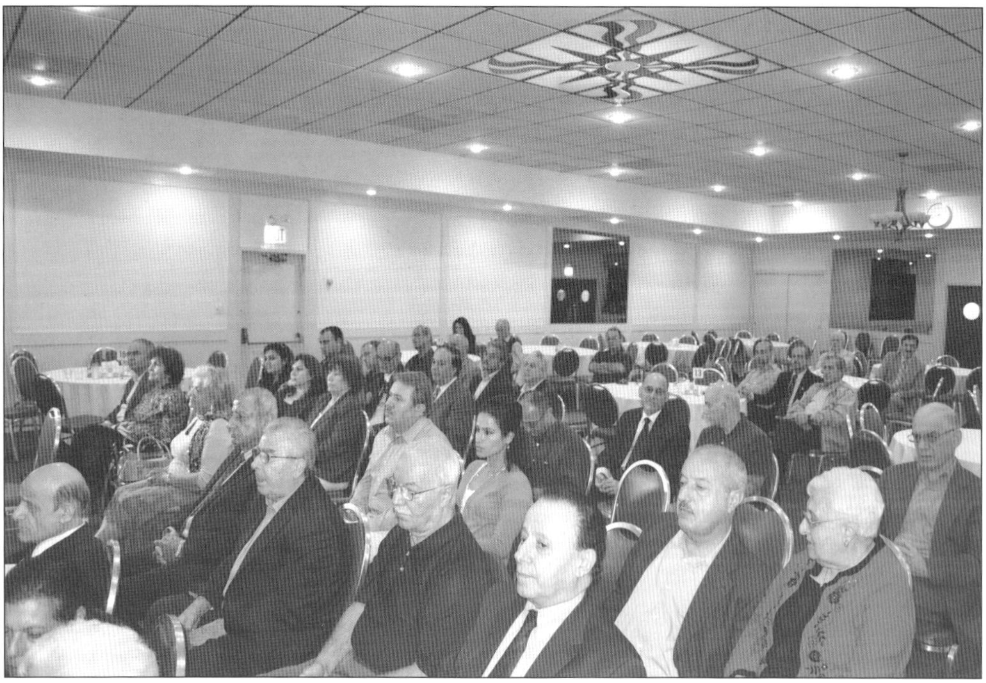

The AAAC lecture hall is always full of people. The association hosts all kinds of lectures, concerts, rallies, and shows. (Author's collection.)

Professor and linguist Robin Bet Shmoel from Iraq was invited to give a lecture entitled "Assyrian language Development" on March 9, 2014. (Author's collection.)

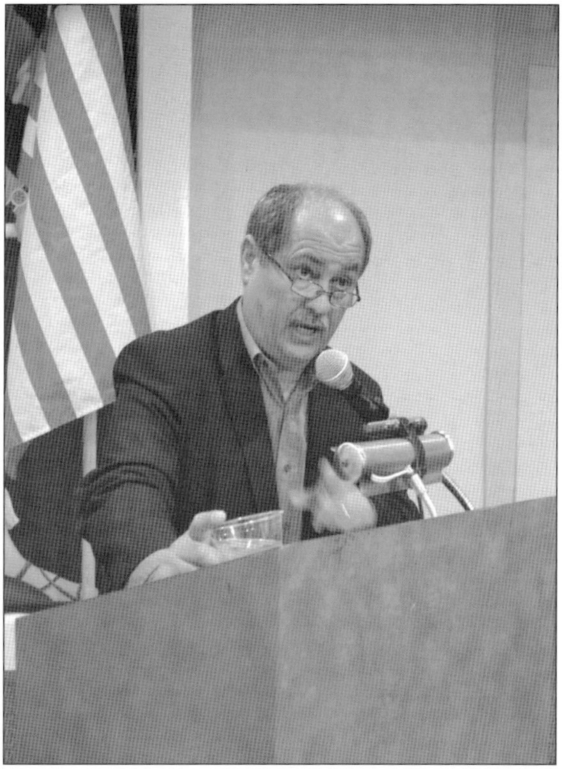

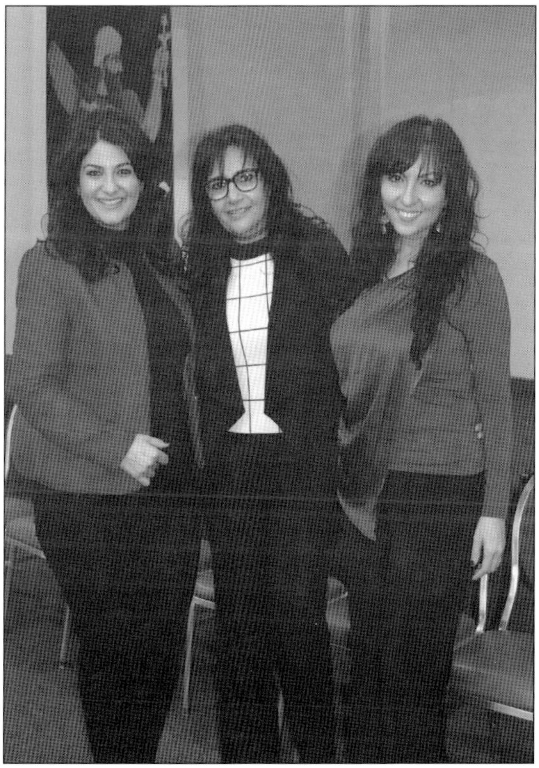

Pictured here is an intellectual trinity. From left to right are Matyam Shamalta, Shamiram Media; Violet Khamoo, actress and community activist; and Juliana Taimoorazy, founder and president of the Iraqi Christian Relief Council in 2016. (Author's collection.)

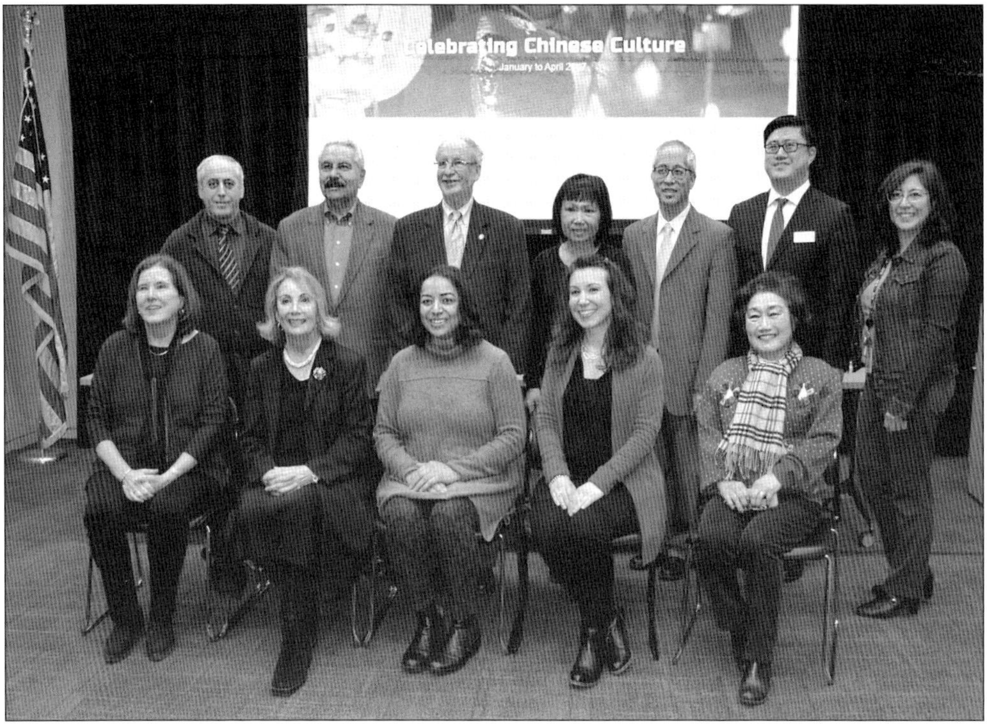

This is a committee of the annual cultural program Skokie Coming Together in the village of Skokie and Niles Township, with AAAC members Vasili Shoumanov (second row, far left), Edward Nadirsha (second row, second from left), Skokie mayor George Van Dusen (second row, third from left); and first lady of Skokie Susan Van Dusen (first row, second from left). This photograph was taken at the Skokie Public Library in 2017. (Author's collection.)

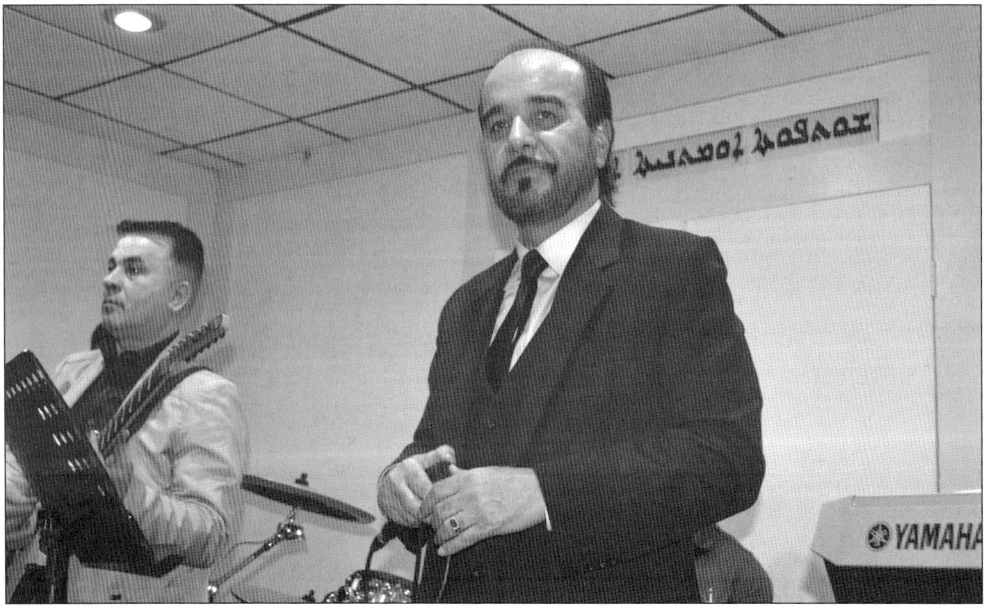

Pictured here are popular Assyrian singers on the AAAC stage: Salem Sefo (left) and George Jindo. (Author's collection.)

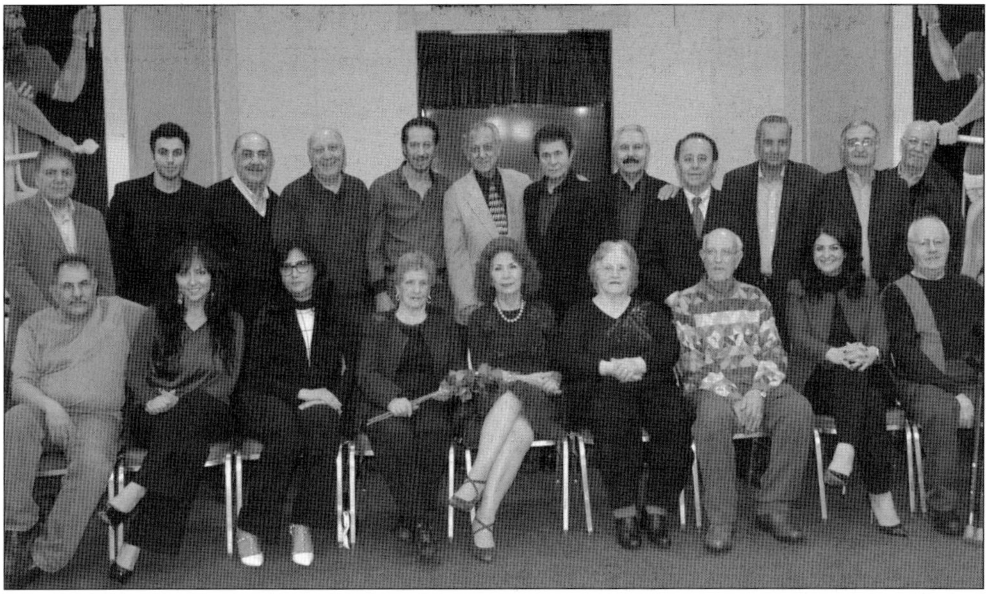

Hollywood filmmaker Henri Charr (second row, seventh from left) meets AAAC members after a screening of his docudrama *A Man Before His Time* in Chicago in 2016. It is a story about poet, doctor, and politician Freydun Atouraya. (Author's collection.)

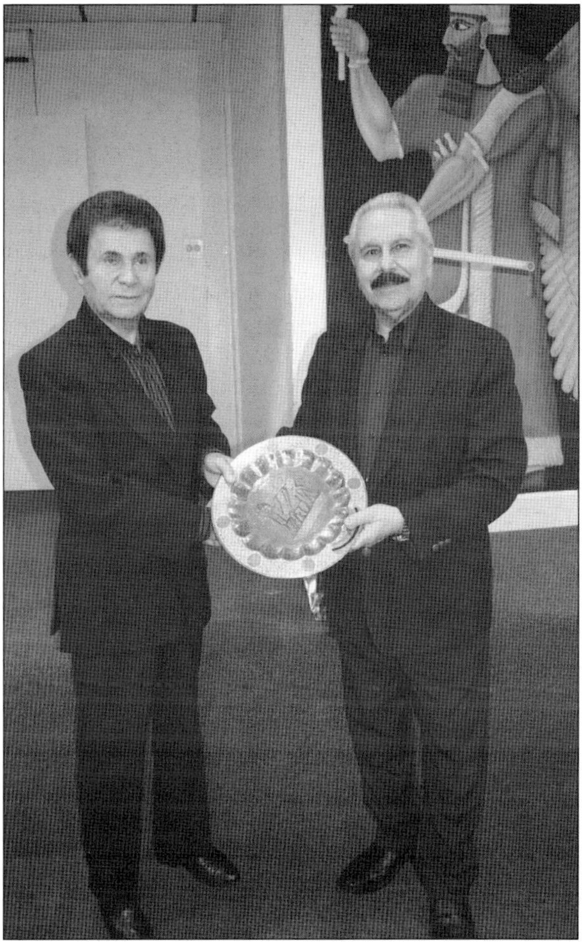

Pictured here are Edward Nadirsha (right), AAAC vice president, and Henri Charr, Hollywood movie director. Charr is being awarded for his new movie production in 2016. (Author's collection.)

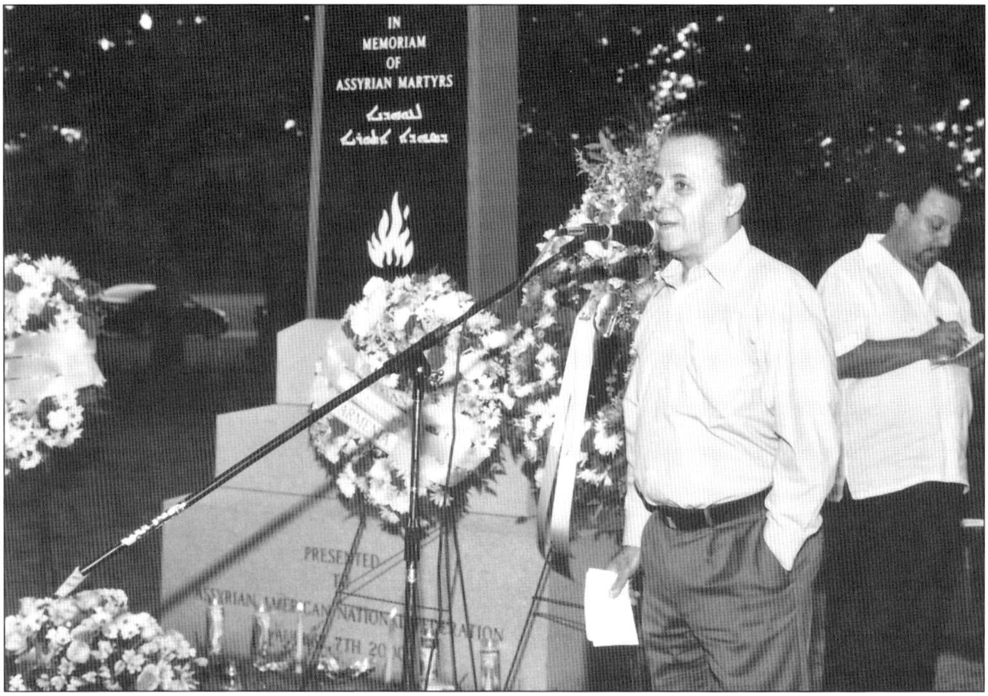

Glen Younan delivers his Memorial Day address to the Assyrian community, presented at the Assyrian Memorial Park at Montrose Cemetery in Chicago in 2016. Memorial Park was founded by Dr. Norman Solhkhah. (Author's collection.)

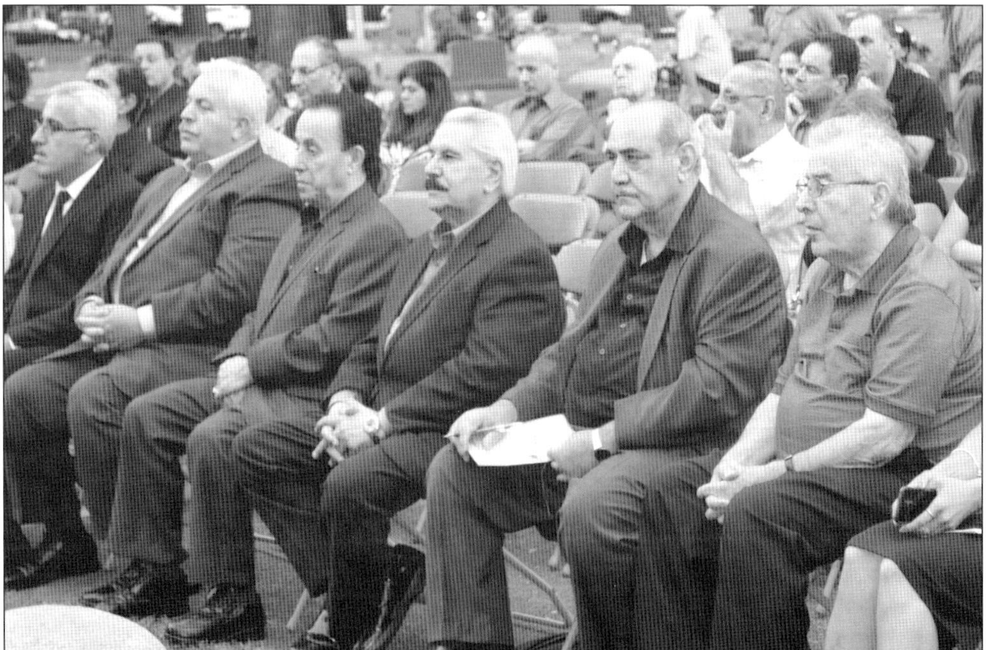

This photograph was taken during the Annual Assyrian Memorial Day at Montrose Cemetery on August 7, 2017. August 7 has been designated as a day to commemorate the massacres of Assyrians in the Middle East. (Author's collection.)

Four

The 100th-Anniversary Celebration

For the past 100 years, the Assyrian American Association of Chicago has provided a strong support system not only to the Assyrian community, but to the city of Chicago and its multiethnic population.

In September 2017, the AAAC received honorary plaques from the Assyrian American National Federation in recognition of the organization's efforts for the Assyrian community and 52 years of being on the air with the *Voice of Truth* radio program at the 84th annual national convention of the Assyrian American National Federation in Scottsdale, Arizona. It was presented by Martin Youmaran, the AANF president.

The year 2017 marks the centennial of the Assyrian American Association of Chicago, a nonprofit, tax-exempt, interdisciplinary organization. Over 100 years, AAAC has enriched its community and added luster to the organization's reputation with multifaceted cultural and social activities, including art, education, sports, music, poetry, history, and literature.

Emanuel Isho was appointed the celebration chairman, and the event committee included Linda Dekelaita, Teena Khaee, Raman Oshana, Emanuel Bet-Somo, Vasili Shoumanov, and Edmond Hasso.

To commemorate the centennial, the AAAC presented a special program that lasted three days. The AAAC brought together friends from all Chicago organization and churches, including the Assyrian American National Federation, Assyrian National Council of Illinois, Assyrian Universal Alliance (Chicago chapter), Assyrian Universal Alliance Foundation, Assyrian Civic Club, Assyrian AID Society, Mar Zaya Organization, Assyrian Athletic Club, Assyrian Democratic Movement, Assyrian Academic Society, Assyrian American Police Association, Assyrian Teacher Association of America, Assyrian Church of the East, Ancient Assyrian Church of the East, Assyrian Evangelical Church, Chaldean Catholic Church, and guests from California, Arizona, Nevada, and New York. All AAAC past presidents attended as well, including Steve Younan, David Youkhanna, Sunny Abraham, Bishop Mar Giwargis, Emanuel Isho, Mar Poulus, Glen Younan, Edward Nadirsha, Pius Hawel, Ben Benjamin, Francis Yoseph, and Shlimon Shlimon.

On Saturday, November 14, *Shotaputa*, a historical drama, was presented. It was based on the historical background of the Assyrian American Association and written and directed by Neenos

Elnaya. The performance featured an ensemble cast of gifted players, including Zaya Marogel, Violet Khammo, Ashur Khubyar, Fuad Tammo, Helen David, and Steve David. The play has been a great success on the AAAC stage. The audience received it with great gravity—a few with tears—but after, they laughed and applauded loudly. The second part of the program was a performance by a new folk dance group of Assyrian youth directed by Linda Dekelaita and assisted by Andre Eramia. This talented group worked hard to put its show together, presenting the traditional dances sheikhane and khegga. The group made a memorable debut and included members Dezarre Tammo, Mariella Khosho, Destiny Tammo, Gabriela Anail, Briana Bou-Malhab, Eva Mishow, Moreen Georges, Andrew Ishaya, Martin David, Ashur Somo, Aurinella Daniel, and Mariam Betyo.

The Jubilee Gala was held on Sunday, November 15, 2017, at Crystal Palace Banquets in Mount Prospect, Illinois. It was attended by around 500 guests and opened with a delightful cocktail hour, during which a new AAAC anthem, "Shotaputa," was performed by two famous Assyrian singers, Fatin Shabo and Sargon Youkhanna. They presented an exquisite composition written by two extraordinary artists—poet Ninos Nirari and musician Sargon Gabriel—providing a truly spectacular opening.

One of the climactic moments of the anniversary opening ceremony was the keynote speech delivered by AAAC president Glen Younan about the organization's background, covering its early life, the time during the Depression and War World II, its rise and fall, and the cause of today's successes. He received an enthusiastic ovation from the audience. Among the honorary guests attending the ceremony and delivering their anniversary speeches to the AAAC were Patrick O'Connor, alderman of Chicago's city council; Diane Pathieu of ABC 7 TV in Chicago; Robert R. Yohanan, managing director and CEO of First Bank & Trust; Sargis Sangari of the Near East Center for Strategic Engagement; and Robert R. Yohanan, managing director and CEO of First Bank & Trust in Chicago.

The anniversary was an exciting blend of Assyrian food, dances, music, and songs drawing on Assyrian traditions, the combined talents of the present day, and the imagination of guests across all ages. The food was prepared by Hany Baba, Ninos Lazar, floor manager Raman Oshana, and past members of the AAAC soccer team.

The gala concert featured many performances from internationally famous musicians and singers from the Chicago area and abroad, including Janan Sawa, Lazar Malko, Odi Simon, Sargon Yukhanna, and Fatin Shabo, all from Chicago, and Madlen Ishoeva from Moscow. The celebrity event was recorded by Hermiz and Edward Hasso of E&H Video Productions and independent cameraman Hanna Moshi.

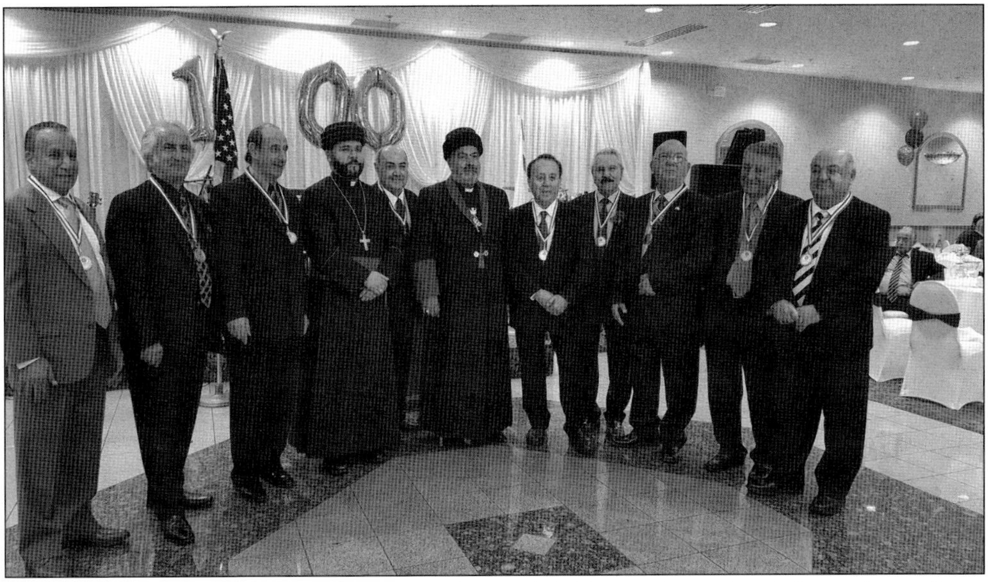

Pictured here at the 100-year celebration are former AAAC presidents; from left to right are Steve Younan, David Youkhanna, Sunny Abraham, Bishop Mar Gewargis Younan, Emanuel Isho, Bishop Mar Paulus Benjamin, Glen Younan, Edward Nadirsha, Pius Hawel, Ben Benjamin, and Francis Yoseph. This image was captured at Crystal Palace on October 15, 2017. (Author's collection.)

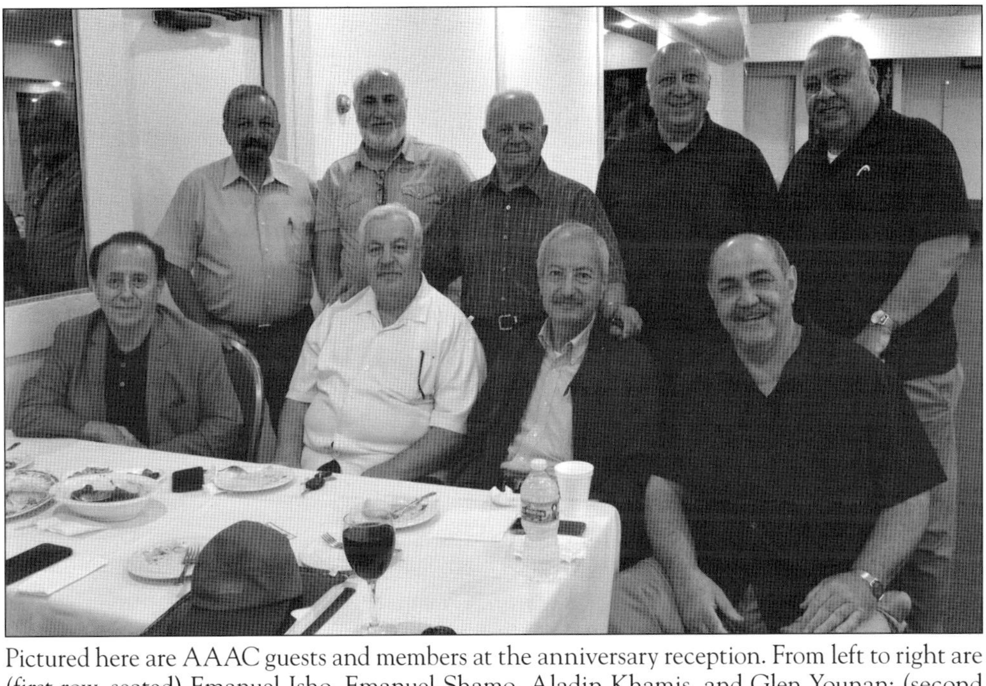

Pictured here are AAAC guests and members at the anniversary reception. From left to right are (first row, seated) Emanuel Isho, Emanuel Shamo, Aladin Khamis, and Glen Younan; (second row, standing) Eddie Zomayah Emanuel Tamo, Dr. Norman Solhkha, Salam Mousa, and Raman Oshana. (Author's collection.)

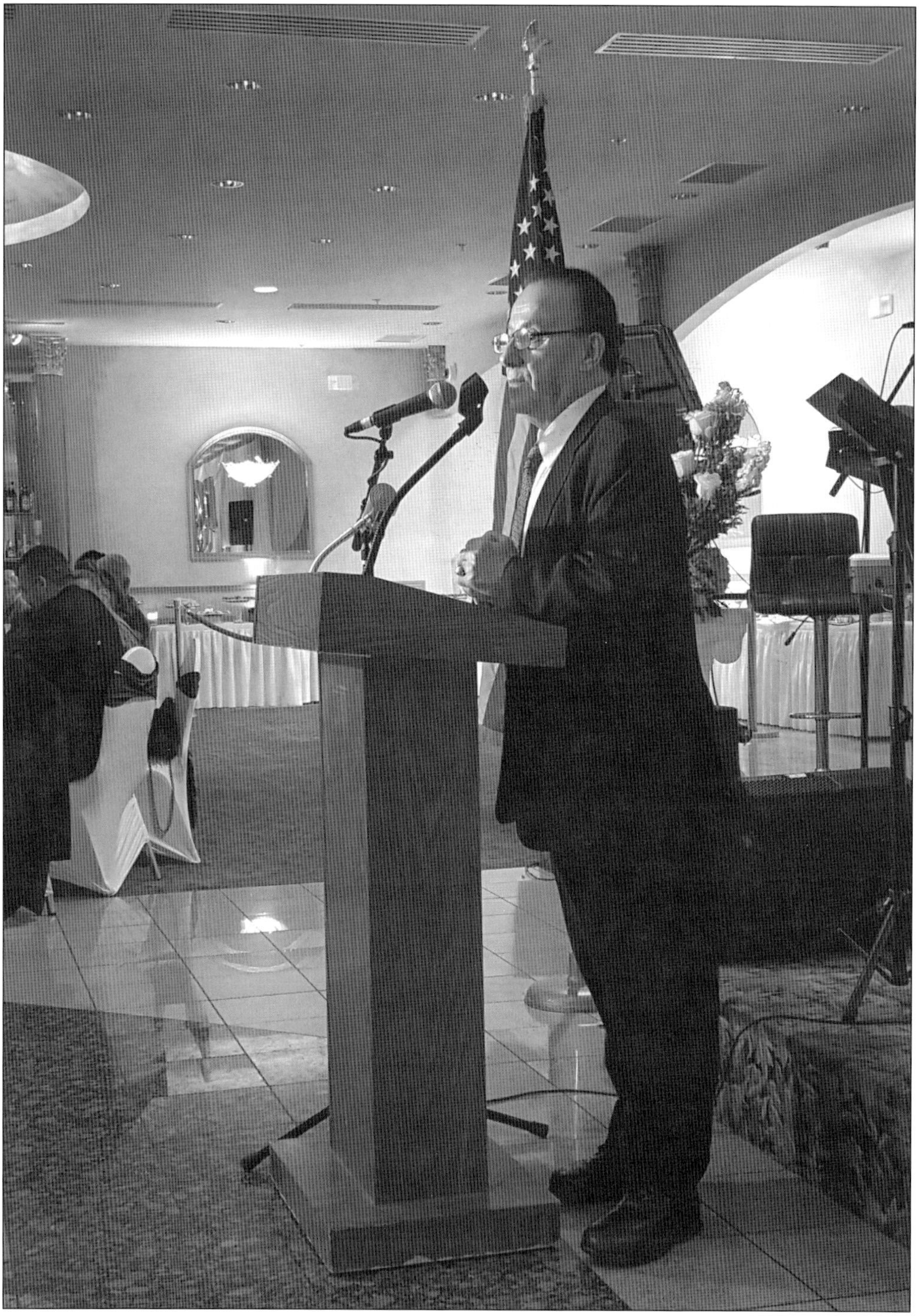

Glen Younan, current president of AAAC, delivers a speech during the anniversary. He was AAAC president in 1987 and was reelected in 2016. His speech contained a brief history of the establishment and formation of AAAC. (Author's collection.)

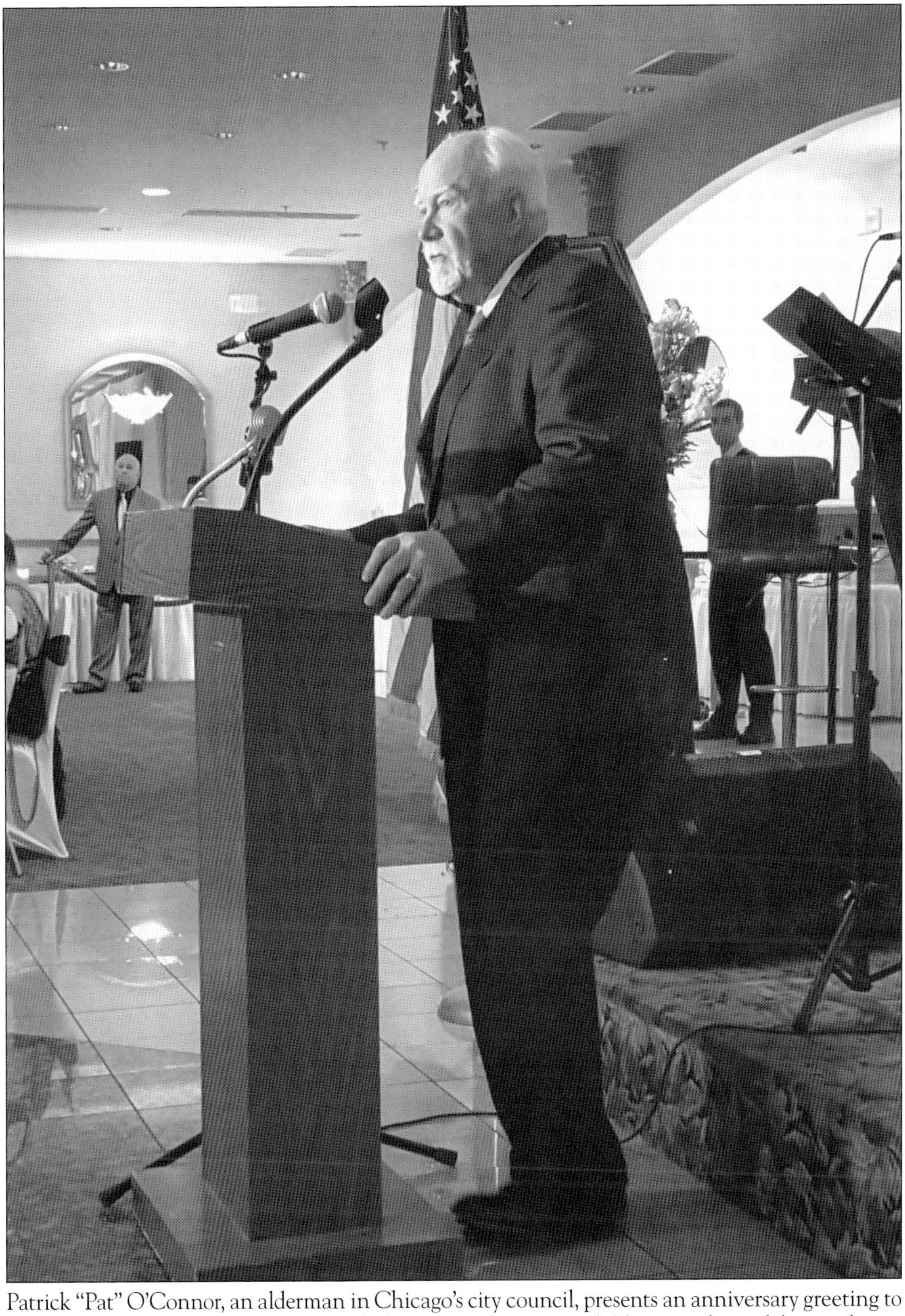

Patrick "Pat" O'Connor, an alderman in Chicago's city council, presents an anniversary greeting to the Assyrian American Association of Chicago. O'Connor is a lifelong resident of the northwest side of Chicago and has represented the city's 40th Ward on the city council since 1983. Alderman O'Connor is committed to understating the needs and concerns of all ethnic communities of Chicago, including Assyrians. (Author's collection.)

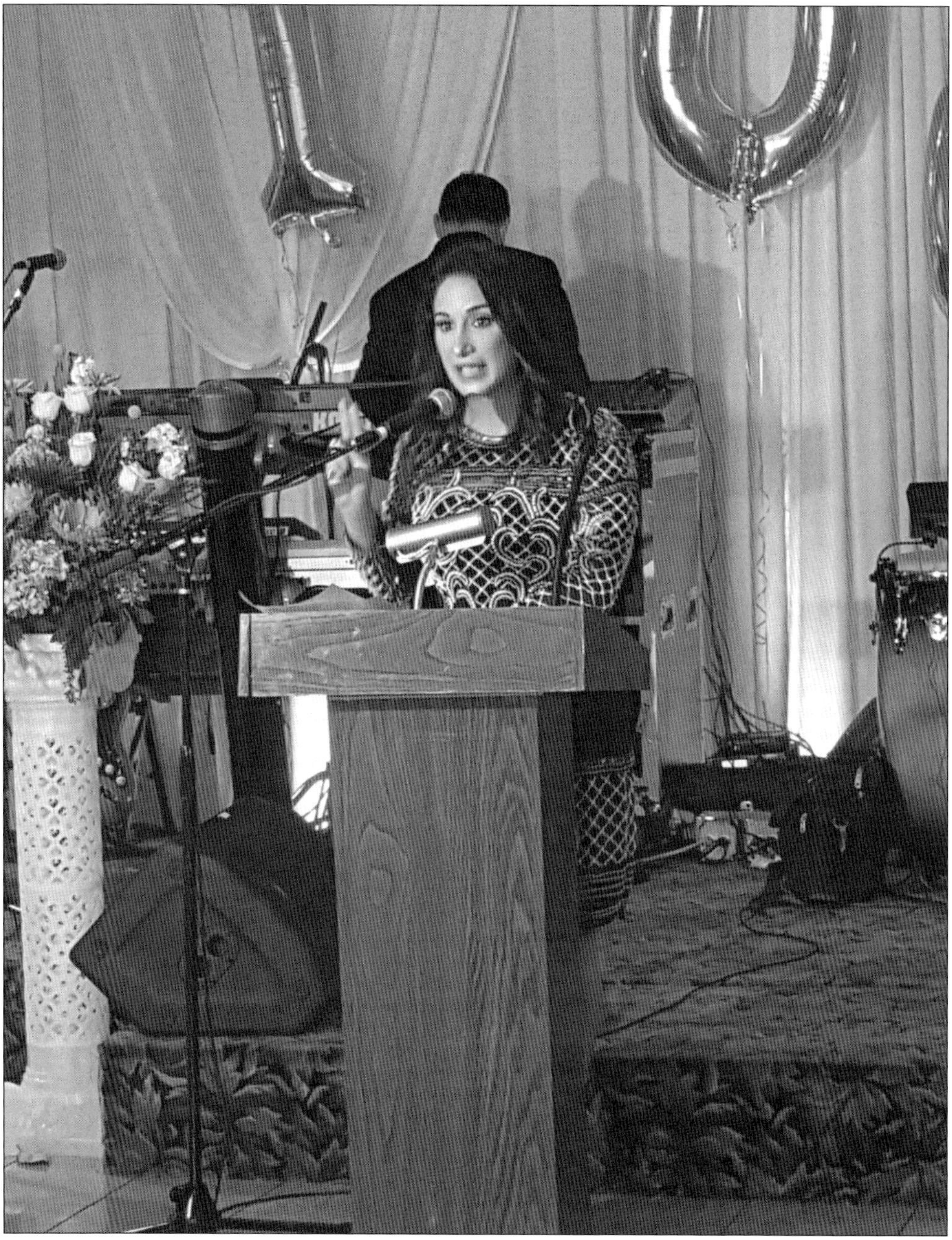

Diane Pathieu, an Emmy-nominated news reporter with ABC 7 Chicago, speaks during an event to mark the 100th anniversary of the AAAC. Pathieu was born to an Assyrian family in the Rogers Park neighborhood of Chicago. Her mother is an immigrant from Syria, and her father is an immigrant from Lebanon. In 2001, she graduated from Columbia College. She worked as a general assignment reporter in Cedar Rapids, Iowa, and at KFXB-TV in Dubuque, Iowa. In 2005, she accepted a position at WTMJ-TV in Milwaukee as a reporter on the morning newscast and as an anchor for the noon newscast. In December 2011, she moved to WLS-TV, where she serves as weekend morning anchor and general assignment reporter during the week. (Author's collection.)

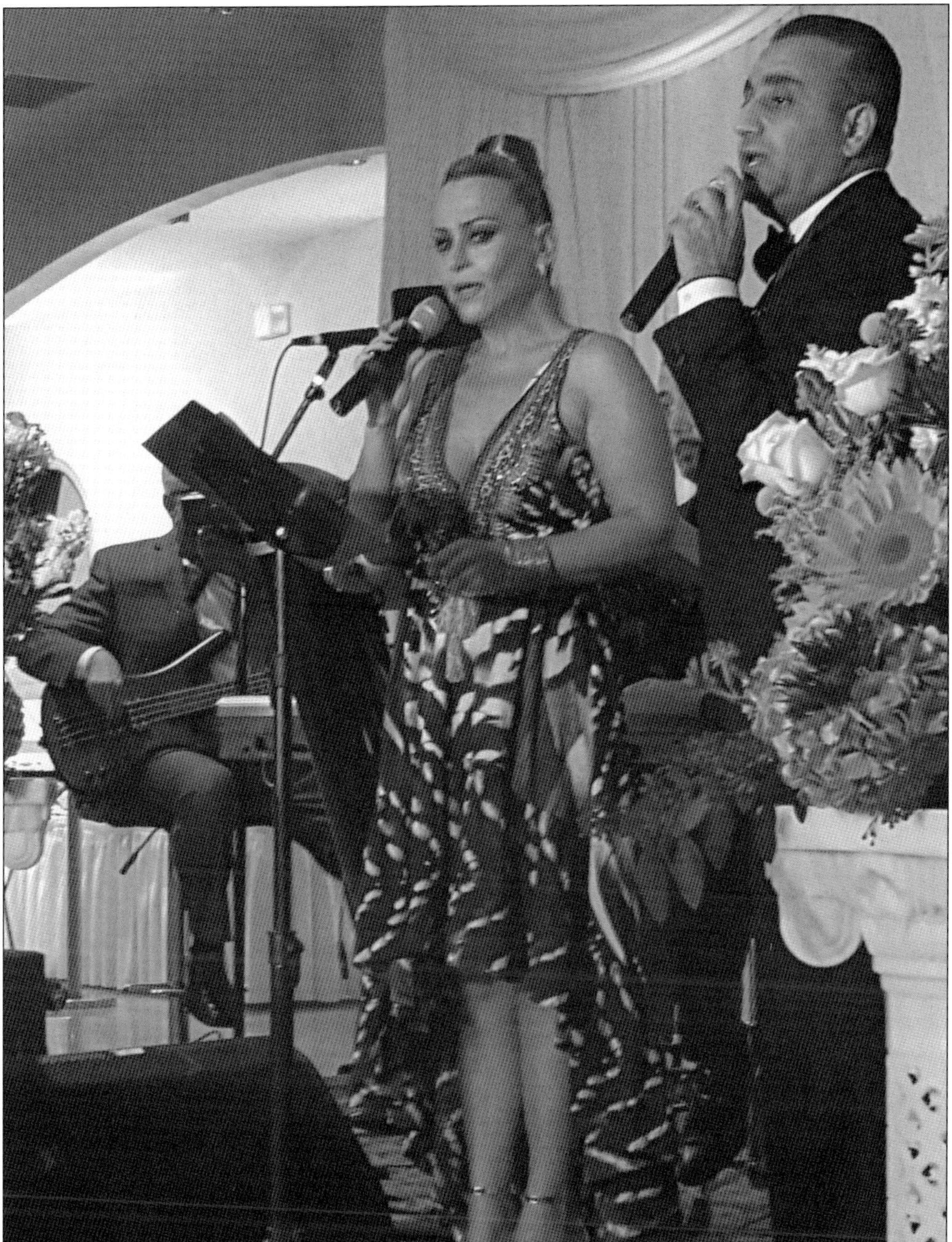

Pictured here from left to right are Assyrian superstars Fatin Shabo and Sargon Youkhanna performing "Shotaputa" during the 100th-anniversary celebration; it was written by poet Ninos Nirari, and the melody is by Sargon Gabriel. Fatin grew up in Sweden, and in the 1990s moved to Chicago. Sometimes called "the Goddess of Pop," she gained popularity in the 1980s all over Europe. She is known for pushing the boundaries of lyrical content in mainstream Assyrian traditional music as well as visual imagery in her music videos and on stage. Sargon, an actor and public activist, was named Entertainer of the Century by the AAAC in 2012. (Author's collection.)

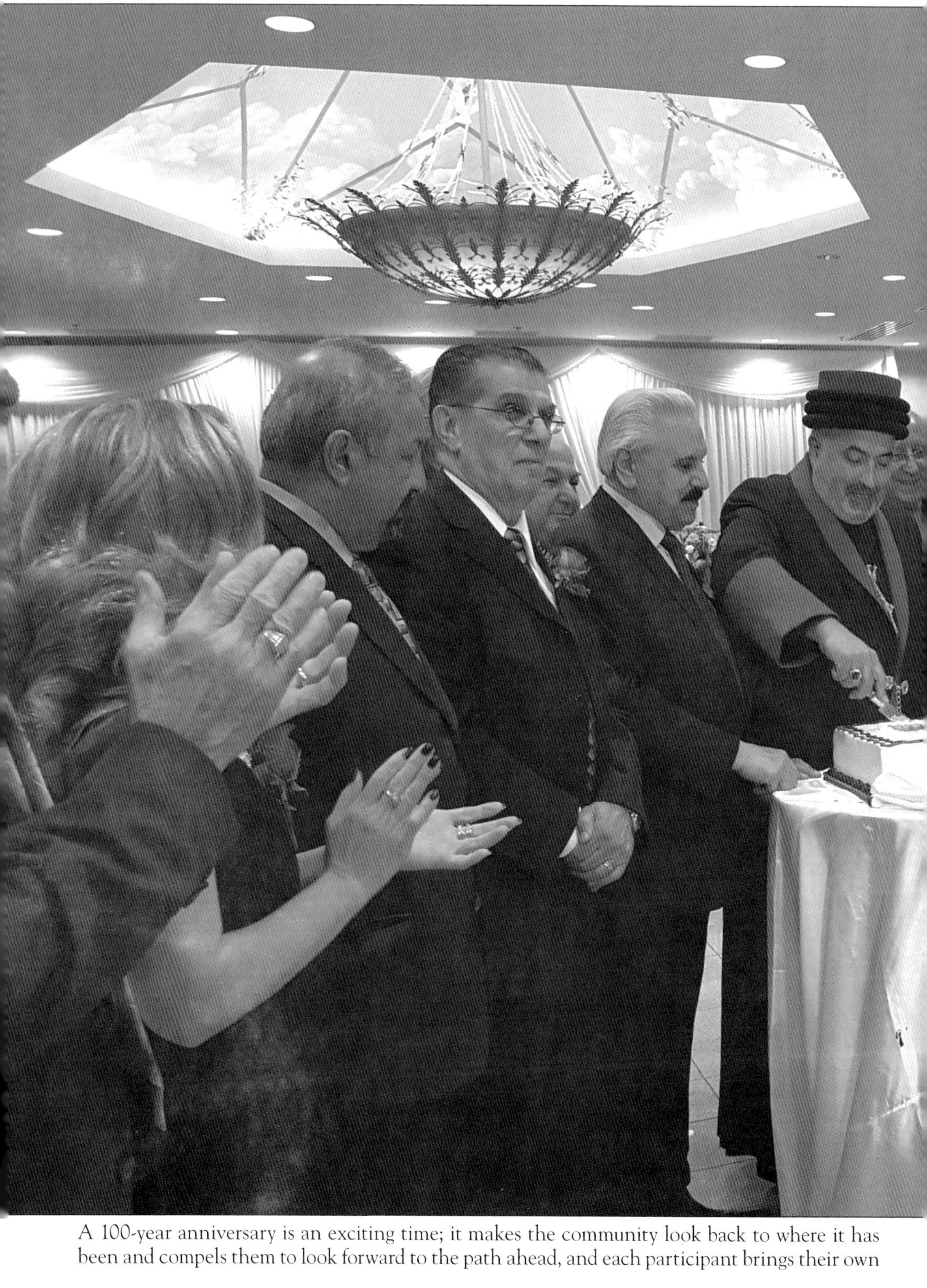

A 100-year anniversary is an exciting time; it makes the community look back to where it has been and compels them to look forward to the path ahead, and each participant brings their own

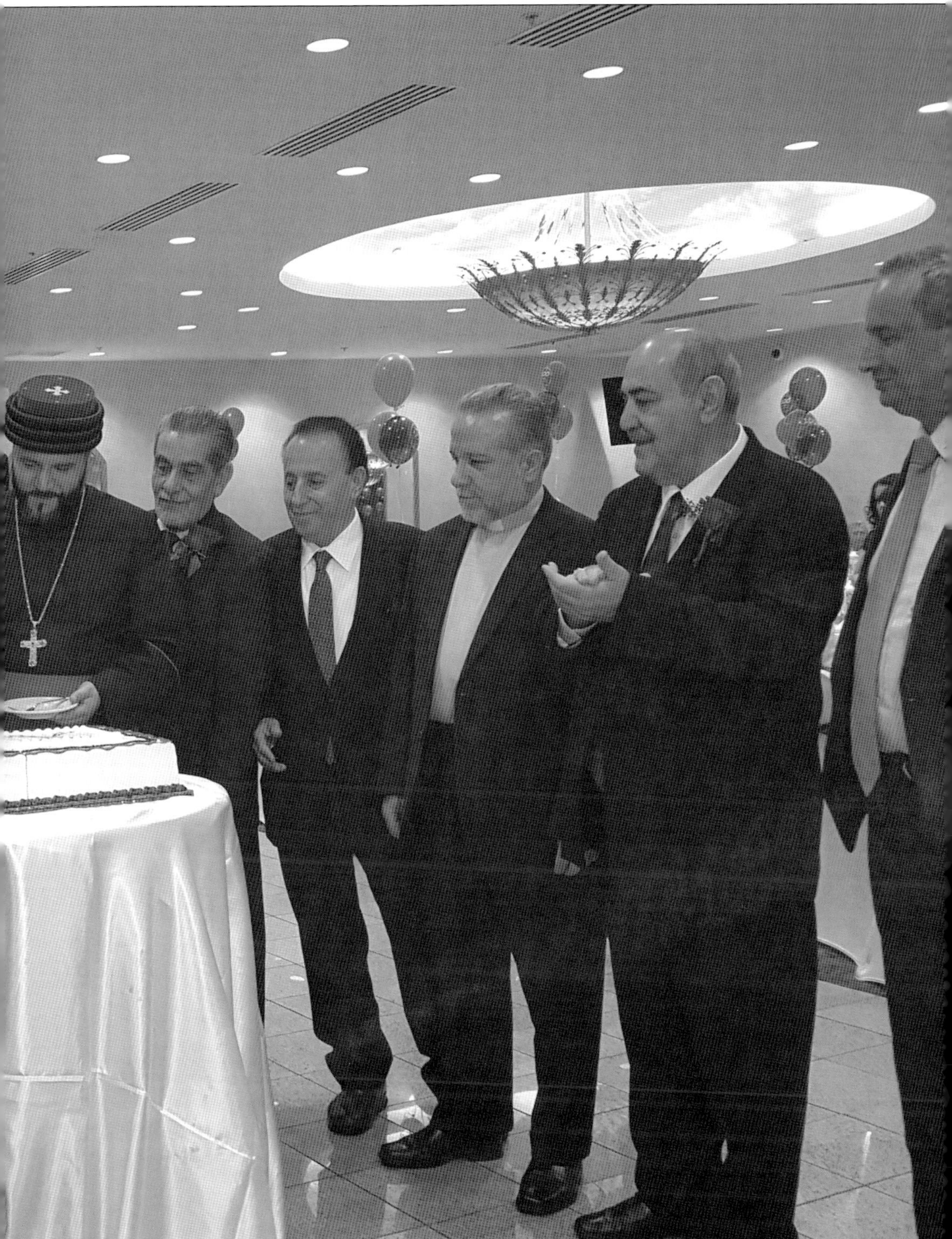

perspective. This is a photograph of a cake cutting at the celebration. The association has been in existence for 100 years. (Author's collection.)

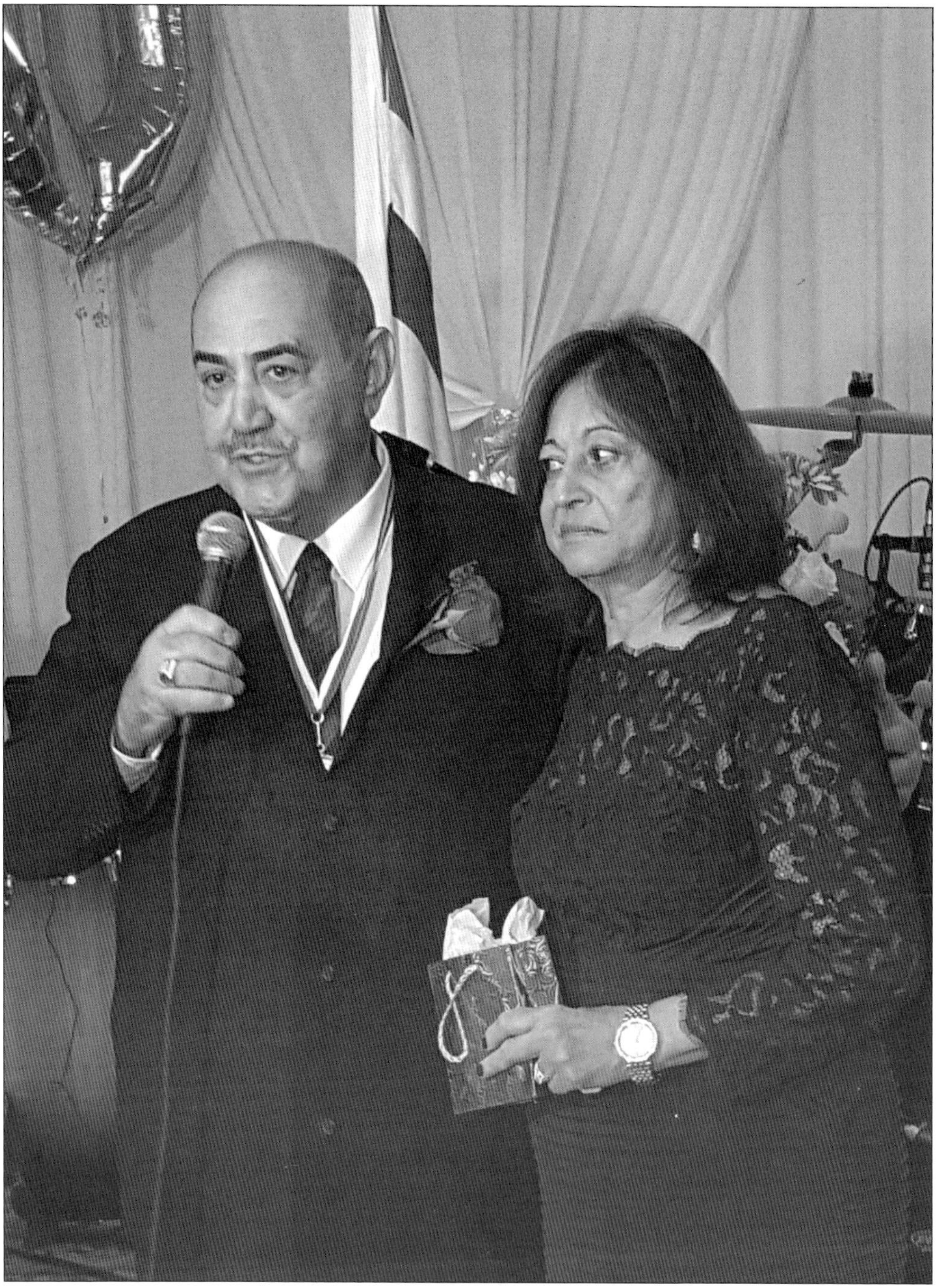

Pictured here are Emanuel Isho, the anniversary chairman, and his wife, Maria Isho. Emanuel received an award for Long Time Achievement, the organization's highest individual volunteer recognition for his longtime work in radio broadcasting, academic, and social programs of the AAAC. (Author's collection.)

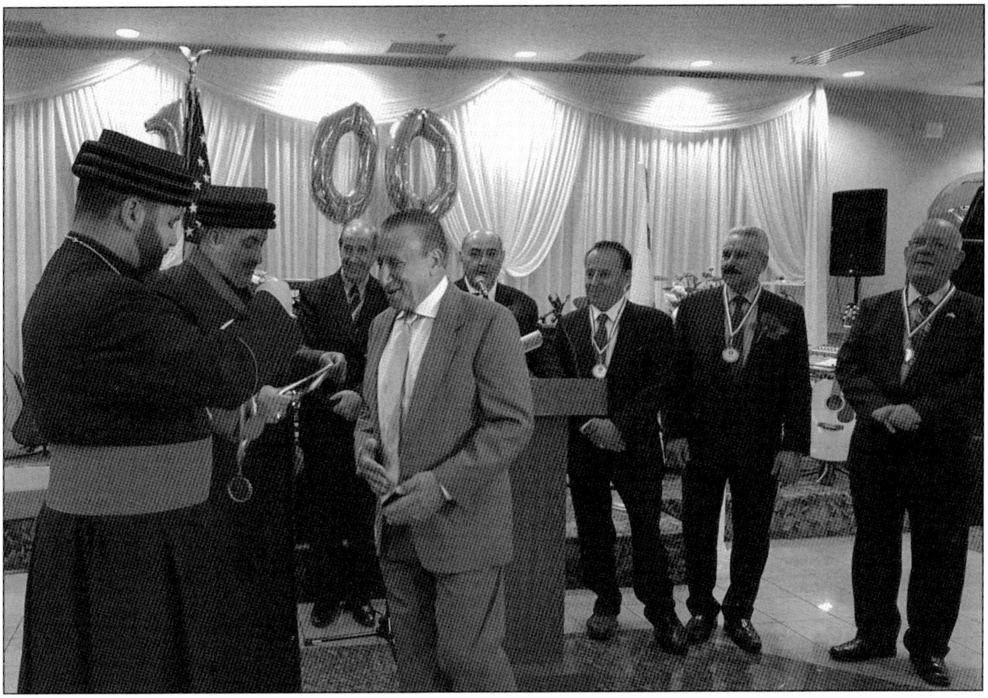

This photograph was taken during a significant moment of the celebration: two bishops of Chicago, His Grace Mar Giwargis and His Grace Mar Paulus, give former AAAC president Steve Younan the Medal of Honor. Younan was elected president of the AAAC in 1984. (Author's collection.)

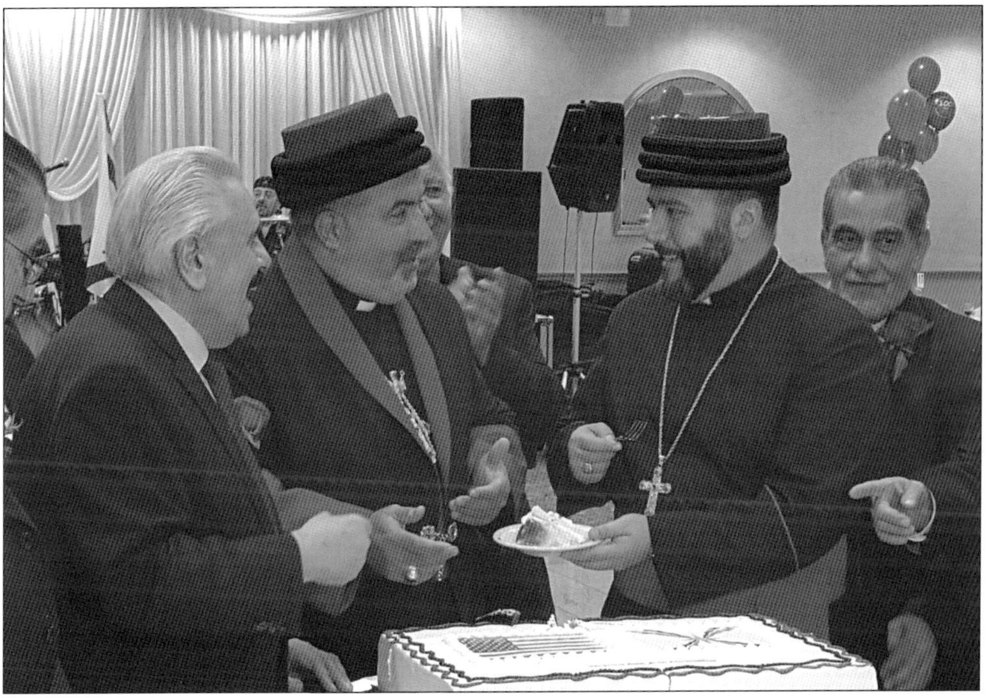

Bishop Mar Paulus Benjamin (left) and Bishop Mar Gewargis Younan are pictured with friends at the 100 Years Celebration. (Author's collection.)

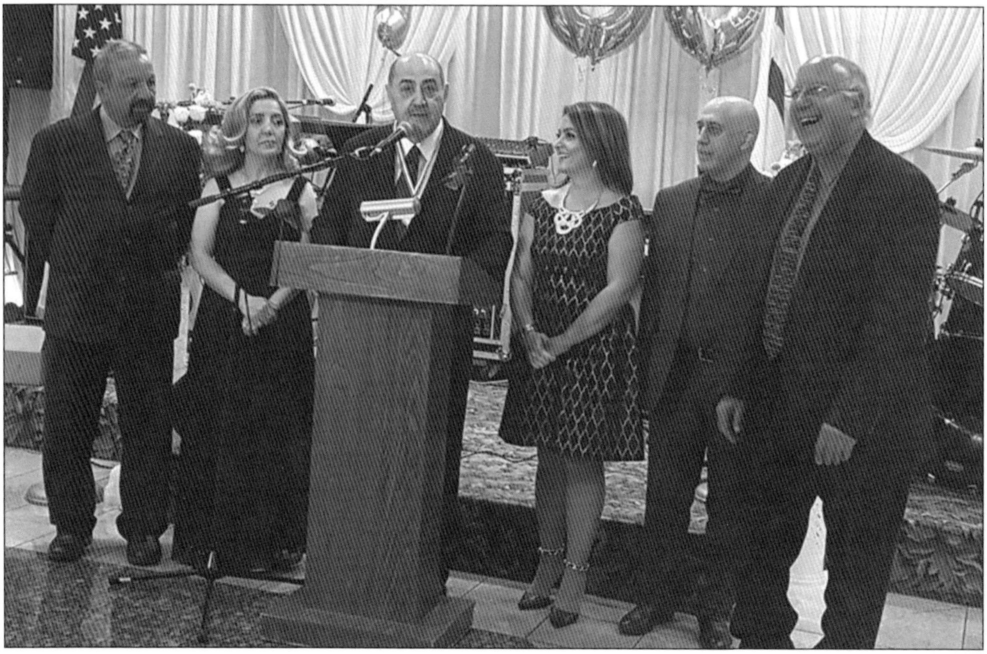

AAAC members used this opportunity to spruce up their capabilities for Shotaputa gatherings. This is a photograph of the anniversary celebration organizing committee; from left to right are Raman Oshana, Teena Khaee, Emanuel Isho (chairman), Linda Dekelaita, Vasili Shoumanov, and Emanuel Bet-Somo. (Author's collection.)

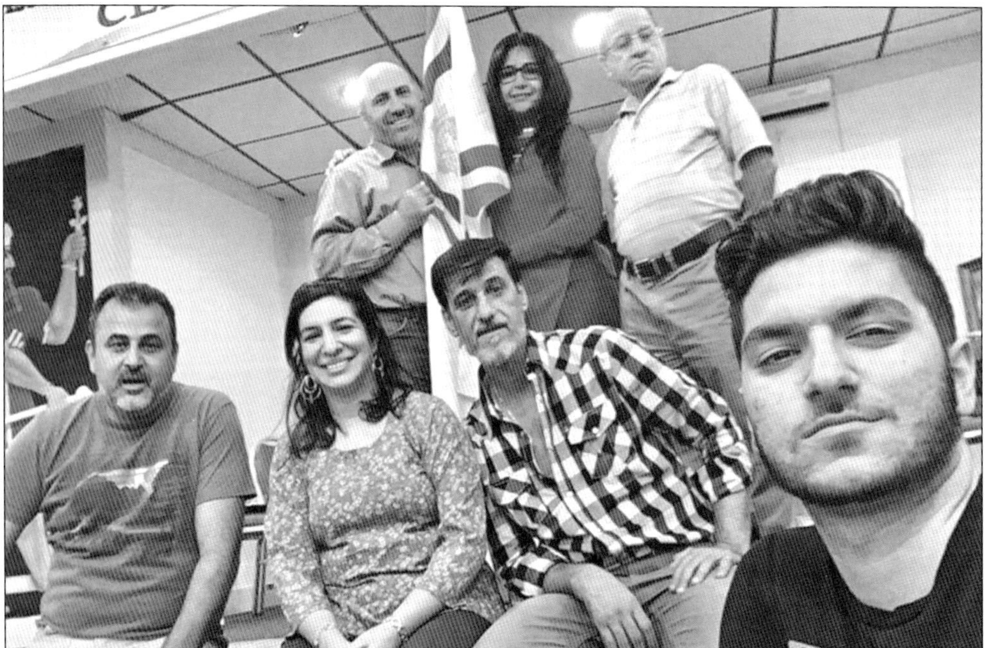

Pictured here is a theater troupe of the association. From left to right are (first row) Ashur Khubyar, Helen David, Neenos Elnaya (director), and Steve David; (second row) Fuad Tamo, Violet Khammo, and Zaya Marogel. (Courtesy of Violet Khamoo.)

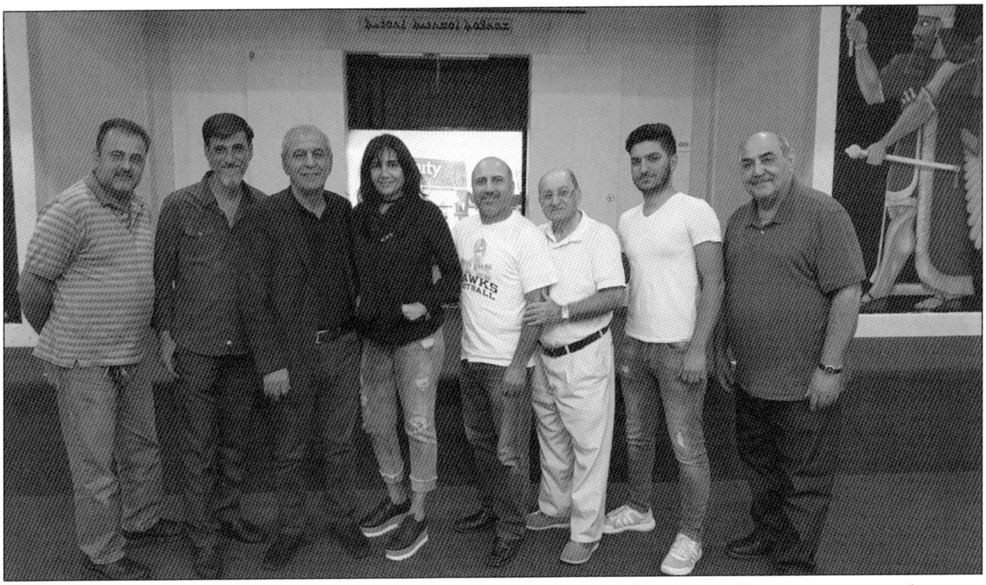

Old photographs in the AAAC archives shows a history of theater performances over the past 100 years. Seen here is a theater troupe of the association performing the play *Shotaputa*. The play was inspired by Emanuel Isho but written and directed by Neenos Elnaya. The first play took place on Saturday, October 17, 2017. From left to right are Ashur Khubyar, Neenos Elnaya (director), Sami Yaku, Violet Khammo, Fuad Tamo, Zaya Marogel, Steve David, and Emanuel Isho. (Author's collection.)

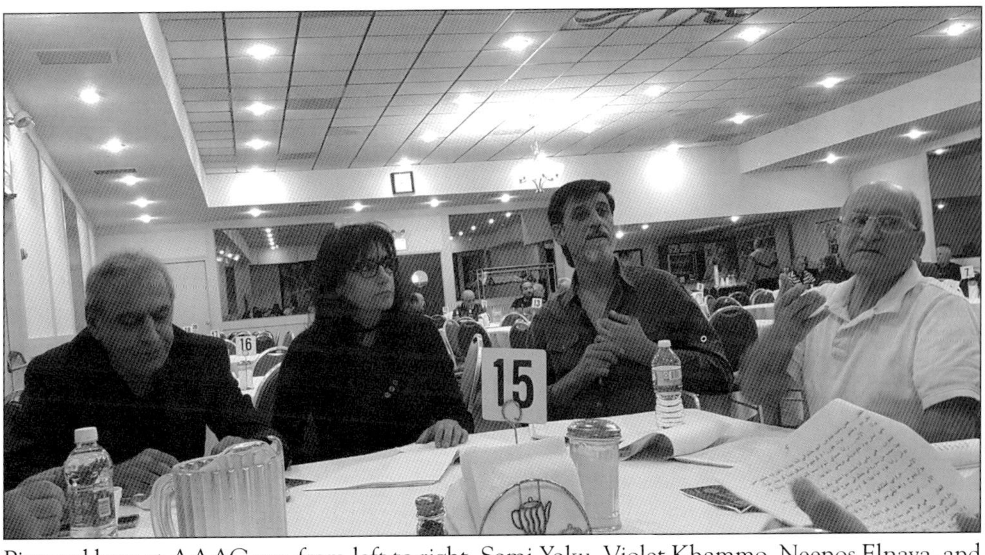

Pictured here at AAAC are, from left to right, Sami Yaku, Violet Khammo, Neenos Elnaya, and Zaya Marogel. (Author's collection.)

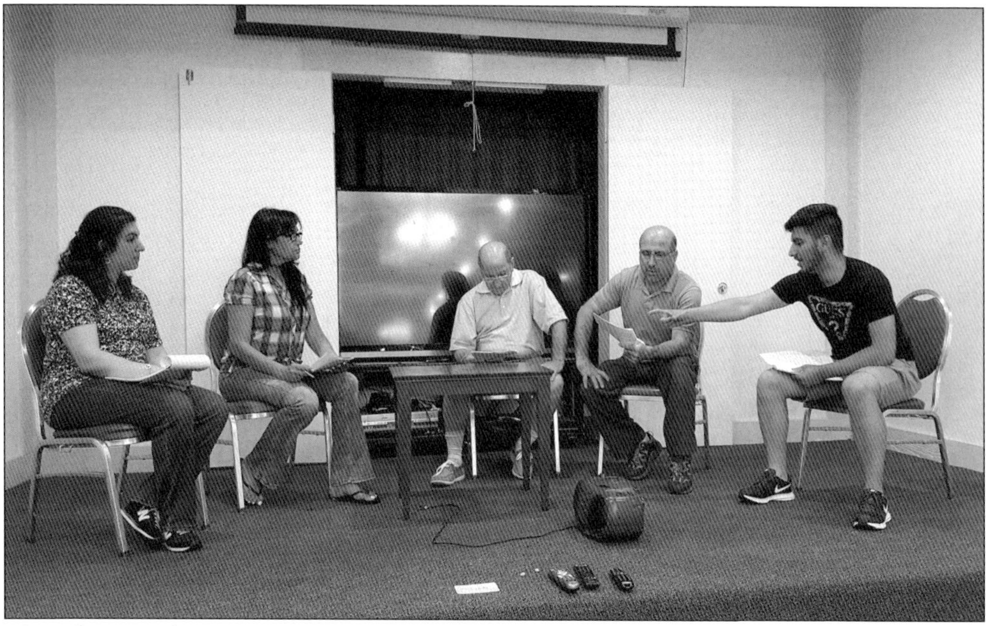

This photograph was taken during the final rehearsals before anniversary day; from left to right are Helen David, Violet Khammo, Zaya Marogel, Fuad Tamo, and Steve David. (Author's collection.)

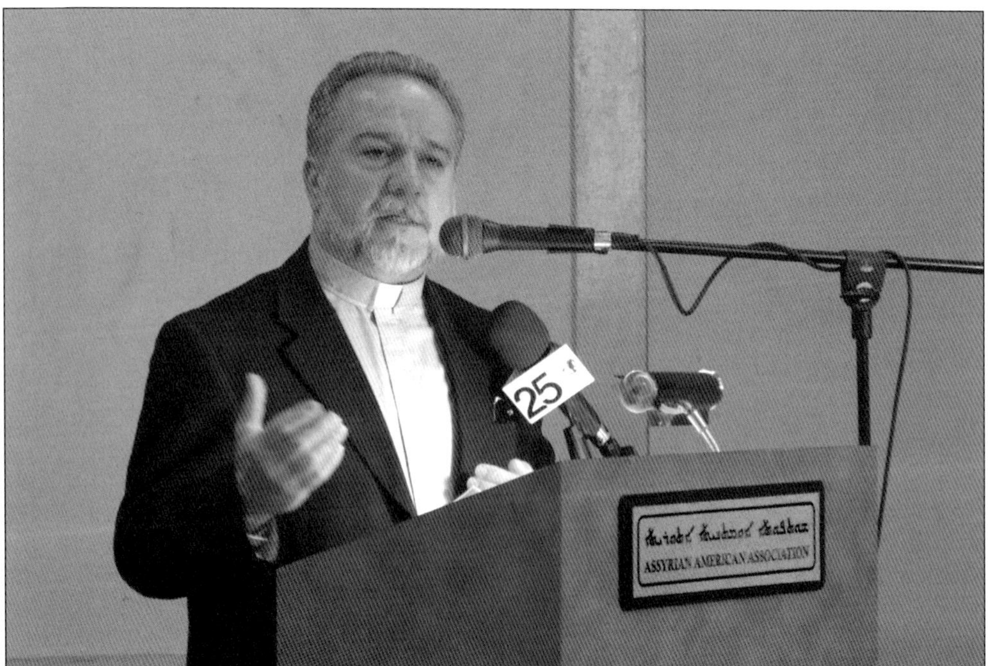

Educator and cleric Rev. Antwan Latchen of the Assyrian Church of the East was the personal secretary of His Holiness Mar Dinkha IV, catholicos-patriarch. (Author's collection.)

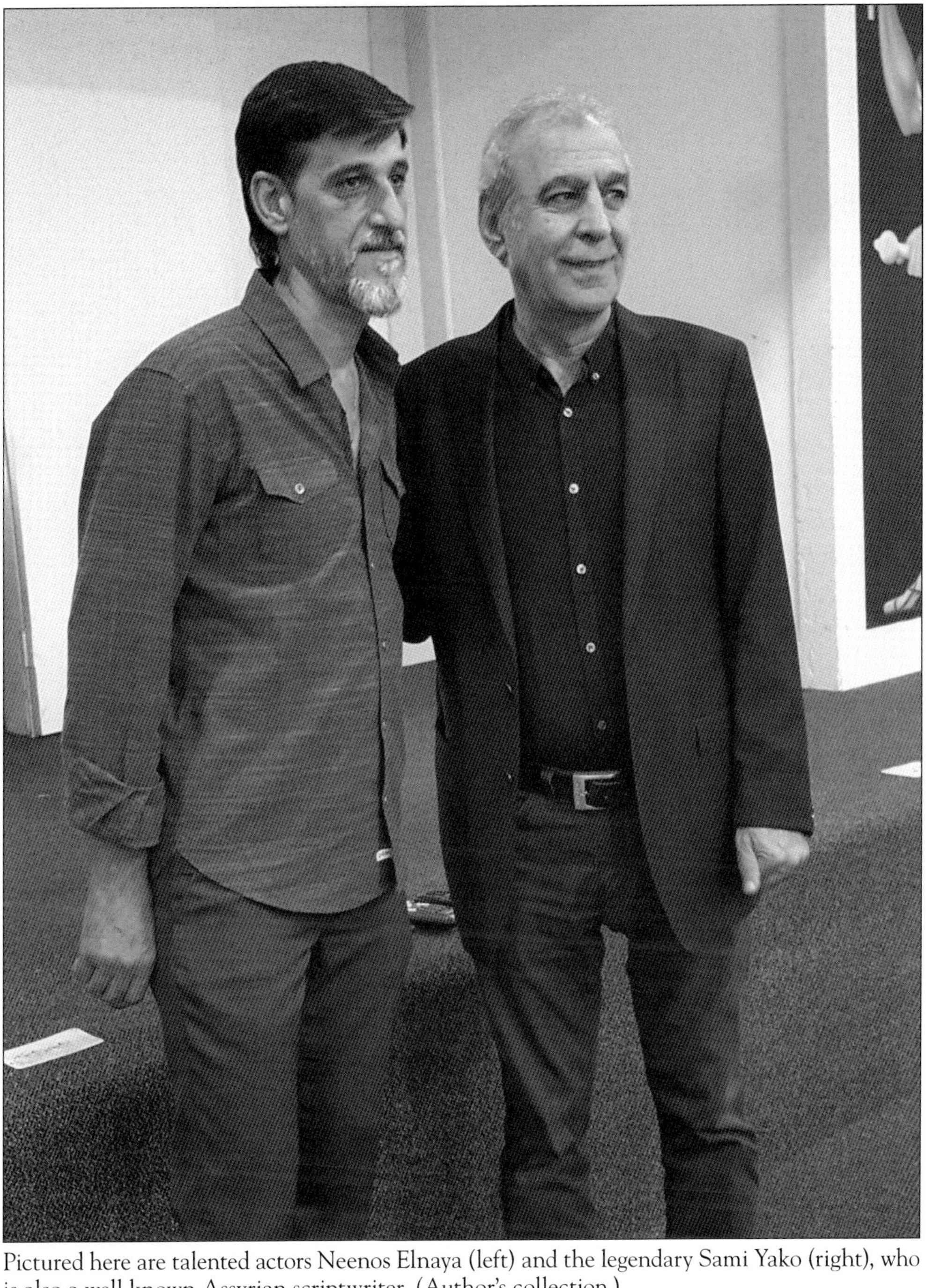

Pictured here are talented actors Neenos Elnaya (left) and the legendary Sami Yako (right), who is also a well-known Assyrian scriptwriter. (Author's collection.)

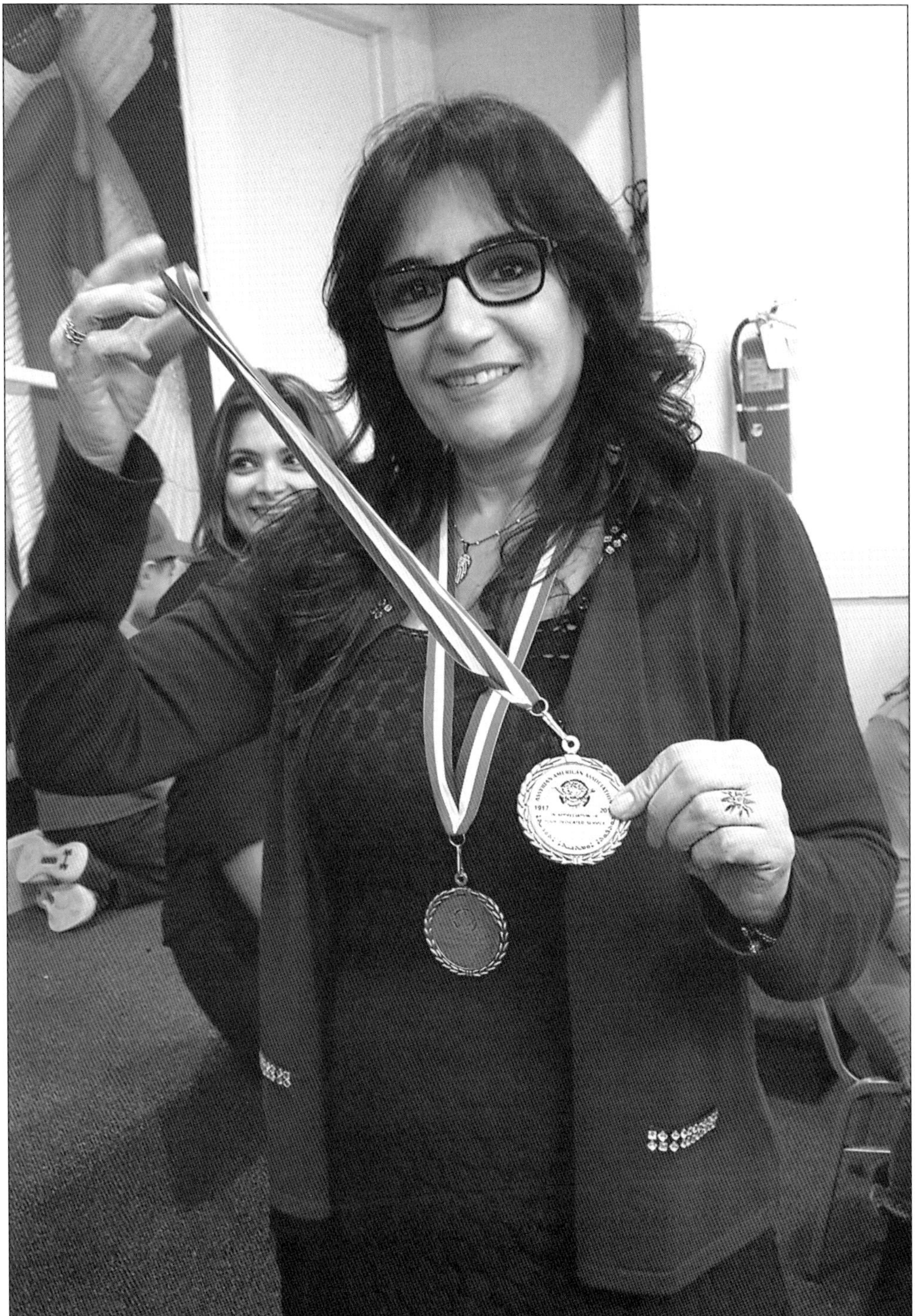

Violet Khamoo, a consistent supporter of the international Assyrian community, is also a talented actress. She is seen here displaying her award presented by the Assyrian American Association of Chicago in 2017. (Author's collection.)

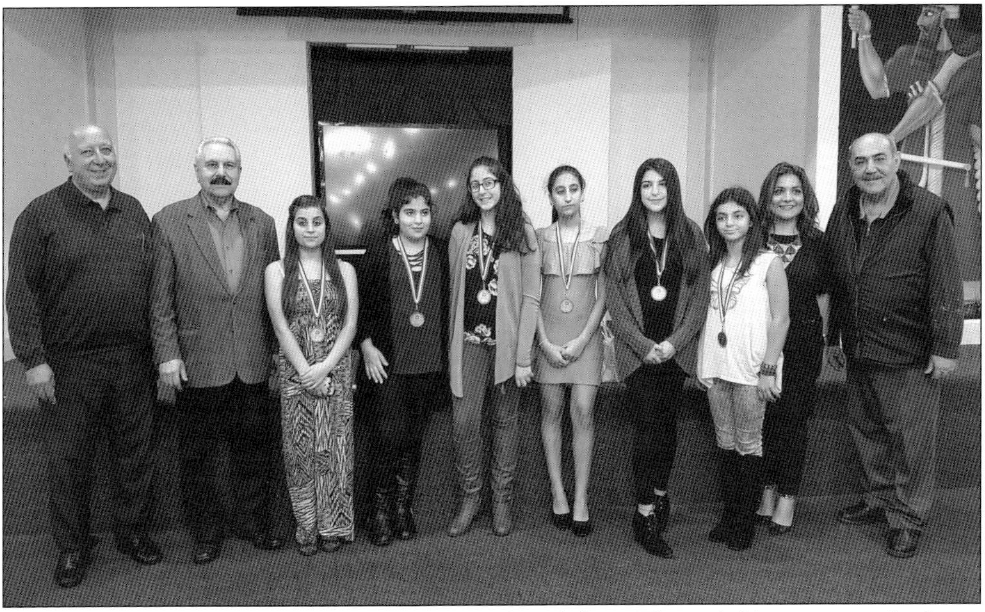

Seen here is the Assyrian folk dance group of Linda Dekelaita. These children presented a dance performance during the 100th anniversary of the AAAC. From left to right are Emanuel Bet-Somo, Edward Nadirsha, Olivia Khoshaba, Dezarre Tammo, Destiny Tammo, Mariam Betyo, Brianna Bou-Malhab, Mariela Khoshaba, Linda Dekelaita, and Emanuel Isho. (Author's collection.)

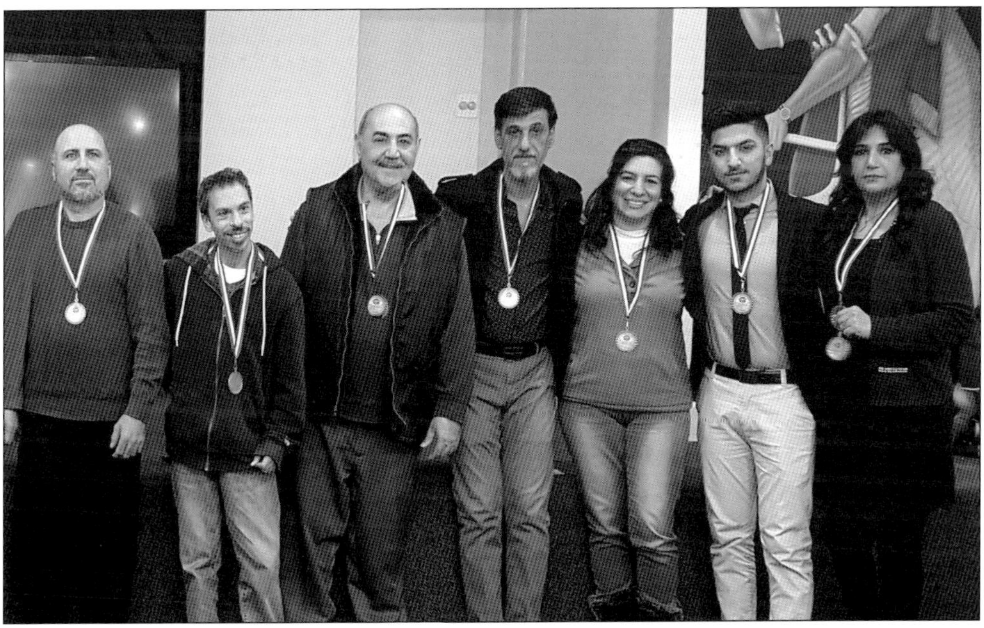

The Assyrian theater troupe was awarded at the 100 years celebration by AAAC. (Author's collection.)

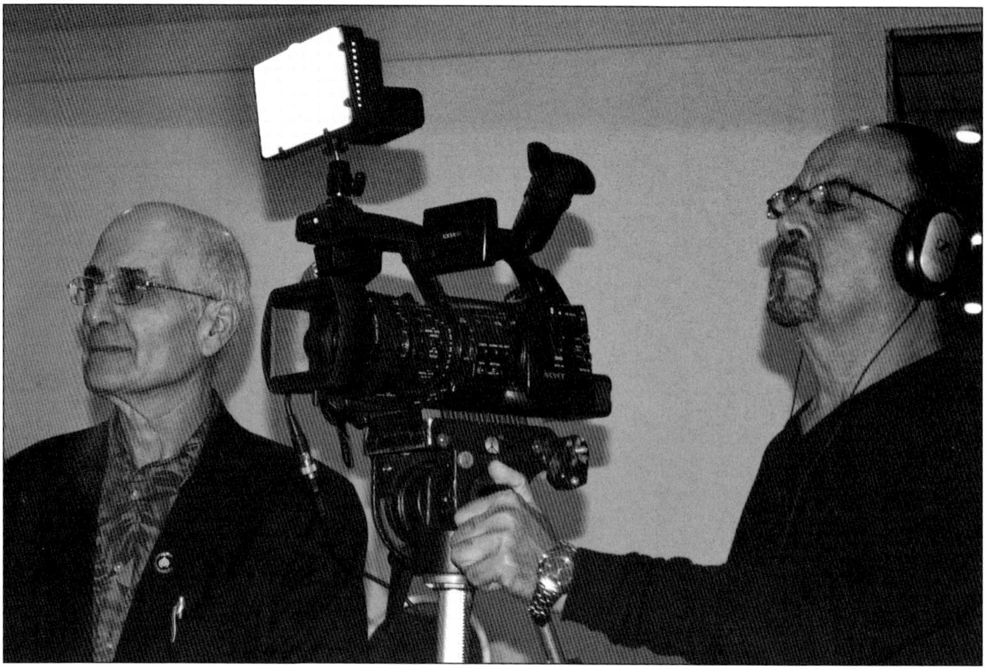

Brothers Edward (left) and Hermiz Hasso are veteran photography and video journalists and filmmakers with more than four decades of experience. They began their career in Iraq. When they immigrated to Chicago, they worked with channel 25 and established a new television program, *Assyrians Around the World.* (Author's collection.)

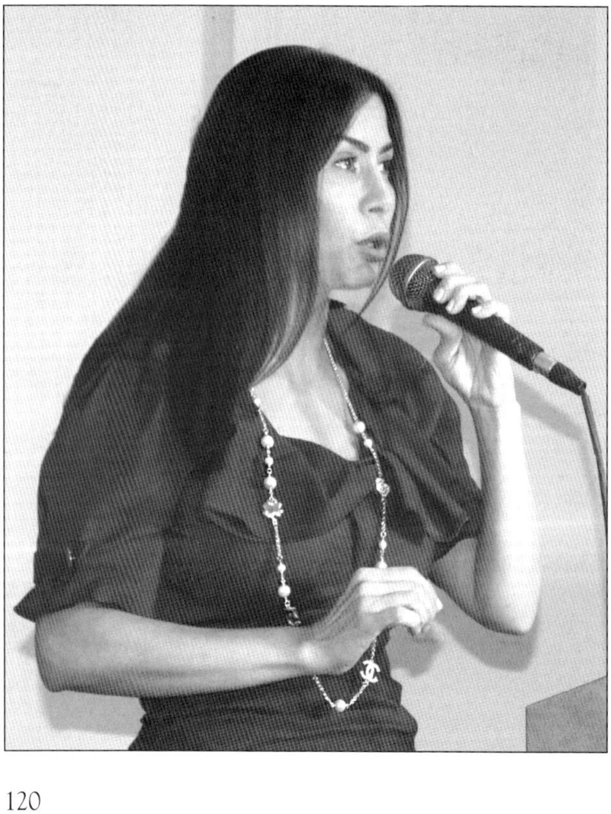

Linda George gave a soulful performance on stage during a concert at the AAAC. She started her career as a church singer and gradually became the most famous Assyrian singer. Since 1980, she has sung in different musical styles, including pop and folk. She continues to attend mass in Assyrian churches and sings at services. She is always welcome at the Shotaputa stage. (Author's collection.)

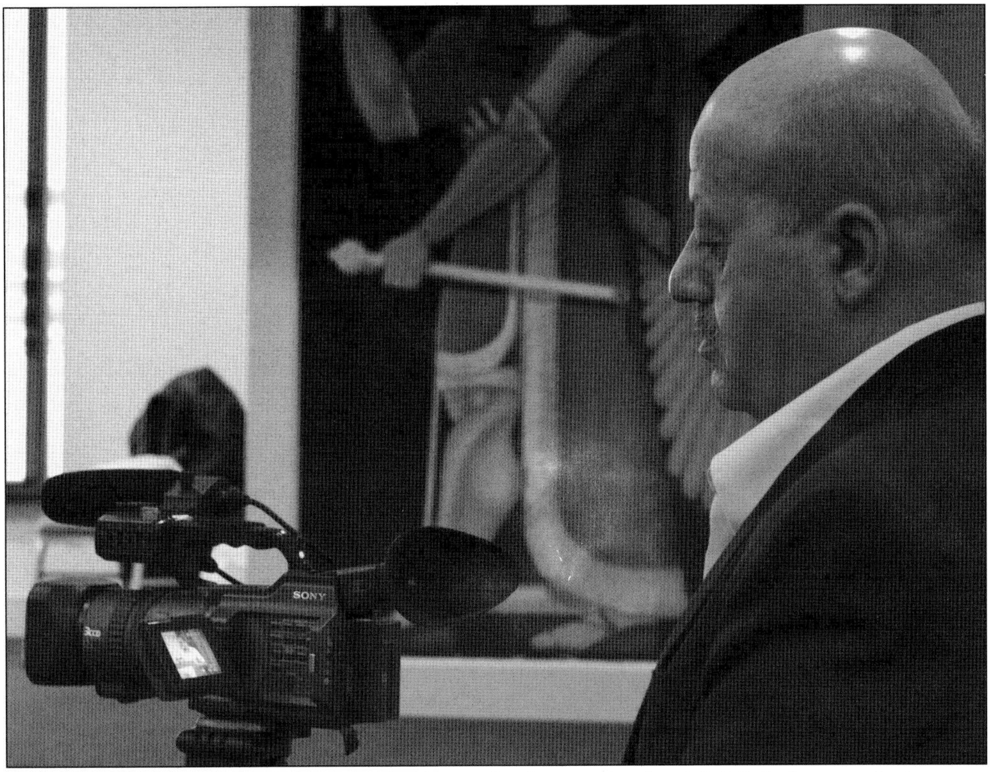

Freelance cameraman Hanna Moshi is a devoted volunteer for the AAAC, helping with shooting video and photographs of public events. (Author's collection.)

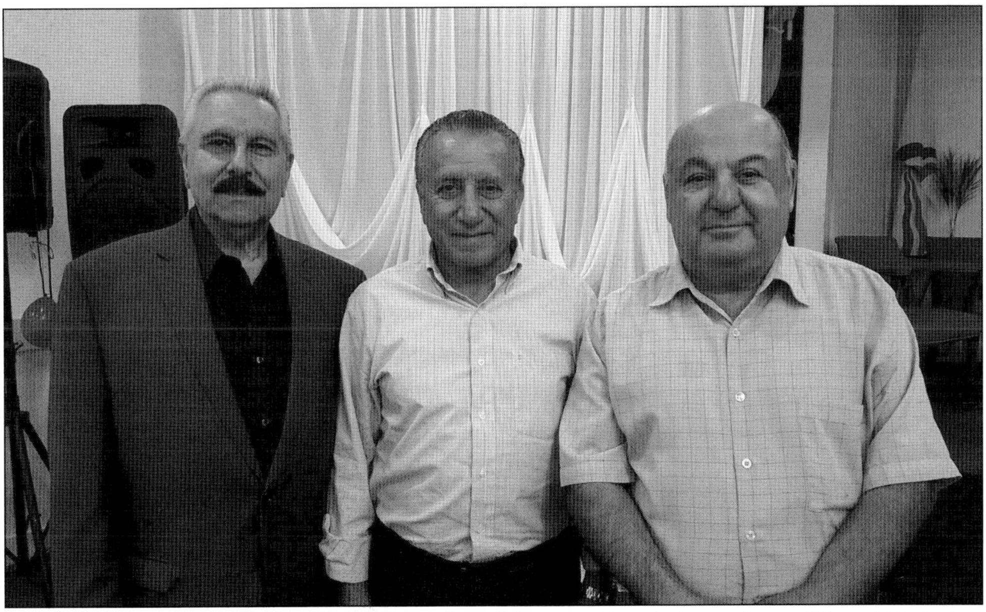

Three former presidents get together during the celebration. From left to right are Edward Nadirsha, Steve Yonan, and Francis Yoseph. (Author's collection.)

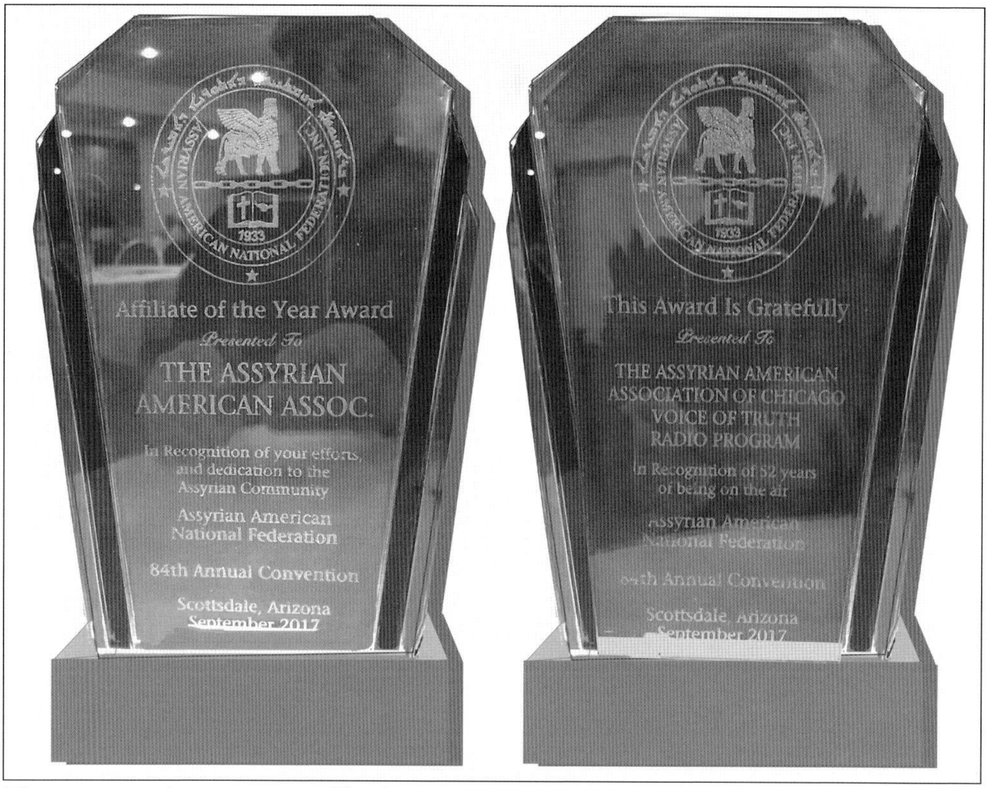

These two awards were presented by the Assyrian American National Federation to the Assyrian American Association of Chicago and the *Voice of Truth* radio program at the 84th annual national convention of AANF in Scottsdale, Arizona, in September 2017. (Author's collection.)

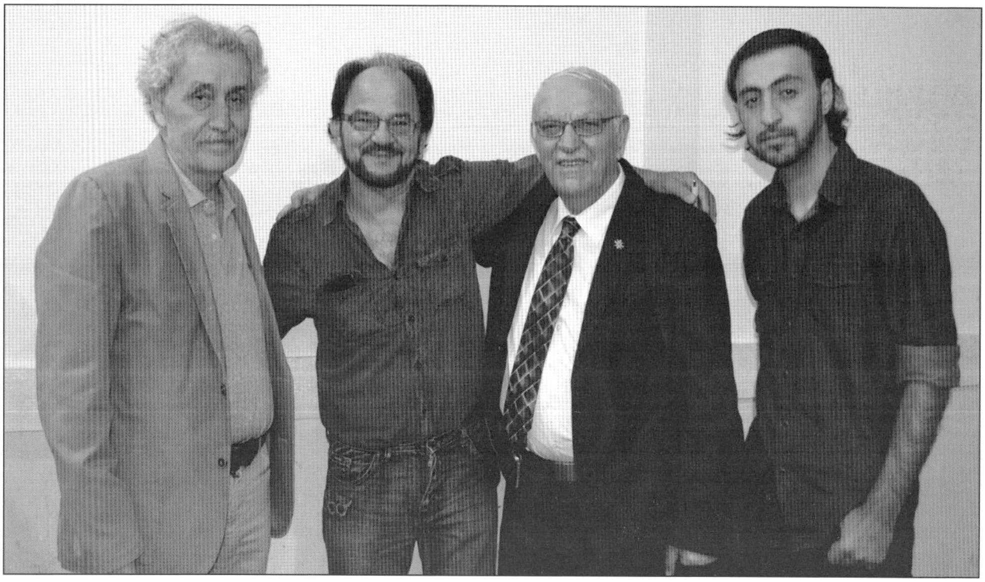

History professor from France Joseph Yako (far left) is pictured at the AAAC with, from left to right, artist Abee Sargis, teacher Michael Mammo from Sweden, and film director Frank Gilbert. (Author's collection.)

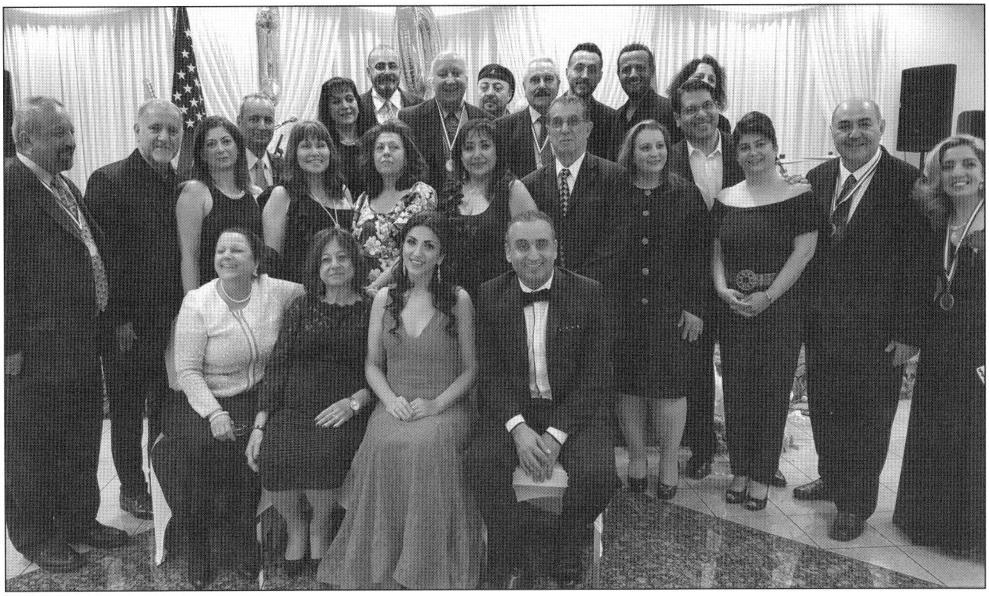

Nearly 300 guests joined the AAAC's 100-year celebration from October 13 to 15, 2017, to recognize special honorees and guests who have been influential in the association's development and to pay tribute to the Shotaputa mission and amazing members who embody it through their personal journeys and their incredible stories of success. (Author's collection.)

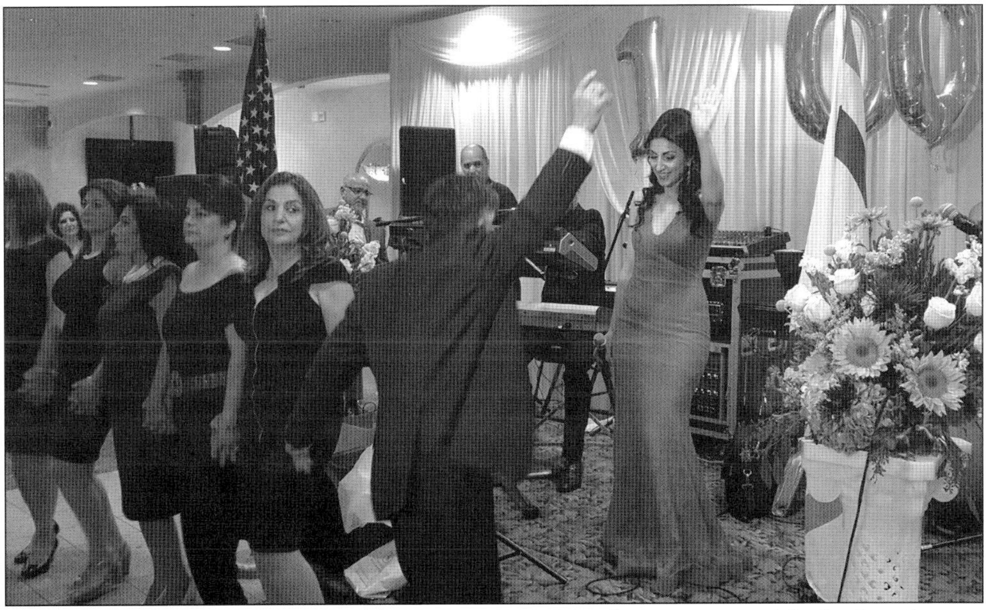

Here, the Assyrian folk dance Sheikhane is performed for the anniversary. The leading dancers are Iosif Gabriel and Russian singer Madlen Ishoeva. (Author's collection.)

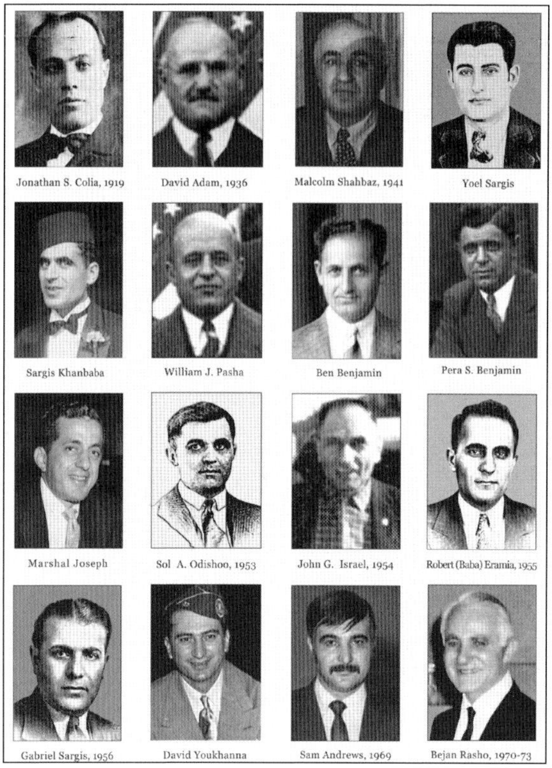

At left are the Assyrian American Association of Chicago presidents from 1917 to 1973; below are the presidents from 1973 to 2017. (Both, author's collection.)

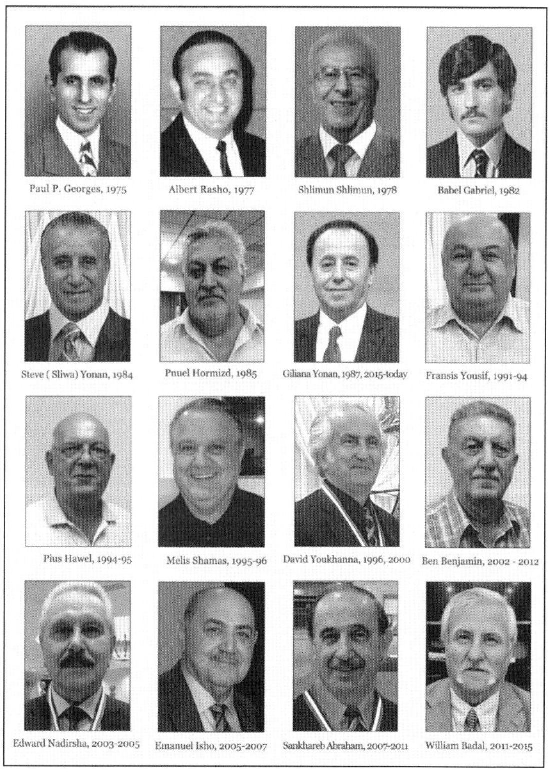

These were the Assyrian American Association of Chicago official logos in 1917, 1953, 1956, and 2017. God is represented as an archer and appears frequently in many Assyrian symbols and iconography. (Courtesy of AAAC archives.).

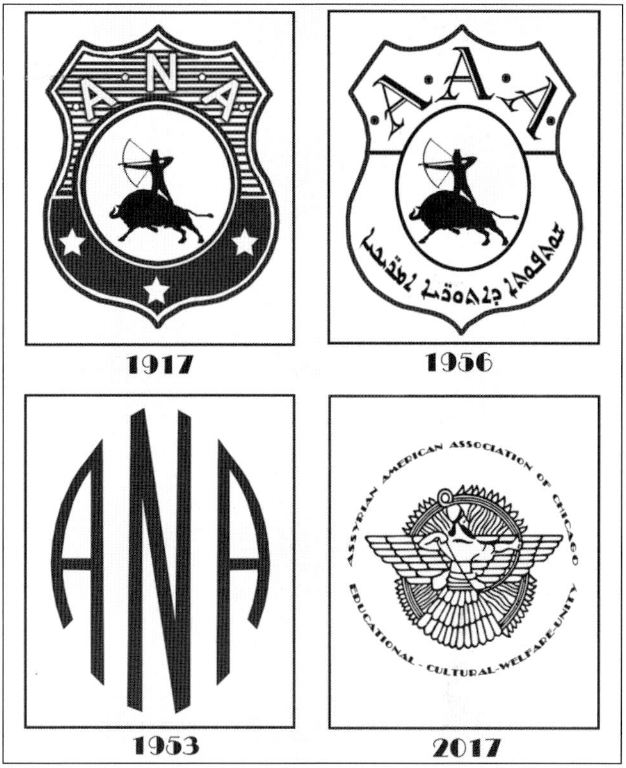

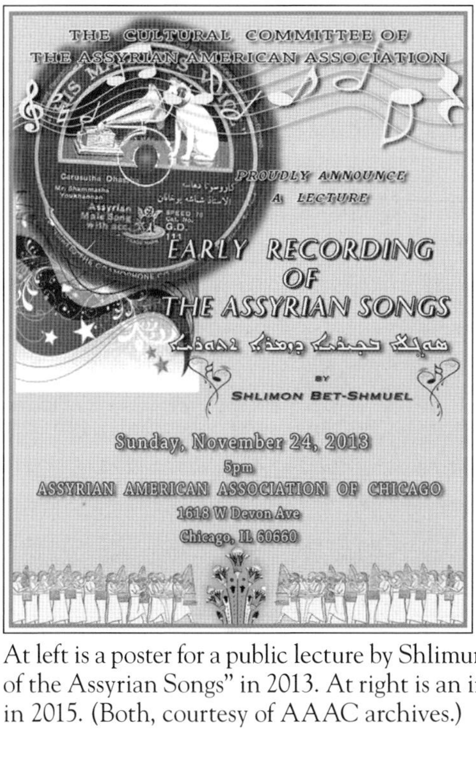

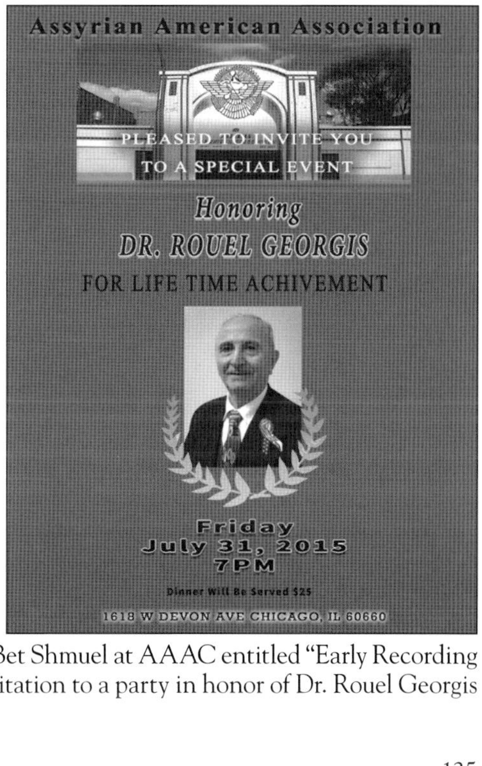

At left is a poster for a public lecture by Shlimun Bet Shmuel at AAAC entitled "Early Recording of the Assyrian Songs" in 2013. At right is an invitation to a party in honor of Dr. Rouel Georgis in 2015. (Both, courtesy of AAAC archives.)

Presidents of the AAAC and Ladies Auxiliary

Sargis Baaba, 1917
Agakhan David, 1918
Jonathan S. Colia, 1919–1921, 1932
Shimshon Gewargis, 1933
Goliath N. Benjamin, 1935
David Benjamin Adams, 1936
Malcolm Shahbaz, 1941
Yoil Sargis
William J. Pasha
Sargis Khanbaba
Marshal Joseph
Bob Newey Baba
Pera S. Benjamin
Narsay Serges
Sol "Saul" A. Odishoo, 1953
John G. Israel, 1954, 1963
Robert E. Eramia, 1955, 1960
Gabriel Sargis, 1956, 1964
Konstantin Aslanoff, 1965
Alexander P. Evans, 1967
Sam Andrews, 1969
Bejan Rasho, 1970–1973
William David, 1974

Paul P. Georges, 1975
Sargon Isaac, 1976
Albert Rasho, 1977
Awisha Hormizd, 1978
Shlimun Shlimun, 1978
Ben Benjamin, 1979, 1981, 1988
Ivan Giwargis, 1980
Babel L.Gabriel, 1982
Henry Moshe, 1983
Steve Yonan, 1984
Pnuel Hormizd, 1985
Kaisar Shahbas. 1986
Guiliana Younan, 1987
Fransis Yousif, 1991–1994
Pius Hawel, 1994–1995
Melis Shamas, 1995–1996
David Youkhanna, 1996, 2000
Ben I. Benjamin, 1979, 1982, 1988, 2000, 2003
Edward Nadirsha, 2003–2005
Emanuel Isho, 2005–2007
Sankhareb Abraham, 2007–2011
William Badal, 2011–2015
Guiliana Younan, 1987, 2016–present

Mary Werda, 1937
Anno Shabaz
Anna Odishoo
Aksana Azra Michael
Murassa Georges, 1956
Sophia Daniel
Helen Sargis
Dorothy S. Peara, 1964

Katryn Nicolas
Sonia Aghakan
Germaine Malik, 1979, 2001
Nellie Ganja Benjamin, 1969
Nina Malick, 1973
German Malick. 2001
Sarah Benjamin, 2002–2003, 2015

Bibliography

Assyrian American Association. *100 Years*. Stockholm, Sweden: Michael Mammo, 2017.

Assyrian American Courier (Izgadda). April 3, 1916: vol. 1.

Assyrian Americans Who Served in the Armed Forces of the United States. Chicago, IL: Assyrian National Association of Chicago, 1993.

Assyrian Monthly (Ktawoona). December 1933.

Assyrian National Association 50th Anniversary. 1967.

Assyrian National Association Meeting Minutes. 1935.

Assyrian Star, 1963.

Banquet in Honor of Mar Dachtou, Archbishop of Urmia and Bishop of Slamas. 1963.

BetGivargis-McDaniel, Maegan. *Assyrians of New Britain*. Charleston, SC: Arcadia Publishing, 2007.

Biennial Report of Secretary of State of the State of Illinois. Springfield, IL: 1919.

Bylaws of Assyrian National Association of Chicago. July 1953.

Full Report of the Fourth Annual Convention of the Assyrian National Association of America. New Britain, CT: 1919.

Journal of Assyrian Academic Studies. 1978.

Journal of the House Representatives of the United States, 67th Congress. Washington, DC: 1923.

Nineveh. 2017: vol. 41, Nos. 3–4.

Shedd, Mary Lewis. *The Measure of a Man: The Life of William Ambrose Shedd, Missionary to Persia*. New York, NY: George H. Doran Company, 1922.

Shoumanov, Vasili. *Assyrians in Chicago*. Charleston, SC: Arcadia Publishing, 2001.

Sparzona. June 1937–1938.

Speer, Robert E. *The Hakim Sahib, the Foreign Doctor; a Biography of Joseph Plumb Cochran, M.D., of Persia*. New York, NY: Fleming H. Revell Company, 1911.

Testimonial Dinner in Honor of His Beatitude Mar Eshai Shimun XXI. October 22, 1940.

The Assyrian National Directory. Chicago, IL: Assyrian American Association of Chicago, 1960.

The Ladies Auxiliary Meeting Minutes. April 7, 1937.

Werda, Joel E. *The Flickering Light of Asia: Or, The Assyrian Nation and Church*. New York, NY: self-published, 1924.

White, Jesse. *Illinois Blue Book, 2009–2010*. Springfield, IL: Secretary of State, 2010.

Zahrera. 1971.